SCIENCE

EVERYWHERE

OPPORTUNITIES FOR VERY YOUNG CHILDREN

SCIENCE

EVERYWHERE

OPPORTUNITIES FOR VERY YOUNG CHILDREN

BARBARA J. TAYLOR

BRIGHAM YOUNG UNIVERSITY

HARCOURT BRACE JOVANOVICH COLLEGE PUBLISHERS

Fort Worth Philadelphia San Diego New York Orlando Austin San Antonio
Toronto Montreal London Sydney Tokyo

PUBLISHER: Ted Buchholz
ACQUISITIONS EDITOR: Jo-Anne Weaver
PROJECT EDITOR: Nancy Lombardi
PRODUCTION MANAGER: Erin Gregg
BOOK DESIGNER: Peggy Young

Requests for permission to make copies of any part of the work should be mailed to: Permissions Department, Harcourt Brace Jovanovich, Publishers, 8th Floor, Orlando, Florida 32887.

Photo Credits: Cover photo and pages 20, 50, 64, 128 by Donna Buie. Pages 2, 5, 16, 26, 31, 34, 36, 44, 56, 59, 68, 71, 78, 83, 90, 95, 100, 103, 112, 117, 122 by Glen Anderson of Instructional Media, Brigham Young University.

Chapter Opening Illustrations by Darrel Kolosta. Part IV illustrations by Clifford Dunston of Instructional Media, Brigham Young University.

Address for Editorial Correspondence: Harcourt Brace Jovanovich, Inc., 301 Commerce Street, Suite 3700, Fort Worth, TX 76102.

Address for Orders: Harcourt Brace Jovanovich, Inc., 6277 Sea Harbor Drive, Orlando, FL 32887. 1-800-782-4479, or 1-800-433-0001 (in Florida).

ISBN: 0-03-054194-8
Library of Congress Catalogue Card Number: 91-78063
Printed in the United States of America

3 4 5 6 7 8 9 0 1 2 090 9 8 7 6 5 4 3 2 1

PREFACE

This book is the result of working with very young children for many years and watching their expressions as they become involved in scientific phenomena. The second stimuli is working with student teachers for many years and seeing, in general, their reluctance and fear when confronted with requests or assignments to prepare some scientific experiences for young children. I have been aware, especially over the last decade, of the excitement children between the ages of 18 and 36 months exhibit when they make simple discoveries. It is amazing to see how much time and interest can be involved in events that are seemingly common, and even boring, to older children or adults, such as using magnets to attract paper clips, being mesmerized by water, building up and knocking down blocks, or pouring rice between containers while listening to its crisp sound and watching its jumping action.

Science is all around us. We cannot escape it. And it is the magnificence of science that urges us to always move forward while we examine and use the opportunities around us.

It is not the showing or telling of science by adults that holds the interest of the children, but the exploring, doing, and discovering that make science so fascinating. Likewise, it is not the rigidity of science, but the flexibility and possibilities that have charm. School-age children think that science belongs in the "magic" category; younger children think science was made for them to discover and explore.

In order for science to be exciting and challenging during our lives, it must be exciting and challenging for our youngest children. Teachers and parents can help youngsters to cultivate these attributes by **appreciating their curiosity, providing opportunities, encouragement, time, materials, peers (when appropriate), and then sharing their successes, excitement and knowledge.**

Adults in various roles (teachers, parents, and others) need to recognize the importance of science in the daily lives of each of us. They need to know that "teaching is not always telling and learning is not always listening." They need to appreciate that young children have a learning style that is individual and that is different from older children and other adults. Young children learn in a friendly environment through their senses, through discovery, and through encouragement.

While language, motor and social skills are yet immature, young children do and say marvelous things. They express themselves simply based on experiences and available vocabulary; they are often clumsy and even anti-social. But these traits will develop as the children form personal attitudes about themselves, people around them, and acceptance of them and their ideas and attempts. They need a loving, patient, optimistic environment. Adults who know how young children learn can provide this wholesome atmosphere.

Because individuals learn through various sensory modes, they need multiple opportunities to stimulate each mode—not to the extent of overwhelming them, but repetition so they can clarify and solidify their thinking or make necessary modifications. Therefore, adults should be aware of the kinds of opportunities provided as well as the preferred learning mode of the individual.

When planning activities, especially when young children are involved, there always needs to be attention given to the safety and health of the children. More experience, practice, and benefit will come from opportunities that result in happiness, success, and encouragement. Let there be emphasis on the rewarding feelings, but also appreciate that road blocks (failures, if you will) can be excellent learning experiences if they are handled in a constructive way. When things don't work out the planned way, make modifications and try again—and don't give up or turn your back. Think it through carefully. What learning was gained from the deviation? What do you need to modify, add, or delete? Perhaps more learning and enjoyment was created from the deviation than if the activity had gone perfectly the first time. That's what science is all about—at any age.

As you approach this text and as you plan activities for young children, look at their individual needs and interests. This book is intended to stimulate adults to create ideas appropriate to the interests and needs of the individual children with whom they come in contact and not a "cook book" with all the recipes and ideas. Be creative! Enjoy children and science!

TABLE OF CONTENTS

I Laying the Foundation

II How Children Learn

III   Preparing and Disseminating Information

IV   Concepts and Activities

Laying the Foundation

1

Overview

Not long ago, a popular television show featuring adolescents pictured a science classroom with the teacher seated at a desk at the front of the room reading a chapter aloud as the students followed in their texts. The students, who were fully capable of reading themselves, made silly comments, were totally uninterested, and considered the assignment juvenile and boring. The teacher tolerated no interruptions and gave a sigh of relief when the bell rang. Because of the teacher's inflexibility and the student's total disinterest, it is doubtful their learning was increased. A similar situation could occur with teachers of young children, unless teachers present materials that are developmentally designed and have personal child involvement and meaning. The children can develop positive or indifferent attitudes toward the subject, the teacher, or the learning process based on their early experiences. Teachers need to make their subject *alive* and help students want to learn.

Technically, the period of early childhood education extends until the child is about eight years of age; however, the focus of this text will be on children ages two through five. During this time it is important that the developmental and personal needs of each child be identified and met as closely as possible. It should be a period when children gain competence and confidence in themselves and others who are important to them, and learn to handle and welcome new experiences. As Rachel Carson states,

> If a child is to keep alive his inborn sense of wonder without any such gift from the fairies, he needs the companionship of at least one adult who can share it, rediscovering with him the joy, excitement and mystery of the world we live in. I sincerely believe that for the child, and for the parent seeking to guide him, it is not half as important to **know** as to **feel.** If facts are the seeds that later produce knowledge and wisdom, then the emotions and the impressions of the senses are the fertile soil in which the seeds must grow. The years of early childhood are the time to prepare the soil. Once the emotions have been aroused—a sense of the beautiful, the excitement of the new and the unknown, a feeling of sympathy, pity, admiration or love—then we wish for knowledge about the object of our emotional response. Once found, it has lasting meaning. It is more important to pave the way for the child to want to know than to put him on a diet of facts he is not ready to assimilate. (1956, p. 45)

Children are eager learners. Their surroundings are new to them; the people they meet may be friends or foes. How are the children to know without experience and guidance from others who are more knowledgeable? But one must be cautious in both the approach and the content. Froebel, the father of kindergartens, writes,

> "For the purpose of teaching and instruction is to bring ever more *out of* man rather than to put more *into* him; for that which can get *into* man we already know and possess as the property of mankind. On the other hand, what yet is to come *out* of mankind, what human nature is yet to develop, what we do not yet know . . . " (1899, p. 279)

PRINCIPLES

In this text certain principles will be introduced and discussed. These principles apply to good teaching practices for young children in all settings; however, emphasis will be upon a science curriculum.

Different theorists have proposed assumptions about the nature of the individual under varied circumstances. For example, Gilbert, Osborne, and Fensham (1982) identify three assumptions about **science learning** in children (ages discussed are vague but possibly apply to elementary or older students)—those with no prior knowledge (blank-minded), those with some conceptual view but little understanding (teacher dominance), and those with strong science views that persist and interact with science teaching (student dominance). Examples using number concepts and young children could include:

a. No knowledge. Numbers are not used and have no meaning.

b. Concepts with little understanding. Rote memorization with no understanding of quantity or symbols.

c. Strong views. Not yet mastered by young children.

In working with young children, the first assumption seems to be logical—that the learner's minds are blank and in need of information and experiences even though some children have more experience and knowledge than others. Therefore, adults need to listen to what children say, to be observant of children's interests, to value the children's contributions, and to explore and explain science so young children can form new and accurate concepts.

For example, children who have daily contact with animals have a greater knowledge about animals than children who only see them occasionally or in restricted circumstances like the zoo or the pet store. Information can be obtained from the more knowledgeable children so the teacher can slightly increase the knowledge and experience for all children. Perhaps a discussion or activity will include how animals help people by providing food, transportation or security. For less knowledgeable children, the teacher will start with some very basic experiences—maybe with replicas or pictures—and build up to having a live animal in the classroom. Regardless of the knowledge of the children, the teacher helps them solidify accurate concepts and increase their learning.

Environments that favor process learning (as opposed to product learning) include opportunities for self-selection and choices for children. Young children should savor the use of materials and activities (the "how" and the "why") over having a finished product (the "what"), which some parents value. Process learning, or open environments, where children are encour-

Children enjoy new experiences at a safe distance.

aged to meet their needs and desires, require more careful planning than those environments that are teacher-dominated.

Piaget's Theory

Piaget's theory provides a sound basis for selecting and planning experiences appropriate to the general cognitive abilities of a young child with experiences formulated to enhance the child at each age level. Repetition is common; familiar and concrete experiences are used as a foundation for new concepts. Children are actively involved in sensory experiences, and open-ended questions help children to experiment and formalize their ideas.

Hands-on Experiences

When children manipulate (or act upon) objects, a **mental action** is performed which increases or decreases the social context of the classroom. Children become mentally passive,

take no stands, exchange no points of view, and feel no consequences of their own decisions in classrooms where the teacher holds the power of decision making (Williams and Kamii, 1986, p. 26).

Dawes (1987) conducted a study supporting the use of a hands-on approach in science teaching with young children. Goals of the study included having teachers develop their ability to teach science, spending more time teaching science to young children, and helping students and teachers develop a positive attitude toward science. All three goals were met and a positive attitude change was noted in both children and teachers.

Whitehead advocates first-hand knowledge as the ultimate basis of intellectual life. He argues that the world offers too much second-hand knowledge thereby breeding mediocrity rather than seeing immediate events as instances of general ideas in one's life (1959, p. 79).

Research for more than a half century has pointed to the importance of children under a mental age of six having first-hand experiences of learning; therefore children in kindergarten (or higher grades) need lively play activities, interesting projects, others with whom to converse, appropriately planned environments, and time to enjoy them. Unfortunately, "If some children do not progress satisfactorily, it is assumed that the children have failed, rather than that the system has failed to meet their needs" (Hendrick, 1987, pp. 32–33).

Total Needs of the Child

While this text focuses on science, attention will also be given to providing an integrated curriculum and promoting physical, social/emotional, and intellectual growth in a pleasant atmosphere free from pressure, time, and performance restraints. Problem solving, language in its entirety, social skills, physical development, and relationship building with others and oneself will be important components (see Chapter 9).

Some children learn best through one approach while others learn through a different one—auditory, visual, physical, and so forth. By using various approaches, children have a chance not only to strengthen their most effective mode, but also to practice using other modes that may presently be less effective (see Chapter 5).

The developmental areas of a child's growth are often uneven—she may be advanced in some areas and slow in others. Therefore, all areas of development need attention and opportunities

> **PRINCIPLES RELATED TO EARLY CHILDHOOD EDUCATION**
>
> - **Piaget's theory identifies the cognitive abilities of young children.**
> - **First-hand experiences are beneficial for young children.**
> - **Each child's personal and developmental needs are considered.**
> - **Children show interest in their surroundings.**
> - **Curriculum for children should be versatile in content and support various areas of development.**
> - **Each person in a teaching/learning situation is important.**
> - **Preassessing current knowledge before teaching a topic helps the teacher plan meaningful activities.**
> - **Pressure on young children to perform or accelerate learning should be avoided.**

to improve. Early childhood professionals know from training, as well as instinctively, that it is primarily not *what* you teach, but *how* you teach that makes for success or failure (Hendrick, 1987, p. 32; Eliason and Jenkins, 1990, pp. 27–28).

Interest in Immediate and Expanding World

The younger the child, the more his interests are involved with self, immediate family, and familiar surroundings. However, with motor skills, language, and additional experiences, the child will want to explore outside environments and relationships.

Adults should consider local resources, topics, events, and individuals when planning meaningful experiences for young children. Certain occupations, such as fishing, sports, or farming, are dependent upon weather; unusual animals are raised in specific locations; children living in desert areas have different interests and experiences than those living near bodies of water; large industries have an effect upon lives through employment, politics and community support. As stated by Ziemer, "Our world is a huge hands-on museum, a well-stocked laboratory, a fascinating never-ending field trip" (1987, p. 45). It is in this type of environment that our children can mature with the right kind of nurturance (see Chapter 5).

Schultz states, "We cannot expect children to grow up valuing trees, spiders, and snakes without positive experiences that touch them personally. Young children's direct contacts with nature awaken them to its beauty and the pleasure it offers" (1985, p. 49). Schultz shares a classroom experience in which a teacher created a science corner with magnifying lenses, magnets, fish, and other objects. Children added specimens, such as frogs, ants and pretend snakes. Of the children who participated in the classroom experience, Schultz reports an 86-percent improvement in science concepts, 167-percent improvement in science vocabulary, and 15-percent improvement in perceptual skills over preinstruction scores. And in addition, Schultz noticed a decrease in both teachers' and children's fear of animals as their interest rose.

Rather than emphasizing teaching facts to children, Neuman (1978) contends that teaching should involve them in understanding their world through observing, manipulating, and interacting with science activities and materials. For Neuman, the benefits of science for young children include the promotion of intellectual growth, greater potential for success in school, and opportunities for the development of positive self-images.

Varied Curriculum to Promote Development

From the activities, materials, interactions, and opportunities provided, children are encouraged to observe, explore, inquire, question, combine, incorporate, and make generalizations. The curriculum should include opportunities for creativity, affective expression, psychomotor practice, critical thinking, good citizenship, expanded career choices, awareness and diminishment of stereotyping, and other ways to help children live fully and well in their environment. Such meaningful experiences sharpen their senses and skills while they gain scientific knowledge.

Value of Each Person

In a teaching/learning situation, responsibility needs to be acknowledged and shared by both children and teachers. In this way they both benefit from the environment and the people within it.

Every adult dealing with young children should have a general knowledge and understanding of how young children grow and develop. Adults who are committed to children allow the children enough time to live fully within each stage of development. Children of the same chronological age may be ahead of or behind norms. "Early childhood learning activities must be appropriate to the child's *age and stage and personal interests* to promote success" (Bredekamp, 1986, cover). One must continually ask whether children are being prepared for the program, or if the program is being prepared for the children. Another question about early education may be "Ready or not?, or Ready for what?" (Buckner, 1988, p. 69). Elkind reminds early childhood educators that good experiences for children are an outward extension of the home rather than a downward extension of the school and that the "best measurement of children's adjustment and learning is obtained through careful observation by skilled observers who know the child well, and not by the children's responses to standardized tests" (1987b, p. 69).

We as educators of young children know it is our ethical responsibility to stand up for what we know is best for them. Connell states, "But the misuse of these early years—through curricular content or teaching methods that inappropriately emphasize intellectual achievement, narrowly defined—can waste the promise of early childhood education" (1987, p. 15).

Valuing each person includes dispelling stereotypes. Harlan writes that actions and beliefs of teachers, whether negative or positive, contribute heavily to the self-attitudes being formed by their students and are the single most cru-

cial force in shaping what an individual is able to accomplish (1988, p. 33).

She further suggests that teachers should give more attention to girls and minorities (rather than just Caucasian boys) by verbal and social encouragement, new opportunities, use of bulletin boards, media and visitors, combatting crippling stereotypes, and modifying difficult activities as needed. Harlan states, "It is important not to give up on science activities because of an occasional unexpected outcome. Keep in mind Thomas Edison's observation that a mistake is not a failure if we learn how not to do it next time" (1988, p. 37).

Investigators have been trying to discover why more males do better in science than do females. They looked at, but could not find, any biological (genetic or anatomical) or intellectual causes. Of great impact on female performance in science are cultural biases, many of which begin by the age of 11. Young children retain their natural curiosity about the world with few differences between boys and girls during the preschool years, but an attitude change creates a clear diversification in interest (Peltz, 1990, p. 44). As children get older, attitudes that discourage girls from science participation include teachers not expecting girls to excel in science, families encouraging boys and discouraging girls from taking science classes, and differences in teachers' treatment of girls and boys. Scientific texts reveal a highly disproportionate number of pictures and references to males (Bazleer and Simonis, 1990, p. 26). Henniger is quick to note that both young men and young women who have sound math and science backgrounds have many more opportunities and career choices which are not available to those who lack such training and interest (1987, p. 167). Make science exciting!

In their chapter "Girls' stuff, boys' stuff; young children talking and playing," Browne and Ross (Browne, 1991) report some interesting sex-related observations and conversations from 29 different schools for young children, such as:

1. Children as young as three were conscious of toys and activities as "for girls," "for boys," and those that were gender neutral (pp. 38–39).

2. The children had firm ideas about how resources were to be used by each gender (p. 40).

3. "Territories" or "domains" varied by the confidence and assertiveness of the children depending upon whether they were in or out of "their" territory (pp. 42–43).

4. "Many girls did not passively accept the gender-based boundaries and developed their own strategies to gain access to 'boys' activities" (p. 44).

5. No evidence existed that girls or boys chose activities based on their cultural, linguistic, or religious background. Rather, when new activities were presented, the children were drawn to familiar things to build confidence to try something new (pp. 45–46).

6. "Girls were very adept at sabotaging teachers' efforts to ensure that they engaged in any activity they would not normally choose" (p. 46).

7. "Children's attitudes towards science and technology reflect deep-seated social patterns and therefore cannot be modified by a single, simple strategy" (p. 51).

From Browne's report, and other similar ones, it appears that teachers and parents of young children need to make conscious efforts to involve children of both sexes in many different kinds of activities, including science opportunities, so they can diminish barriers and territories and gain more experience and pleasure from their everyday world (see Chapter 9).

I thought my classroom provided young children with a good balance between "masculine" and "feminine" toys, materials, and activities until one of the four-year-old boys marched right up to me, put his hands on his hips, looked me right in the eye and said: "I'm so tired of all these girl things!" I was shocked, but quickly glancing around the room I noted many "boy things." I recovered quickly and said, "Well, what do you think we could change?" Without hesitation, he said, "If you'll let us make doughnuts, I'll show you how." And even though his gender "things" were not the same as mine, the next day we did make doughnuts and he did show us how! This example may be a good reminder for teachers to look around their classrooms to make sure they are providing what they think they are providing—materials, toys, and activities that are not gender-oriented.

Most of my experience has been with children in family groupings—mixed (2-year span) rather than chronologically. When children are grouped chronologically, there are undoubtedly differences in size, skills, emotional maturity, interests, and so forth. I prefer children of mixed ages because it gives the older children an edge in some developmental areas (even if it is only in their minds) and it gives the younger children a model or challenge to do more things. Likewise, family grouping takes into account younger children who may be more advanced than their chronological counterparts and older children who are less advanced than their chronological counterparts. This is where I see children in their development of scientific concepts—some are more advanced and others are less advanced. Wherever they are, they can *be* models or they can *seek* for models. Each child has worth.

Planning Meaningful Experiences

In order to plan stimulating and challenging science experiences for children, teachers need a basis upon which to begin. Those who determine what the children already know can plan activities to solidify that knowledge (provided it is correct—or correct it if it is inaccurate) and move the children one step further in this knowledge or integrate it into other aspects of the childrens' lives. Those who plan science experiences without ascertaining the present knowledge of the children may confuse the children with bits and pieces of information.

Based on a study of teaching science to preschoolers, Iatridis emphasizes the appropriateness of the educational materials selected. It may be challenging to properly identify the abilities and interests of young children, but the experience should contribute to their cogni-

tive growth, their interests, and their physical environment (1981, p. 25). In the study, Iatridis reports, "Children exposed to the science-based curriculum increased their self-directed discovery (active, child-initiated exploration rather than aimless handling of materials) and verbalized curiosity more often than the control children did" (p. 26). The study encourages science studies that begin in preschool, supports the notion that even a modest, inexpensive curriculum can increase preschoolers' cognitive development, and claims that disadvantaged students and girls may show special benefits from an early science program.

Frequently teachers ask, "How can I find out what children know?" Their first inclination is to quiz the young children as they would older children. Forgetting that young children have difficulty combining language and ideas, teachers assume that because of weak or no responses to their questions, the children know nothing and that leaves the field open for teaching. Often the questions asked by teachers are so broad that even an adult ponders about responding. Rather than asking, "What do you know about cows?", ask more specific questions (*if* asking is the best approach): "What do cows like to eat?", "What color are cows?", "Who has been up close to a cow?" Better still, have some books out on cows and talk informally with the children about the pictures, or sing songs about cows and then talk about cows. You could also place toy cows in the block area while you casually observe the children playing and listen to their conversations. A trip to a local farm or dairy may be possible. Or play a word game with the children, "I know an animal that has a long skinny tail to brush away flies, it has four legs, it has horns, and sometimes provides milk. Guess what it is?'' Then show a picture or replica and talk about the cow. In other words, questioning of young children may be the least effective method of determining their present knowledge. But when questioning *is* appropriate, make sure the questions are simple, clear, and pertinent (see Chapter 11).

Once present knowledge is assessed (and with a group of children there will be those who have much information and those who have little information), begin putting ideas and activities into a teaching format. Knowledgeable children can help less knowledgeable children to understand the concepts. An attempt should be made to raise each child's knowledge just slightly—not to make it easy on the teacher because he only want to teach about cows *once*! The teacher should take it slowly and gradually, planning on repeating and advancing the information periodically.

Preassessment is valuable and should be used as the basis for providing information and activities. Teachers who decide prematurely what they will teach before preassessing are promoting their own ideas and whims rather than meeting the needs of the children (see Chapter 10).

Avoid Pressure/Acceleration
There is increasing emphasis on early education programs. Some advocate a developmental approach while others argue for better and faster academic learning. Voices are heard on both sides of the fence. Some children are being rushed into this and that and from here to there and back again.

There has been talk about mandatory full-day programs for four-year-olds. The media bombards parents and teachers daily to buy commercial materials in an effort to accelerate the children's learning. Elkind (1981b) argues against ''hurrying'' children. Buckner asks about some early childhood educators being on the ''fast track'' because they do not object or are not verbal about acceleration in preschool or are ''too accommodating to those crowding and hurrying us up a road that from our experience and research we believe to be the *wrong* road (1988, p. 5).'' Wanting to get children off the fast track, he challenges us to shift gears and wave a red flag rather than merely being spectators while the race continues. He suggests that, ''Perhaps preschool teachers should stage a 'sit-in' at kindergarten, kindergarten teachers at first grade, and so on up the line until some of the many recommendations are enacted that allow children to be themselves—and not little adults'' (1988, p. 5). After the advent of Sputnik, curriculum began to be moved to the next lower grade. ''Children at this grade level (not necessarily at this *developmental level*, of course) were then expected to learn in 1 year what had formerly been taught in 2,'' reports Connell. She further states, ''The records show that during the past 30 years not a few children have failed to thrive with these sharply higher, and often inappropriate, expectations. Potentially eager little learners have floundered and 'failed' first grade!'' (1987, p. 30)

Textbook publishers and material suppliers compound the problem. They proliferate rote learning of letters and numbers, endless paper-and-pencil skill drills, and responses to achievement tests. Learning of this type, while it can be achieved, is not of primary importance for children between the ages of two and five.

Worksheets, another means of group teaching, do not allow the child or the teacher to measure the child's understanding.

> "Young children cannot think very well when they sit silently. However, movement, manipulation, and noise in themselves are not necessarily educational. The teacher who stops using worksheets is taking a step in the right direction, but this is only the first step. We must replace the worksheet with an environment that offers ample opportunities for children to think as they manipulate objects . . . remember to use your own initiative to encourage children's thinking." (Williams and Kamii, 1986, p. 26)

Some children are anxious to move ahead quickly—even faster than adults think they should. These children also need to be kept interested and stimulated but not encouraged to move so quickly that they out-distance peers or experience early burn-out.

SUMMARY

For science to be valued by young children, experiences must be developmentally and personally appropriate.

Young children have limited but varying amounts of experiences and knowledge.

Giving first-hand opportunities to young children that support their immediate environment, are of interest to them, and include variety and personal

involvement stimulate the children to participate while interacting with their peers.

Environments should be nonsexist.

Pushing children or putting undue pressure on them discourages rather than encourages their learning ability.

EXERCISES
study/discussion questions

1. Describe a good learning environment for young children

   a. at home with parents.

   b. in a classroom with teachers.

2. Explain the differences between "blank-minded," "teacher dominance," and "student dominance" science learning. Give examples of each.

3. Choose one of the principles beginning on page 4 and elaborate upon it. Why is it important? How do you address it in a classroom of young children?

4. What has been your experience with gender and science? Suggest ways to encourage *all* pupils (regardless of sex, age, socio-economic status, or culture) to become involved in and enjoy science learning and teaching—for we are all learners and teachers!

5. What could you do to discourage adults from pressuring young children before they are ready for or ca-

pable of handling some concepts or activities?

6. Study the "Sequential, Procedural Teaching Model" presented on pages 14 and 15; then give additional examples for each principle.

A SEQUENTIAL, PROCEDURAL TEACHING MODEL _____

PRINCIPLE	DESCRIPTION	EXAMPLE
Identification of meaningful information or problem	This involves getting clues from children about their interests or proposing information or problems from which children could benefit.	When children continually mention something they are interested in (or have concern about), teach about it in a logical, responsible way so all children will benefit from it.
Various means of preassessing current knowledge	Rather than gaining information only through pointed questions with specific answers, one should use a variety of means to find out the current knowledge of children regarding a certain topic. Questioning is one way; others are through observation, demonstration, role playing, discussions, curriculum opportunities, integration of information, building on prior concepts, and others limited only by the creativity of the teacher and the situation.	Consider whether the children are interpreting your methods the same way you are interpreting them. Did they give a "dumb" response because the request was not understandable or because their thinking was incomplete?
Outlining ways to present experiences	When teachers have a plan, they are more likely to deliver information and experiences in a logical, sequential manner. Without a plan, information may be misleading, incomplete, inaccurate, too complex, or inconceivable.	Are you beginning at a certain point because you know background information or do you need to lay a better foundation?
Ways of integrating experiences	Information that is complete, understandable, and valued has the possibility of being retained. For young children, exposure to an idea only once or from a limited viewpoint may confuse them. Rather than teach some information in a rote, structured, or narrow manner, teachers should look for variety, flexibility, and integration.	Some children remember a situation because it had rhythm, some because they tied it to one or more familiar situations.
Availability of materials and experiences	Teachers need not be concerned about purchasing elaborate or expensive materials to provide meaningful experiences for children. Familiar materials and experiences are more likely to cause children to show interest and connection between ideas.	Raw materials are likely to appear in the cupboards, files, and shelves of most teachers. Take a look at the items you discard from your classroom or home. Could they be "treasures" not trash?
Observation and participation with children	Too often teachers concoct situations for children without considering the children either individually or as a group. Through astute observation and participation with the children (listening to their conversations and watching their actions and interactions), teachers gain insights into how the children think, thereby increasing their planning skills and interpretation of the young children's behavior.	A child may do or say certain things because that is a family pattern or because personal skills are immature.

PRINCIPLE	DESCRIPTION	EXAMPLE
Evaluation of children's experiences	Just planning different experiences for children is not enough—these are not mere time-consumers. Teachers must carefully examine how the experiences are received and utilized by the children. If we are not teaching the "right" things to children, then we must be doing an ineffective job of teaching.	Does the situation need minor or major modifications—or should it be replaced entirely? Did the children develop correct concepts upon which to build?
Building upon previous experiences	Teachers should review carefully the previous experiences they have provided for the children. How could these experiences be built upon or integrated with other concepts? Use the prior concepts as a preassessment or foundation and then enhance.	Suppose you had taught about seeds and the children had actually had a planting experience. As a follow-up, talk about the growth process of plants, what makes them survive, what plants grow in your vicinity, what parts of the plant are edible—followed up by tasting opportunities. Children need repetition to make their ideas concrete and to lay the foundations for future learning.
Planning for follow-up on information or problems	Get clues from children regarding concepts or experiences presented.	Perhaps you had a baker come into your classroom or you took a field trip to a bakery. You plan a baking experience within the classroom. The children are disappointed that the procedure goes so slowly and that their product does not turn out like the baker's. What do you do: 1. Make excuses? 2. Try baking again with some modifications? 3. Ignore the problems? 4. Tell the children they will do better when they get older? 5. Encourage them to buy at the bakery? 6. Decide never to bake in the classroom again?

2

Theories

Several theories have been advocated for use in planning and describing curriculum for early childhood education. The theory of Piaget is a preferred one by this author, and the theories of Bruner and Gagné will be briefly compared to Piaget, followed by a short note about direct instruction and philosophical roots.

Piaget's Stages

Piaget is known for his observation of children and his stages of cognitive development. His influence has been great upon teachers designing and presenting curriculum to young children. As a refresher, his stages of cognitive development with characteristics of each stage are given on page 18.

Of most focus for the purpose of this book will be the second quadrant, the preoperational stage; however, it is important for the reader to note the stages that precede and follow the ages represented in this text. It is also important to note that these characteristics are general and not specific, and that children of a similar chronological age may not be in the same developmental stage. Each characteristic should be interpreted as a trend from less mature to more mature behavior. For example, one characteristic states, "Makes great strides in language development." This could be interpreted for two different ages as follows:

TWO-YEAR-OLD	SEVEN-YEAR-OLD
• has little command, but enjoys books and conversation	• is quite verbal, experiments with language, is interested in print
• possesses a small amount of knowledge	• knows more facts
• lacks in experiences	• builds upon past experiences and explores new ideas
• is often insecure	• depends on peers for security

PIAGET'S FOUR STAGES OF COGNITIVE DEVELOPMENT

SENSORIMOTOR STAGE

(Birth to Age 2)

The child (with differing intensities and abilities):

- Relies heavily on his/her five senses
- Is preverbal
- Deals with real objects
- Associates objects with actions and events
- Learns object permanence
- Learns to identify objects
- Distinguishes familiar people
- Does not plan actions or goals—accidental happenings
- Imitates others
- Shows appearance of make-believe play
- Engages in solitary play
- Has a here-and-now frame of reference

PREOPERATIONAL STAGE

(Age 2 to 7)

The child (with differing intensities and abilities):

- Acquires symbolistic thought (ability to use mental images and words to represent actions and things not present)
- Engages in sociodramatic (make-believe) play
- Is ego-centric (self-centered in thoughts and actions, and leads to animistic thinking)
- Makes great strides in language development
- Is unable to reverse thinking
- Thinks mainly in the present; some ideas about near past and future
- Begins to expand into neighborhood and community
- Centers thoughts narrowly (cannot decenter)
- Makes judgments primarily based on how things look

CONCRETE-OPERATIONAL STAGE

(Age 7 to 11)

The child (with differing intensities and abilities):

- Increases use of language (written and oral)
- Performs operations: combining, separating, ordering, seriating, multiplying or repeating, dividing, and substituting
- Can classify ideas, variables, objects
- Can reverse thinking
- Ties ideas together and can organize time and space
- Can conserve substance
- Begins to think in abstract terms

FORMAL-OPERATIONAL STAGE

(Age 11 and Above)

The child:

- Begins to think about thinking (hypothetico-deductive reasoning)
- Thinks in abstract terms (single propositions and relationships between two or more propositions)
- Hypothesizes
- Questions values and ethics

Young children who are in the sensori-motor and preoperational stages according to Piaget's theory are unable to perform mental operations such as adding, subtracting, multiplying, dividing, performing correspondence, ordering, substituting, and reversing.

Piaget's time table for gaining formal operations correlates with junior and senior high school students, but at all ages there are students who have or have not reached the levels indicated. The role of teachers of students at any age is to adjust their teaching to meet the needs and abilities of their students.

> Example: Several three- and four-year-old children were discussing the nursery rhyme, "Hey, diddle, diddle." When asked about the characters and their actions in the rhyme ("Could a cow really jump over the moon?"), two children promptly said, "Yes." Further discussion involved, "How would he do it?" The two looked at each other, then backed up, took several running steps and then a leap. "Just like that!" they replied. Children in the sensorimotor and preoperational stages lack experiences and language to describe ideas—but they can "show." These children can explain better by using a replica (or physically demonstrating as these two children did) rather than verbally. The teacher for these ages should not expect too much or rely on verbal learning only. Older children, who use abstract thinking, could organize ideas and give verbal responses—a more appropriate method for them than to use demonstration.

Knowing the expectations of children at different ages helps teachers plan science experiences that have appeal and meaning to these children.

In Piaget's theory each person must, through interaction with the environment, *construct her own intellect*. Knowledge is constructed in the mind through actions of the individual. Children are not **passive receptors** but **active agents** in developing their own minds. The child holds the power to form her intellect; knowledge is not somehow stored in the content and techniques of a subject.

Piaget believes that there are three kinds of knowledge: **physical,** which develops through the child's observation and interaction with objects and is involved in science education; **logical-mathematical** or reasoning, a reflection of one's actions related and organized in the mind, and part of math; and **social,** which evolves from personal interaction.

Knowledge comes from two sources: external and internal. As Williams and Kamii state,

> The source of physical knowledge is partly external to us, but the source of logicomathematical knowledge is internal . . . We used to think children acquired knowledge only through their senses. Piaget extended this belief by showing that children can obtain sensory information only when they act on an object physically and mentally. Physical knowledge is acquired when children handle objects and observe how they react. For example, children discover the properties of balls by holding them, dropping them, rolling them, and throwing them. This is why *manipulation* is essential for children—and adults— to acquire physical knowledge. (1986, p. 24)

Interaction increases social skills, knowledge, and enjoyment.

Franklin and Biber agree that learning is an active process and that knowledge is constructed rather than acquired. Therefore, the child must be in an environment that furthers his own natural tendency to explore, manipulate, and experiment by acting on and with objects (1977).

The idea that direct exploration and handling of objects are vital elements in early education is a Piagetian perspective of cognitive development. Proponents of Piaget also support the stage theory of development, "that individuals pass through different stages in such areas as cognition and moral development as they mature, and they have documented examples showing that children actually do think differently than adults" (Hendrick, 1990, p. 11).

Morrison states that Piaget's theory is used heavily because it "is the only theory that explains fully and in detail human intellectual development." However, Morrison does report weaknesses in Piaget's theory, including the informality of experiments, Piaget's intolerance of other ideas on intellectual development, the use of his own children in his studies, and the difficulty of interpreting Piaget's writings (1990, p. 65). Morrison also notes that Piaget was more concerned with characteristics of behavior at a particular stage than with rigid age/time frames. Others believe that experiences of training, education, and feedback may play more important roles in cognitive development than Piaget did.

Nevertheless, Piaget is regarded as a leader in the field of cognitive development: His ideas are important in the teaching of science to young children.

Bruner

"Jerome Bruner more than any other person has successfully applied the principles of Piaget's child development theories to the education of children" (Esler and Esler, 1984, p. 41). This type of learning is often called **discovery learning.** The basic tenets of Bruner's theory are threefold: the involvement of the child with the learning process; the interaction between the child and teacher, who is a guide and advisor rather than an expositor of information; and involvement of concrete materials (see Chapter 7).

As defined by Bruner, the advantages of discovery learning include helping the child learn independently, shifting motivation for learning from external rewards to internal satisfaction, giving the learner practice in solving problems, and assisting the learner in retention and recall (1961).

Besides promoting Piaget's ideas in the United States, Bruner has also developed his own theory of intellectual development in children. Like Piaget's, Bruner's theory states that children pass through age-related and biological stages and that learning depends on the child's developmental level.

Differences are noted between Bruner and Piaget with regard to the child's readiness for learning. Piaget concludes that the child's readiness for learning depends on maturation and intellectual development. Bruner believes there is always readiness in the child for concept learning, and he states, "Any subject can be taught ef-

fectively in some intellectually honest form to any child at any stage of development".

According to Bruner, a child can only learn science concepts according to her present intellectual development. The teacher can help the child by providing challenging but usable opportunities and problems. The child can then progress from one stage of intellectual development to another by acquiring deeper understanding of science concepts and conceptual schemes. It is vitally important that the science program be built around major conceptual schemes, skills, and values of society, and it should be taught as early as possible in a manner that is consistent with the child's present stage of development and forms of thought (Victor, 1985).

Gagné

Known in America for his hierarchy of learning levels, Robert Gagné believes, "Learning is the establishment of a capability to do something that the learner was not capable of doing previously" (Victor, 1985). Where Bruner emphasizes the *process*, Gagné emphasizes the *product* of learning, whether it is learned through discovery, review, or practice. Gagné emphasizes learning itself; Bruner places emphasis on discovery learning.

Differences between Views

Victor notes differences between Piaget, Bruner, and Gagné in their attitudes toward the child's readiness for learning. For Piaget, it depends upon the child's maturation and intellectual development. Bruner finds that the child is always ready to learn a concept in some form or manner. Gagné relates readiness to learn to successful preliminary subskills and subconcepts rather than to the child himself (1985, p. 30). It should be noted that Piaget, Bruner, and Gagné speak more to the teaching of science for elementary and older learners than to preschool and kindergarten ones; however, these theorists state that the concepts to be learned and the sequencing of them should proceed from the very simple to the most complex, and be appropriate for the age group addressed.

DIRECT INSTRUCTION

Another type of learning, **direct instruction,** differs in organization, goals, and usage from discovery or developmental learning. Direct instruction (sometimes called "psychometric learning") involves rote learning, is often used with groups of learners, and assumes that each child learns in a similar manner. Esler and Esler state,

> Recent research on effective teaching has indicated that when highly specific information that might be committed to memory is the desired learning objective, direct instruction is the most efficient mode. The current model or direct instruction includes the parameters of whole class instruction as compared to group or individual instruction, maximizing children's time engaged in tasks that represent easily attainable goals, and providing constant feedback to children on their completed tasks. The direct or verbal learning model is more effective with primary-grade children who are being taught the basic skills of reading and mathematics. (1984, p. 42)

Example: Direct instruction would be advocated by some in the teaching of the alphabet, numbers, mathematical concepts, and specific facts to be memorized. Accomplishment of the task would be evidenced by verbally repeating the information, by performing worksheets correctly, or completing a specific project.

PHILOSOPHICAL ROOTS

Teachers of young children may have philosophical preferences. To accommodate their views, they must know their specific role in planning and delivering the information, what they expect of the children in their classrooms, and how to evaluate the effectiveness of their teaching.

Three major viewpoints apparent in early childhood education today are **behaviorist-environmental, maturationist,** and **comprehensive-interactionist.** Teachers of young children, especially those educators in science and mathematics, must be prepared to work within each of these viewpoints. (See the Planning Essentials box.) "Most likely, the maturationist view will be predominant. A behaviorist-environmental view is likely to be the second most common view. Many teachers will not rigidly adhere to one view but will combine elements of different views with the maturationist view" (Sunal, 1982, p. 6). Sunal concludes:

> Science and mathematics education for the young child cannot have one philosophical basis if it is to be effectively implemented into existing early childhood programs. Three sets of program goals and objectives need to be developed to fit in with current early childhood philosophies. In order to accomplish this, science and mathematics educators must become familiar with the philosophies influencing early childhood

1. Note the interest(s) of the children and provide opportunity where they can solidify their ideas or learn more about the topics. What and how much do they know about things that interest them? At what cognitive level are they functioning?

2. Provide concrete, hands-on experiences as often as possible. A little imagination can make this very appealing to children. Use referents such as objects, pictures, and replicas to provide realism and value.

3. Plan activities and provide materials that:

   a. appeal to both boys and girls, encouraging a non-sexist attitude toward science and other learning

   b. include variety in use and for enjoyment

   c. appeal to each sense—some learners use one sense more than another

   d. are versatile in the amount of time and space needed, and to solitary and cooperative play

   e. help children understand their immediate world and people

4. Be patient when presenting ideas. Anticipate and handle questions and problems with ease.

5. Be near enough to observe but not too close to intrude.

6. Use appropriate words, terms, questions, and responses to enrich the experience for the children.

7. If children don't ask questions or show interest in their environment, find ways to stimulate their play. Help them to use their minds.

8. Allow time for contemplation, evaluation, and sequential planning. One exposure to a topic or material will not help the child develop secure concepts.

9. Consider and implement ways to assist children to replace misconceptions with accurate information.

education and with some of the model programs which reflect these philosophies. (p. 7)

This text is based on the developmental, or hands-on, method involving discovery learning; however, it is possible to see parts of other theories as they support this method. Strong perceptual props such as material to be handled, replicas, pictures, and real objects help the child build concepts through conceptual experiences. Also, when activities encourage cooperation and interaction, the children gain from the experiences by asking questions, making suggestions, trying ideas, listening, and watching others.

SUMMARY

The question of pushing learning experiences on young children is a current and serious one. Whether young children can learn more or faster than they do is debatable. Perhaps a more important question to ask is whether they are interested in what they are doing and whether they are enjoying it. "Piaget believes that involving students in rich experiences at their level of development provides a firm foundation for later stages of cognitive growth. The quality of experiences at each level is more important than quantity," write Carin and Sund (1985, p. 36). Teachers should consider their major task as designing activities so their pupils can perform mental operations comparable to their abilities. (Review the Planning Essentials box on p. 23) When teachers do this, they make the "difference between teaching as a professional and as a technician" (Carin and Sund, 1985, p. 36).

EXERCISES
study/discussion questions

1. Study Piaget's four stages of cognitive development, focusing mainly on the Preoperational Stage, but becoming familiar with the stages that precede and follow this stage in order to recognize characteristic development through the child's life cycle.

2. Observe a two- or three-year-old child for a twenty minute period. Make notes of the language used, if any, or how the child interacts with others. Observe a four- or five-year-old for a twenty minute period. Make notes of the language used and how the child interacts with others. Compare the language of the younger child to the older child in terms of length of sentences (responses), frequency of verbalization, and purposes of verbalization.

3. Select a child between the ages of two and five. Provide a developmentally appropriate toy or activity (preferably one that is unfamiliar to the child). Without pressuring or bombarding the child with questions, casually interact with (or watch) the child as she explores the object. From the child's comments or actions, does it appear to you that the child is actually "constructing" her own knowledge about the object? Record your interpretation of the experience.

4. How are the theories of Piaget, Bruner, and Gagné alike and different?

5. Describe direct instruction (or psychometric) learning. Design an activity and tell how it would appear in both direct instruction and developmental learning. When is direct instruction effective?

6. Make a point to identify and research several teaching theories in early childhood education.

Thinking

Early thinking about intelligence, later found to be incorrect, was that an individual possessed a finite capacity for intelligence at birth, determined by genetic inheritance. Brain cells continued in gradual, predictable growth only until about age eighteen, maintained that pattern through adulthood, and then began gradual deterioration that resulted in senility.

In fact, intellectual development in young children is vital. It is the belief of Bloom (1964), White (1975), and others that the most crucial period of intellectual development is from birth to age three. Epstein (1978) acknowledges the importance of early intellectual development, but points out that growth spurts occur at approximately two-year intervals through at least age eighteen.

The reader is referred to the general characteristics of children (Appendix A), especially to those changes in the quality and quantity of intelligence between the ages of two and six.

BRAIN FUNCTIONS

In recent years, focus has been on left and right brain hemispheres and their roles in development and learning. It is believed that most individuals have a dominant style of learning. For this reason, teachers and parents need to present information to young children in different ways, since some will be visual learners, some audio, and some kinesthetic. **Visual learners** need to see the information in print, or watch a demonstration. **Audio learners** want to hear or be told the information. **Kinesthetic learners** comprehend through hands-on or manipulation experiences.

Springer and Deutsch (1985, p. 237) have identified the characteristics of the two brain hemispheres as follows:

Left Hemisphere
Verbal
Sequential, temporal, digital
Logical, analytic
Rational
Western thought

Right Hemisphere
Nonverbal, visual-spatial
Simultaneous, spatial, analogical
Gestalt, synthetic
Intuitive
Eastern thought

Some child development and early childhood education writers have interpreted these characteristics for use with young children (see the table on pages 28–29).

Memory and Thinking
Bruner discusses that memory, the retrieval of information, is a process of problem-solving and that attitudes and activities can help make material more readily accessible. Bruner suggests that material has the best chance

of retrieval when it is organized in terms of one's own interests and cognitive structures (1961, p. 32).

Eliason and Jenkins propose three main processes by which young children acquire knowledge and thinking skills: "(1) experiences and cognition, (2) feedback and cognition, and (3) clarifying misconceptions and extending beyond the original concepts. Through these processes, children can acquire process skills such as observing, inferring, reasoning, rationalizing, questioning, exploring, classifying, and communicating" (1990, p. 39).

Other authors offer opinions about thinking and the importance of providing appropriate learning experiences for young children. For example, Fowler states, "The mind is formed by the

FUNCTIONS OF THE BRAIN _____

RIGHT

Theorist	Ideas
Galin	"Very good at perceiving and expressing novel and complex visual, spatial, and musical patterns. The right hemisphere is said to function in a *holistic mode.*" (1979, p. 18)
Herman	Tolerates a lack of closure and ambiguity, desires lots of space, sees the whole problem or situation, appreciates an artistic and aesthetic focus, and enjoys spontaneity. (1981)
Clark	"Involvement with the creation of art, music, the concepts of mathematics, synthesizing, and a more coherent perceptual style. The right brain seems better at passive comprehension." (1986, p. 149)
Harlan	"Tends to multiply similar ideas and mix images, experiences, emotions, and other mental operations in a way that encourages invention. The right brain can take in whole masses of detail at once as images, then recombine the content and create new ideas." (1988, p. 6)
Hildebrand	"Controls the left side of your body." "Is the center for holistic and creative thinking." Gives "support to educators who have long advocated lots of hands-on activities and the use of art materials as vital to children's learning. Hands-on activities, pictorial, and three-dimensional figures . . . are processed in the right side of the brain. Such right-brain activities can also aid in the learning of *digital* information such as numbers, letters, and words which are left-brain activities." (1991, p. 296 and 195)
Harris and Liebert	"Specializes in non-verbal things such as spatial ability, perceptions of patterns and melodies, and the expression and recognition of emotions." (1991, p. 273)

LEFT

Theorist	Ideas
Galin	A cognitive style that is verbal-analytic. (1976, p. 18)
Herman	Preference for written directions, structured places, organized tasks, lists that can be crossed off as tasks are completed, successful results, control, and closure. (1981)
Clark	"Is most responsible for linear, sequential, analytic, rational thinking" and "seems better at active articulation." "Reading, language, the computational aspects of mathematics, the inquirer, and the critic." (1986, p. 149)

effects of environmental stimulation on the brain, working through the sensory and motor systems" (1980, p. 7).

Osborn and Osborn, contending that children's concepts are based on their experiences, write, "Activity is a vital part of cognitive development. . . . When one becomes mentally and motorically involved, learning and understanding are increased. . . . For young children the most effective learning settings require activity and concrete experience" (1983, p. 15). Osborn and Osborn add that it is not effective to *tell* children about a concept; rather, they must have an opportunity to verify for themselves through active manipulation and sensory experiences.

Wadsworth writes, "Possibly the most important and most revolutionary

Theorist	Ideas
Harlan	"Specializes in processing verbal, step-by-step, symbolic thought such as that involved in reading, mathematics, and other logical, analytical tasks." "The productive planning details depend upon the left brain." (1988, p. 6 and 7)
Hildebrand	"Controls the motor functions of the right side of your body." Functions in an "*analytic, logical mode,* for which words are an excellent tool." "Controls both language and analytical thinking." "Caution must be taken that the left brain is not the only hemisphere stimulated in the new computer age." (1991, p. 18, 296 and 195)
Harris and Liebert	"Specializes in producing and understanding speech and in reading and writing." (1991, p. 273)

BOTH HEMISPHERES

Theorist	Ideas
Clark	"Each function is intricately interdependent on each other function; any methodology that focuses only a part of the brain process on the learning task is inefficient at best and, at worst, wasteful of human talent and ability. The vast resources of the brain/mind complex are best developed when opportunities are made available for that interdependence." (1986)
Galin	"Healthy people use both sides." "If we want to cultivate creativity, it appears that we must first develop each mode, both the rational-analytic and intuitive-holistic; second we must develop the ability to inhibit either one when it is inappropriate to the task at hand; and finally we must be able to operate in both modes in a complementary fashion." (1976, p. 18)
Harlan	"Two systems of processing information do not function in isolation . . . multiple neural connections between brain halves make it possible for the two processing styles to evaluate and integrate information simultaneously. Putting creative thinking to use is an example of integrating right- and left-brain functions." "Learning experiences that allow the process of the two brain hemispheres to complement each other enhance the learning potential." (1988, p. 7)
Levy	"Two hemispheres do not function independently . . . each hemisphere contributes its special capacities to all cognitive activities." (1985, p. 44)

implication of Piaget's theory is that children construct knowledge from their actions on the environment'' (1984, p. 186).

And Wellman states, ''Children's stimulation for concept development would be limited to their own personal experiences unless they can talk with others about their experiences'' (1982, p. 131). Concepts can be introduced to children and materials can be provided for children to examine, but unless there is conversation or interaction, how can a teacher assume that the concept was clearly delivered and correctly received?

> Example: A kindergarten teacher was teaching the letter *n* to the children. Focusing on the letter, she made a paper nest, placed it on the board, and cut out pictures that started with the letter *n*. The object was to place the *n* pictures into the *n*est. Several situations may occur:
>
> 1. The children will be able to correctly identify the pictures and place them in the nest.
>
> 2. All the pictures started with *n* and the children do not have an opportunity to discriminate between *n* and non-*n* pictures.
>
> 3. The children may not perceive the identification of the pictures as the teacher does. For example, when a picture of a nurse is shown, a child may disagree that it goes into the nest. There could be two problems:
>
>   **a.** The child knows that birds have nests but that a nurse is too large for a nest.
>
>   **b.** The child may be thinking of the nurse as a ''lady,'' a ''mommy,'' or

some other term related to prior experiences. Without probing or giving the child an opportunity to explain, the teacher can call the child ''wrong'' and his confidence is diminished, or the child can question the teacher's thinking—often non-verbally.

Discussion would give the teacher and the child an opportunity to clarify their ideas.

Children often misunderstand pictures, words, and ideas. Unlearning and relearning is difficult for children, just as it is for adults. Those who learn a concept or skill one way find the transition to learning a new way difficult, and often pause to consider which is the correct response—the old one or the new one? Misconceptions can last a lifetime. As Eliason and Jenkins state, ''The assimilation of incorrect information makes it difficult for the child to develop congruity in the world'' (1990, p. 43). How often have stories (in books or on the flannelboard) been interrupted by children questioning the proportions, sizes, personifications, or even content? (''Look! that chicken is bigger than the farmer.'' ''The mouse is the same size as the elephant!'' ''Do animals *really* wear clothes and go shopping?'')

True concepts need to be constructed by these young, pliable minds during planned activities and those wonderful spontaneous, teachable moments, ''when a child's curiosity and initial interest in a subject provide fertile ground for the planting and nurturing of clear understandings. One must be alert to the ever-questioning and investigating young mind, and be prepared to assist the child in furthering

An adult can encourage cooperation among children.

knowledge and comprehension of the surrounding world" (Eliason & Jenkins, 1990, p. 44).

In an earlier writing, Gilbert (1971) identified the amount of learning perceived through the senses as:

From sight	83 percent
From sound	11 percent
From smell	3.5 percent
From touch	1.5 percent
From taste	1 percent

Because sight is a strong sense perceptor, if the child's eyesight is deficient, learning could be reduced. Demonstrating and describing simultaneously would be an excellent way to deliver information. Montessori reminds us that the combination of senses makes the learning more meaningful for young children.

Example: Some students were asked to explain how the use of the senses could enhance language arts. One student said, "I just can't think of a way to include smell or taste." Agreeing with the first student, a second student said, "I can't think of a way, either." "You can read about how things smell or taste, but you can't actually experience them," they both insisted. An exploratory discussion followed which revealed the limited way they were interpreting "language arts." Language arts was broadly defined as reading of symbols (print and visuals), reading to others, listening to information, writing information, and a combination of ways people communicate. As the students dealt with the broader definition, they talked about written descriptions of all senses (the "odor" of this, the "sight" of that, the memories and experiences they had in both good and bad situations) and soon realized that even though they may not experience tasting and smelling directly, their abilities to abstract and recall did enhance all their senses.

Abruscato (1988, p. 15–19) suggests specific goals of science education which include the different domains:

cognitive: knowledge, comprehension, application, analysis, synthesis, evaluation

affective: positive attitude toward science, schooling, and development of appropriate relationships with others and the natural world

psychomotor: ability to operate their bodies in such a way that they can manipulate their environment—gross and fine motor abilities

In their writing, Benham, Hosticka, Payne, and Yeotis agree that early childhood learners are in the preoperational stage identified by Piaget. These children need to learn by making mistakes, seeing the consequences of these mistakes, and revising their views and theories of the world to include the new information gleaned from mistakes. In order to facilitate this learning process, the teacher needs to provide an interactive environment for children and help them focus on what they see and do. This environment must be constructed with care so that erroneous authoritarian views and theories are not formed through inadequate feedback. The teacher should help focus, not dictate, the learner's attempt to give structure to what is observed. "This view suggests that what is formally presented to the learners must be within the realm of their ability to understand, and not just for the exhibition of a non-meaningful behavior. Teaching at this level should aim at the exposure to content, not to its mastery" (Benham, Hosticka, Payne, and Yeotis, 1982, p. 55).

Gelman (1979) is concerned that demonstrations of cognitive abilities by young children may be interpreted to mean preschoolers are miniature adults where their cognition is concerned. Gelman cautions, "This is not what I want people to conclude, and should they so conclude it would not be in the best interests of either those who study cognitive development or the child. . . . My message is quite straightforward. We should study preschoolers in their own right and give up treating them as foils against which to describe the accomplishments of middle childhood" (p. 904). Progress in brain mapping points to implications for parents and teachers of young children. An important implication is the variety of cognitive styles or individuality in young children. Hildebrand states: "The challenge is to stimulate both hemispheres of each child's brain and help each child use the style appropriate for each new situation" (1991, p. 230).

SUMMARY

What do brain functions, memory, and thinking have to do with teaching science to young children?

1. Most children have a dominant cognitive style of learning, so teachers and parents should plan to present science experiences using different methods to enhance the visual, auditory, or kinesthetic learning of each child.

2. The right hemisphere of the brain functions in a holistic mode; appreciates an artistic, musical, and aesthetic focus; enjoys spontaneity; seems better at passive comprehension; encourages invention; and aids in learning digital information (left-brain activities).

3. The left hemisphere of the brain specializes in verbal, symbolic thought; controls language and analytical thinking; prefers written directions and lists that can be crossed off; and seems better at active articulation.

4. For optimum growth, all areas of development must be exercised. This means independent use of each hemisphere when appropriate, and the interaction between both hemispheres.

5. Teachers and parents who plan science and other curriculum for young children should make sure to provide a variety of activities for the development of the total child. Aesthetic and social activities are as important as cognitive and physical ones.

EXERCISES
study/discussion questions

1. How do early theories differ from current ones on the development and importance of the brain?

2. Some individuals do not give much credence to the brain theories. However, for this exercise, assume they are true. Describe the functions of both the left hemisphere and the right hemisphere of the brain.

3. Formulate a one-day plan, noting which activities stimulate the right hemisphere and which stimulate the left hemisphere of the brain. Explain how both hemispheres support each other and why it is important to include both hemispheres when planning activities for young children.

4. Referring to the table ''Functions of the Brain'' in this chapter (and other resources), try to identify if you are a right- or left-brain learner. What differences does this knowledge make regarding your own personal learning?

5. Design an activity for young children in your classroom where the five senses are involved. If possible, present the activity to the children and note which senses are most used.

6. Checking additional sources, define *visual*, *auditory*, and *kinesthetic* learning. Give examples of each and how they could be used in a classroom to ensure that all children have an opportunity to learn through their best mode.

4

Safety

Whether or not a teacher is intending an activity to be "science," accidents do happen. Teachers should know proper procedures to ensure children's safety and to handle accidents and injuries calmly. How an adult acts in an emergency will have great impact on how a child acts. It is therefore necessary to call special attention to safety in science as well as in all classroom activities.

SAFETY FACTORS

Key safety factors that should be established very early when using science in the classroom with young children include:

- What to do in case of an accident, injury, or emergency.

- Who establishes and enforces the rules?

- What kinds of materials and activities can be used?

- Are there special precautions to take?

- Who initiates, sets up, uses, and stores the materials and activities?

- What is the role of the teacher?

- How can the child prevent accidents or ensure safety?

- Are conditions different for indoor or outdoor activities?

Of course, the safety and health of the children is vital in any area of the curriculum; however, when science activities are planned, extra precautions should be taken.

Prevention

The best way to teach young children about science is by having them participate. Because children may be impulsive, enthusiastic, and present-oriented, they may overlook possible problems. This means that the teacher must plan science activities with safety in mind. This may be done through discussion, demonstration, role playing, or supposition.

Example: Suppose the science activity includes the use of kitchen appliances. Many children may not have had any prior experience with such appliances and may not know what to anticipate. The teacher will begin with common appliances, and limit the number used—perhaps a toaster, a popcorn popper, and an electric can opener. These particular appliances are selected because of their differences and similarities: two have cords and heat; one has food placed inside; one has openness and interaction of food with heat; one has a cutting ability; and all are used in food preparation. What safety factors could be involved?

1. Cords can be tripped over. Cords may be frayed. Plugs may cause shocks.

Good environments promote safety and participation.

2. Heat can always be hazardous because it may not give the appearance of being hot.

3. Bread being toasted is not visible. When toast gets caught and fails to pop up, it must be removed.

4. Children are anxious to eat the product (toasted or popped) and may burn their fingers or mouths.

5. Sharp edges cut easily.

To practice safety, the teacher and children could examine the various aspects of the appliances (cord, plug, temperature, removing the products safely, watching for sharp edges, and so on). The teacher makes sure the ideas are simple and clear. Still, accidents can happen.

If children have a positive experience with science, they will be willing to join opportunities, look at science as a fun and rewarding experience, and develop self-confidence.

There are certain activities or situations which are never allowed in a classroom of young children (check your school policies, use your best judgment, and practice safety at all times). Fire of any kind (even birthday candles), sharp objects, long objects (children don't realize their length or power), broken or loose toys, and other items can cause accidents and injuries—even with good supervision.

Children should have many opportunities to practice and talk about safety in the classroom. In this way they will feel more secure in attempting different experiences without fear of failure and harm.

Handling Injuries
Important phone numbers and common procedures should be posted in a conspicuous place in each classroom. This helps the teacher respond quickly.

Even with the best laid plans, accidents can happen and injuries can occur. Teachers and other adults who interact with children should be trained in proper first-aid procedures. Some injuries can be easily handled within the classroom; however, if more serious injuries occur, the teacher must know what to do and whom to call. Proper attention to injuries can reduce further problems. The teacher should first take care of the child's immediate needs and then respond according to the severity of the injury (call for emergency help, calm the child, or whatever else is necessary). The teacher needs to make sure that the parent(s) and school officials are properly notified and that a full report is written and filed.

Serious injuries must receive proper treatment by a qualified person.

Emergency Situations
Besides accidents and injuries, other emergency situations may arise. Children should be instructed calmly about what to do and where to go in case of fire, earthquake, flood, electrical outages, and so on. Children can be prepared for these emergency situations by practicing how they should behave if and when an emergency should arise, but they should not be unduly worried. Even emergencies can be good science experiences if the children have been properly prepared and if teachers act in a reassuring manner. The ages of the children and the physical layout of the classroom, building, and surrounding areas will determine how much and what is taught to the children.

Teach for understanding and not from fear.

Rules
Too often, adults set rules, and if the children can repeat them, the adults assume that the children understand them. Before there is danger or a problem, the teacher should talk with the children about some possible guidelines or precautions. When children understand the rationale, they are more apt to follow instructions (and remember them) than if the rules are automatically and emphatically placed upon them. Talk with the children about the use of a knife before they make sandwiches, talk about awareness of situations (cords, heat, overcrowding, and so on) before the activity begins, and talk about finalizing an activity (putting things away, storage, and future availability). Make the children a part of the whole activity—preparation, use, and clean-up. Each segment of the activity teaches useful science concepts.

Children can help determine the rules of play, such as how many children should play in an area (if toys and space are limited), what to do when a child misbehaves, or safe places for toys. For the most part, teachers and children can work together for acceptable behavior during activities.

Rules for safety and fairness should be discussed and expected, so the children have many opportunities to explore and experiment.

Harmful Substances

Under no circumstances should harmful substances be within reach of young children or be used in scientific activities. Some household or cleaning substances can be very harmful to children if ingested. These should be kept in a locked cupboard outside the room where the children usually participate.

Young children quickly put objects and hands into their mouths. Gastrointestinal problems or poisoning can be avoided by keeping *all* harmful substances away from the children. Also, art supplies and toys should be checked to make sure they are free of lead or other contaminants.

If an experiment calls for any harmful substance, another experiment should be selected. Young children like to touch, taste, smell, and look. A teacher should never take chances.

Most regulations related to conditions for young children forbid fire of any kind—fireplaces, matches, burning candles, science experiences, and fireworks. Violation of this regulation can cause serious and lasting negative effects for both students and the teacher.

Supervision

Adults can be good models in helping children practice safety measures. With certain toys and activities planned for the children, the placement of curriculum areas, the tone of voice, and reactions to children's behavior, adults can establish a warm and friendly atmosphere for children to grow and develop.

Some activities will require continuous and alert supervision—woodworking or food preparation, for example. These activities need not be excluded from the repertoire of young children just because some sharp tools or objects are used. The secret of success here is *supervision*. Talk with the children about the use and handling of the tools, how many children can participate at one time, what to do while one is waiting for a turn, and what to do with a finished product.

The teacher sets the stage through demonstration and instruction, but stays nearby to help the children put the skills and ideas into action.

Even in non-dangerous activities, the teacher should be close by to avoid problems, reassure children, and assist verbally or physically *if necessary*.

In unfamiliar activities or when children get highly stimulated, the teacher may need to reiterate safety rules for some of the children. Sometimes teachers can eliminate problems by demonstrating some parts of the activity or giving some directions *before* the children begin; however, there should be many times when the children are free to explore the media—within reasonable limits.

It is up to the teachers to see that work spaces and play areas are free from overcrowding, overstimulation, or clutter so that the children are safe to play and work. Areas or activities can be limited by children posting their name cards at certain places, by the number of chairs that surround an activity, by the number of props available, or other methods. Children unable to play in an area should be redirected until there is room for them. The overabundance of children at an activity can limit experience and learning, and sometimes cause accidents.

Responsibility of Children

Children need many opportunities to practice the concepts that we seek to teach them. And children are immature in skills and behavior.

Behavior itself is a scientific concept! Teachers should **interact** with the children when appropriate. The teachers are there to help the children participate within safe guidelines—not to boss or direct their play. Whenever possible, the children police their own behavior but they know that when situations get out of hand (when they are hurting themselves, someone else, or destroying property), the teacher will help them bring any inappropriate behavior into safe limits.

When teachers plan and provide for activities that are within the developmental abilities of the children in the classroom, the children can turn these activities into meaningful experiences for themselves. A good science experience is learning how to use materials and how to interact with other children. Therefore, most activities should be child-initiated, but teacher-supported and observed.

Children sometimes have sudden outbursts of emotion. Teachers who know the children well know what situations cause some children to become emotional, aggressive, or withdrawn. The teacher will watch and guide the child in acceptable ways of behaving so the child and others will enjoy being together.

Good Work Habits

During science activities, a good opportunity is provided to help the children develop good work habits—in how they proceed, in what they undertake, and in how they conclude the activity. Feeling good about the experience will help the children feel more secure in their world, in people, and in happenings.

Children who come to a science opportunity where the adult has already done all the preparation and then quickly does a demonstration will only see one segment of the activity, and will miss its planning, preparation, outcome, and termination. These children will miss the important parts of anticipating, participating, enjoying, and learning. They will fail to internalize the process of carrying an activity to completion; they need to help in the total cycle of the activity.

When children experience the whole cycle, they are able to reproduce enough of the steps to make the activity possible in other instances or settings. Children generally want to do things by themselves, and when a good model is provided there is a better opportunity for the children to grow in independence and integrated learning.

Wearing Apparel

Young children and science are inseparable. Where children are, science happens. Unlike lab coats in chemistry or food labs, or goggles and gloves where particles or harmful substances may be present, young children generally wear their regular clothing or put on a cover-up for messy or wet experiments. These covers should be attractive, easily put on and taken off by the children, and hung in a convenient area. They should protect the child during certain play activities. Restrictive, loose, or improper clothing may add danger to movement, interaction, or learning.

Cleanliness

Cleanliness is an important part of science for young children. They enjoy messy activities and the independence of washing and caring for their bodily needs. Children's senses are easily stimulated, and the cleansing process is fascinating to them. At this time in their lives it can be easy to teach them about cleanliness and their responses can help them appreciate being clean.

Teaching cleanliness to young children should be fun and rewarding. They do not need or appreciate long lectures, but can understand basic reasons for keeping their bodies clean—especially when they get to practice on their own.

Rather than making daily demands upon the children, help them to take the responsibility to brush their teeth, wash their hands and faces, take care of toileting needs, and establish some good life-long habits.

Outside the Classroom

While many science experiences are conducted within the classroom, science should be extended to field trips or outdoor activities when appropriate. Special precautions must be taken at these times to prevent or minimize problems or injuries.

On the playground at school or at home, attention needs to be given to types of landscaping, avoiding those that may be harmful (with thorns or poisonous plants, for example). Equipment must be sturdy and in good repair at all times.

SUMMARY

Safety must be practiced at *all* times—in science and other activities, indoors and outdoors, in small and large clusters of children, in every season and setting.

EXERCISES
study/discussion questions

1. Find out what the safety policies are in a school and within the classroom. Who determines the policies? How are they enforced?

2. Make a list of emergency phone numbers, procedures to follow, rules for reporting injuries, and follow-up necessary when injuries and accidents happen in your school or classroom.

3. Take a class (or update) on first-aid procedures, especially CPR.

4. Suppose you are one of three teachers assigned to supervise the playground. The children are clustered in the sand area, on the swings, near the jungle gym, and at the woodworking table. The areas are separated by a distance that would allow a teacher to supervise only one of the activities at a time. Note what hazards are related to each area mentioned. How do you decide where to locate yourself to encourage the play of the children, yet prevent any accidents? Would one or more of these activities need to be postponed? Why?

5. What do you do when a child:
   a. starts choking
   b. gets sand in her eyes
   c. gets a slight cut or sliver
   d. gets bumped—no open skin or bleeding

    e. has his feelings hurt

    f. falls from climbing equipment

6. Evaluate your own feelings about handling emergency situations. How can you better prepare yourself to handle accidents or injuries?

7. Be prepared to step into and resolve a situation where children are:

    a. hurting themselves

    b. hurting someone else

    c. destroying property

How Children Learn

5

Science, Development, and Environment

DEVELOPMENT

For a thorough review of the developmental characteristics of children ages two through five, the reader is referred to Appendix A and is encouraged to spend time with the charts there.

As a quick overview and refresher, a summary of Piaget's stages of mental development is provided here for the preoperational period. Piaget's span is ages two through seven; the focus of this book, and emphasis here, will be an age span of two through five years.

The children:

1. vary in their language use and skills (the younger the child, the less verbal)

2. have immature physical, mental, and social skills

3. remember few instructions at a time

4. need to manipulate materials; perception is important

5. take longer to do things than older children

6. may be easily frustrated

7. often want what someone else has

8. learn by trial and error

9. have difficulty recognizing cause and effect

10. may be impulsive

11. need time to organize, reflect, and absorb

12. may brag about their products or accomplishments

13. may attempt things but not persist or reach adult expectations, such as finalizing a project

14. use actions more than words to solve problems

15. are **egocentric,** seeing things from an internal view only

16. are **static thinkers**—they focus on only one attribute at a time, such as color, size, or shape, but not combinations

17. think more in the present, but can deal somewhat with future and past

18. can follow some processes or sequences, but have difficulty with **reversibility,** such as returning clay shapes to previous conditions

19. have not developed the ability to think logically or abstractly, or through a series of operations

While children between the ages of two and five show some definite differences in their social-emotional, intellectual, and physical development, there are some commonalities that teachers can use as guides in planning science experiences for these children.

DEVELOPMENT AND SCIENCE _____

GENERAL CHARACTERISTICS OF YOUNG CHILDREN

ADULT INFLUENCES TOWARD SCIENCE

Attention Span
Most young children have a limited attention span, because of their lack of experiences, their limited vocabulary, and their egocentrism.

Begin with familiar objects and activities, then branch out by adding more objects or integrating the curriculum as development occurs. Include free play, unstructured opportunities, and many sensory experiences to increase the amount of time children willingly spend in activities. Help them manipulate their environment and make discoveries about it. Alternate activities to avoid boredom and restlessness. Activities should be play-oriented rather than work-oriented. Encourage, rather than discourage, curiosity through interesting activities and opportunities for communication and participation.

Thinking
Most young children cannot deal with abstract ideas; they are here-and-now people. They frequently misconstrue concepts and develop misunderstandings.

Give many hands-on experiences to the children. Avoid things that seem "magical." Give the children plenty of time (and repeated opportunities) to work with the same concepts. Build upon concepts applicable to the present stage of the children. Teaching needs to be concrete, simple, and basic. Give the children opportunities to pretend, dramatize, and be exposed to truths and reality but help them understand when they are pretending. Give them opportunities to explore, investigate, manipulate, make discoveries, and talk about their environment. Provide structure (guidelines) and security by scheduling and sequencing activities. Introduce change only after establishing basic patterns. Provide opportunities for the children to be involved in thinking situations such as brainstorming, drawing conclusions, making and following through on decisions.

Interest
Most young children are curious and inquisitive. Their interests are mainly limited to their immediate surroundings and important people in their lives.

Pay careful attention to the interests and conversations of the children. Provide experiences to support their current interests, but plan to build upon these ideas as the children show readiness. Plan to add new interests to the curriculum on a sequential basis. Provide many opportunities for participation.

Language
Most young children are somewhat nonverbal, carry

Have frequent and casual conversations with the children. Talk about their interests, but

GENERAL CHARACTERISTICS OF YOUNG CHILDREN

on monologues, and misuse grammar. However, they love to talk and to listen to stories. Vocabulary and sentence structure are developing very rapidly. They often talk as they act, and act out their thoughts.

Self

Most young children are striving for independence but lack personal skills. They become frustrated and sometimes strike out verbally or physically. They have difficulty sharing objects and people. They are egocentric and often clumsy.

Interaction

Most young children play by themselves, then beside a child or children, and then with others. This pattern is characteristic and developmental. The younger the child, the more he wants and needs the security of an adult nearby.

ADULT INFLUENCES TOWARD SCIENCE

introduce other things which stimulate their use of language. For example, introduce familiar animals, giving the children an opportunity to manipulate them in different situations (through books, music, movement, play, and visuals). Never talk down to the children or use baby talk. Introduce appropriate new words and give the children many opportunities to practice their meanings through language and hands-on experiences. Give the children something exciting to talk about, to question, and to experience. Give time, provide patience, and be quality language models for children to perfect their grammar and articulation. Give opportunities to follow verbal directions.

Be friendly, cooperative, supportive, and loving. Encourage the children to do things for themselves. Give honest praise and encouragement for attempts and accomplishments. Help the children to see other's points of view through definitions of situations, through modeling, through cooperation, and through means other than aggression or physical attack. Show the children that *sharing* does not mean giving up permanently. Anticipate frustration, mood swings, and behavior changes, but don't dwell on them. Make sure facilities for active physical experiences and quiet areas are readily available to challenge each child at his level. Give plenty of time for activities and interaction. Provide materials and tools for practice with hand-eye coordination.

The children need patience, sensitivity, and kindness, but also firmness. Assist the children to have a positive experience by being good-natured and not letting things get too serious. Redirect children when they are having problems with activities or each other. Provide games with simple rules and help the children understand the purpose of the rules. Encourage the children to give directions to others, when appropriate. Provide opportunities for cooperative interaction.

All young children have universal needs for love and recognition in various forms. They also need teachers who are well prepared. Unfortunately, since the 1960s, children have experienced different kinds of "abuse," according to Elkind (1987a, 1987b). He reports that, "We have been teaching too much, too fast, too soon—and with frightening results." He feels there is a correlation between teaching skills earlier and earlier and the stresses and failures felt by school age children. Curriculum has been pushed to lower grades, where children are unprepared, resulting in academic failure or burnout of children in elementary schools. The typical curriculum for kindergarten children (dramatic play, blocks, art activities, and so on) has been replaced by "workbooks, rote memorization, and high-pressure academics" (Seefeldt, 1985, p. 13). Added to that are computers and other advanced academic materials. Through changes in early curriculum, "We are causing young children to experience all the lowered self-esteem, loss of friends, parental concern, and damaged motivation that comes from school failure" (Connell, 1987, pp. 38–39). Through inappropriate curriculum, interest is lost in learning, stress is unmanageable, relationships are not valued, and children do not develop good thinking skills.

Young children have a natural learning style, different from older children and adults. Curiosity mixed with a zeal for making sense of their environment facilitates spontaneous and self-directed learning. Adults must not try to substitute their own conceptions for those which the learning preschoolers can freely and happily express for themselves.

Young children are going through learning stages. Most important for their current development are opportunities for emotional and social growth—cognitive growth will come later. The development of language during the early years is dramatic. Children move from using single words for items and experiences to the mastery of the "major semantic and syntactic distinctions in their native tongue" (Case, 1985, p. 167).

Using a **developmentally appropriate curriculum,** young children should naturally be attracted to science concepts and activities. The opposite approach, **psychometric curriculum,** based on memorizing concepts, all working together at the same time and pace, and conforming to expectations to produce an acceptable product, often leads young children to become disinterested, discouraged, or frustrated.

Although she writes of teaching science for elementary schools, Wolfinger's concepts are sound for younger children as well. These include:

- **open-ended activities** The child can conclude an activity at will without prodding or judging by the adult.

- **autonomy** The child makes choices of activities and knows where to obtain and replace materials.

- **method** The use of manipulative and sensory materials and involvement of large and small muscles is encouraged.

- **questions** The teacher acts as a guide and encourages investigation.

- **atmosphere** Success is possible and frequent.

- **correlation** Science is integrated into the total activity of the day.

Wolfinger concludes. ''Rather than attempting to compartmentalize science into a distinct aspect of the day for young children, the teacher should use ordinary activities as a means for developing science-related topics'' (1984, pp. 15–17).

Victor looks at the science program for elementary schools by identifying the characteristics of school-age children as egocentric, constantly interpreting the environment, curious, loving to investigate, energetic, persistent, sociable, and needing recognition (1985, pp. 34–36). While these characteristics are similar to those of younger children (review the chart on pages 46–47) elementary school children handle science concepts on a more advanced level than do the younger children. But it is interesting to note that the named characteristics are interwoven into the lives of successful people—at any age.

Science is all around us. It consumes our interest and is an integral part of our lives. Teachers and parents of young children should be constantly aware of its daily influence and make special attempts to help young children understand and appreciate it.

ENVIRONMENT

Young children need to feel secure in their environment. Teachers, curriculum, equipment, toys, and the physical setting must convey a warm, loving atmosphere. The routines should be fairly constant, but flexibility of the program should also be an option. The teacher should plan the program and activities so that concepts and experiences create opportunities for children to learn, explore language, build relationships, and develop good work patterns.

Meeting the Needs of Children

Teachers can create an environment where children enjoy themselves, participate freely, and explore materials and other individuals. Children can learn when teachers carefully observe activities, encourage problem solving, and provide opportunities for interactive communication. Teachers do this by varying the types of questions they ask, by providing appropriate materials and activities, by enlisting the children's participation, by encouraging children to listen and speak to each other, and by allowing plenty of time. The teacher plans for children to get ideas from each other and to express themselves freely.

Often, the physical environment receives more attention than particular needs of the children. And while preparation of the environment is important for the children's learning, the total focus must include the needs of children. Teachers should consider whether the children are overwhelmed by the overabundance (or lack) of activities, materials, choices, pressures, clutter, or time restraints. The environment must be meaningful to the learner.

Classroom Management

There should be enough structure in the classroom so the children have guidelines for participation while enjoying variety, alternatives, time, and friends.

When the responsibility for classroom control and behavior is shared by teacher and children, there is the dignity and respect needed for effective growth (deCharms, 1984). The locus of control within the classroom can be either the children or the teacher. This does not mean that anything goes, or that there is utter chaos. **Internal control** allows the child freedom of choice; **external control** gives power to the teacher through reward systems or group participation (see chapter 8). Children should know when they are out of bounds and how to get back on the path to group participation.

Physical Setting

Children respond to an environment that is inviting. They like vivid colors, grouped activities, materials that can be used in a variety of ways, space to move around in and explore, and peers to share toys and situations.

The teacher should carefully plan science areas within the classroom to encourage the combination of some activities (blocks with housekeeping, for example) and the exclusion of others (water play near the books, or complex activities near traffic patterns). Too many stimulating toys, small spaces, restricted time, broken or unpopular toys, and lack of toys can create problems for both teachers and children.

A careful plan for the placement of activities will also encourage children to participate. The activity placed closest to the children's traffic pattern will be the first, and probably most, utilized. Therefore, a science table near the room's entrance, with a frequent change of items, will entice the children to stop, look, and participate. The playground is an on-going science laboratory. Too often, children gravitate to toys and activities without noticing

Children enjoy playing together in a designated classroom area.

the many wonders of nature. Teachers can plan activities to involve children in the outdoors—places to dig, interesting landscaping and tools, obstacle courses, and many more activities which promote scientific concepts.

FIELD TRIPS

The teacher who thinks planning a field trip is easier than planning classroom activities has not thought the differences through carefully. Field trips can be wonderful learning experiences for children or they can be disasters!

Field trips are an important part of the learning environment. Depending upon the ages of the children, field trips can be timed so that learning from these trips is assimilated into the children's repertoire. Young children would benefit most from short and infrequent visits. Familiar sites are popular. The teacher's preparation before the trip, the trip's purpose, and how well the children are prepared just prior to the trip will all have an influence on the trip's meaningfulness for the children. Teachers who provide good follow-up activities, such as role playing, books, and hands-on experiences, gain a better understanding of the trip's value for the children. Goals may need to be re-evaluated, concepts retaught, and sites revisited.

Sometimes field trips are prohibitive because of school or center policies, lack of transportation funds, insufficient numbers of chaperons, large numbers of children, time or distance restrictions, unwillingness of hosts, inclement weather, or other specific or general reasons. These reasons should not be used as excuses to omit good science experiences from the curriculum of young children. Most of these problems can be solved.

POLICIES Policies are established for good reasons—some financial, some protective, some general. Check before considering any trips away from the classroom. If there is a firm policy of *no* outside trips, consider what guests or experiences could be brought to the classroom. If some trips are approved, determine which ones would meet the needs of the youngsters. If there is a limit on the number of trips taken during a period of time, carefully plan those with the most value for the children involved.

> Example: Could a service vehicle (fire engine, police car, garbage truck, and so on) come to the classroom? Would it be as effective to have a medical person come to the classroom as to visit the hospital, office, or clinic? If field trips meet school policies, which ones would be best to pursue? When field trips are not possible, use the next best resource to teach the desired concepts by using filmstrips, replicas, slides, transparencies, objects, pictures, recordings, videos, visitors, or a combination of other items. Young children learn best from sensory opportunities. Sometimes they are not good audiences even for excellent visuals or demonstrations.

TRANSPORTATION Can the center provide transportation (school bus or licensed vehicle) or are there alternate means of transportation (public carrier, parents, or even walking)? Possibly the best, safest, and least expensive would be vehicles owned and operated by the school. If they are unavailable, what options does the teacher have? Are there substitute experiences that could be brought to the children?

CHAPERONS How many children can an adult safely supervise? Are there any particularly hazardous or potentially dangerous conditions to consider? If additional chaperons are needed, how does the teacher acquire those who are dependable, responsible, and qualified? Is there a cost?

NUMBERS OF CHILDREN Classrooms of children, especially young ones, do not have enough permanent adults to take children on field trips.

> Example: When we take walking trips outside our classrooms with three-, four-, and five-year-olds, we have at least one adult for every four children. We put special name tags on each child that lists our school and phone number. We may assign children to a certain adult with matching color or shape name tags. We also have a dry run, talking with the children about where we will be going, what we will be seeing, and how we are to behave. When we take trips by vehicle (and these are very limited), we have two adults per car—one to concentrate on the driving and a second one in the back seat who supervises *all* children. When we go by public transportation, we have four children per adult and we catch the bus on our property. We have found that campus living gives us plenty of walking trips and we seldom take the children off campus. Other classrooms are not as fortunate: They must arrange for transportation, take walking trips, bring experiences to the classroom, or simulate experiences.

TIME AND DISTANCE Teachers should not only carefully consider the amount of time and distance for a trip, but also which times during the day or year the trips are most safe (avoiding rush traffic, holidays, construction, special events, and other planned and unplanned obstacles), or are of most value to children (when they are refreshed, fed, unrushed, and interested).

UNWILLING HOSTS Unfortunately, field trips can offend hosts, disrupt their production, and cost them money. When these things happen, they are less willing to have a group of young children come for a visit. However, when a host is willing to accept visitors, all courtesy should be shown, such as a previsit by the planning teacher or a thank-you note. Whether children have an on-site visit or a visitor to their classroom, the teacher should plan opportunities for the children to support and clarify the experience through follow-up activities.

INCLEMENT WEATHER Teachers must plan their activities well in advance and may not know what the weather will be like on the scheduled day; therefore, they must have a back-up plan, which could be a supplement related to the field trip or a substitute for it. Even walking trips may need to be rescheduled if inclement weather occurs on a trip day.

CONDITIONS These conditions may appear in expected or unusual ways, and each situation will need to be handled individually. Some common conditions caused by last minute emergencies could include not enough adult supervision, absenteeism of children, lack of parent permission for the children, an unexpected need in the school, bad weather, and so on. It is difficult to predict specific conditions, but some cases might include danger at the site, strikes, or outbreak of disease. This is another situation where a back-up plan would be priceless!

The field trips most enjoyed by children include familiarity or interest (on their developmental level), preparation (what to expect), close proximity, security (friendly teachers and peers), protection (no harmful or frightening experiences, no loud noises), time to absorb, and follow-up experiences to practice what has been seen (or learned).

Becoming more prevalent and popular are museums and exhibits specifically designed for young children. Before taking a group to a public exhibit, the teacher should visit it and decide whether the experience would be a good field trip for the children or whether the experience would be better for the children if their parents took them. (For planning a field trip, see Cohen, 1989; Danilov, 1986; Dunitz, 1985; and McNamee, 1987. For the responsibilities of the teacher, and fur-

ther explanation and examples regarding field trips, see Taylor, 1991.)

Community Resources

Going to a museum may not be available or appropriate for a group of young children. But there are many everyday places that have value, for example, a grocery store, bakery, or gas station. The teacher should look for interesting occupations or professions that could be child-centered, such as a dentist's office, a farm, a fire station, or a barber shop. Often, many residents of the community are employed in similar jobs, such as construction, mining, or manufacturing. Young children could benefit from visiting any of these sites. The object is not "We need to go on a field trip. Where can we go?" but rather, "What field trip would help the children to understand more about their family or community?"

Following are places to consider, remembering the readiness and safety of the children as well as the resources available.

Transportation	Community Services	Suppliers
airport	ambulance	dairy
boat harbor	fire station	dept. store
bus terminal	medical services	grocery/bakery
car wash	police station	factory
RV park	post office	farm
train depot	sanitation dept.	laundry
Housing	**Recreation**	**Nature**
apartment	bowling alley	garden: flower/food
construction	dance studio	lake/dam/river
dormitory	library	nursery: plant/seed
nursing home	pet store	orchard
residence	spa	park
trailer	sports field	woods

Follow-up after a field trip or classroom visit by a resource person is just as important as preparation for the experience. A similar activity could be promoted at school, such as a grocery

store with money, produce, canned goods, clerk and bagger. The classroom could simulate a farm or a fire station. The children could be encouraged to use tools, wood, or blocks in a construction project. Giving the children an opportunity to re-play the experience can help teachers get a better vision of what it meant to the children. Were there any misconceptions to handle? Did the experience enhance or cloud the thinking of the children?

Resource persons should include more than the teacher, the children, and their parents. But in selecting those who will provide information or props, careful planning needs to occur. Scientific concepts need to be identified, and selected resource people should be informed of them along with the interest span and language level of the children, the classroom expectations, and how the experience can benefit the children.

> Example: Suppose the goal is to acquaint the children with sound and vibration. A cellist is invited to share her talents with the children and to provide an example of vibration. The cellist is asked to give simple explanations to the children and to demonstrate the vibrating of the strings. The teacher can help the children relate the experience to their own lives by singing some familiar songs accompanied by the musician rather than expecting the children to sit long periods of time while the visitor demonstrates skills unappreciated by young children.

Fulghum sums up field trips by saying, "When you go out into the world, watch out for traffic, hold hands, and stick together" (1989, p. 7).

SUMMARY

Children of all ages are interested in scientific concepts. Depending upon their ages and skills, young children can participate in and benefit from varied science experiences.

By referring to the table, "Development and Science" on pages 46–47, the teacher can plan meaningful experiences which relate to the children's attention span, thinking, interest, language level, self-awareness, and interaction.

Through inappropriate curriculum, interest is lost in learning, stress is unmanageable, relationships are not valued, and children fail to develop good thinking skills.

Internal control allows the child freedom of choice; external control gives power to the teacher (reward system or group participation).

The physical environment encourages children to participate in science exploration and enjoyment of their world.

Field trips, resource people in the classroom, and simulated experiences help the children become more familiar with their environment.

Careful planning by the teacher—evaluating the resources available, the readiness of the children, and follow-up activities—can ensure meaningful field trips for young children.

EXERCISES
study/discussion questions

1. Compare and contrast the developmental abilities of children of ages two, three, four, and five.

2. Explain the terms **egocentric, reversibility,** and **static thinkers.** Give an example of each term as it applies to young children (see page 45).

3. List differences between "attention span" and "interest span." Is one more important than the other?

4. Explain Elkind's reference to "abuse" of children. How could you help teachers and parents reduce the amount of stress placed upon young children?

5. Give some suggestions for beginning teachers to establish good classroom behavior. Are rules necessary? If so, who decides what they are and how they are enforced?

6. What field trip policies exist in your school or in a school with which you are familiar? How well do you understand the rationale for the policies?

7. Recall any field trips you have taken with young children. What aspects of the trips were successful? What suggestions can you make to ensure success on future trips?

8. Make a list of nearby places you could take children to enlarge their science repertoire. Rank the places according to appropriateness for young children. Plan at least four follow-up activities for the classroom.

9. Make a list of resource people who could be invited into the classroom. Plan at least four follow-up activities for each visitor.

10. Suppose you have been on a field trip or had a resource person in your room. In evaluating the experience, you discover the children have misconceptions and frustrations about what occurred. How would you go about correcting the misconceptions and turning the experience from a frustration to an enjoyment?

11. What tips would you give a person who is going to conduct an on-site trip or be a resource in the classroom? In other words, how could you ensure that the trip would be rewarding to the person as well as the children?

6

Curiosity

Adults who interact with young children need to be constantly aware of ways to enliven the curiosity of children. It should be done with truth and excitement, based on the present environment, and with a positive attitude. This will help young children in their observation, invention, exploration, and discovery of the world and people around them. Children have an innate curiosity to find out, imitate, create, test, handle, belong, and watch.

A curious child will:

1. react positively to new, strange, incongruous, or mysterious elements in the environment by focusing attention on them, moving toward them, manipulating them, and seeking information about them.

2. persist in examining and exploring stimuli in order to know more about them. (Berlyne, 1960; Maw and Maw, 1961)

   Example: One day Val entered the preschool, walked up to the teacher and stated, "Today I am going to make light blue paint!" The teacher replied, "I'd really like to see it when you get it made." With that, Val went to the sensory table where cans of dry paint, containers, water, brushes, and tongue depressors had been set out. He busied himself and the teacher became occupied with other children. Time passed and finally he brought a bottle to the teacher. "See," he said. "I made light blue paint!" The teacher responded, "Well, how did you do it?" He proceeded to tell her that his first attempt, by mixing all the colors on the table, had resulted in "yucky brown." He continued, "So I dumped it out and mixed blue and white. That's how I made light blue."

Several theories important for the overall development of young children attempt to describe, explain, and predict curiosity behavior in children. These theories view curiosity "as a prerequisite to learning, reasoning, problem solving, and/or functioning as a competent, self-sufficient human being" (Bradbard and Endsley, 1980, pp. 22–23). Teachers are encouraged to make their classrooms interesting places, with opportunities for children to explore and inquire, thereby facilitating curiosity.

CURIOSITY AND QUESTIONING BY CHILDREN

Some children rarely ask questions about novel objects encountered, while others have continuous questions.

Example: One child in a preschool group, soon to enter kindergarten, was so quiet that his teachers accepted a challenge to bring new stimuli that might increase his verbalization. Day after day, they brought things they thought would get Billy to verbalize (a puppy, a new toy, sensory materials, food for preparation and so on). Day after day, Billy watched the other children but remained nonverbal. Intrigued by his continual silence, one teacher stood outside the gate as Billy's mother picked him up one day. Just as soon as the gate closed, Billy's excited chatter began and continued until they were in the car and down the driveway. More curious than ever, the teacher contacted the parent for an explanation. Why could Billy recite all the songs and fingerplays, relate the activities, add personal comments, call all the children by name, be aware of the day's happenings and yet be *totally* nonverbal at school? The mother reported that Billy had said, "I'm not going to talk at preschool, but I am when I get to kindergarten!"

Do children ask questions out of curiosity, to socialize, to capture one's attention, to practice speaking, to project solutions to problems, or because they are trying to relate to a situation? Maccoby and Jacklin (1974) report studies that show preschool boys are generally less reluctant to explore objects and toys than are preschool girls, with girls preferring more social objects and boys preferring novel fixtures and nonsocial toys and objects. Endsley and Gupta (1978) find that children in smaller groups ask more questions than they do in a larger group, and further, more questions are asked when there is a one-to-one relationship between an adult and child. And novelty aids question-asking. Children ask more questions when things are interesting, when toys and activities are rotated, when the environment reflects changes (bulletin boards, schedules), and when new combinations are tried. A word of caution: the teacher should avoid too many, too drastic, and too frequent changes, which can add to a child's uncertainty. Changes and repetition need to be handled sensitively by adults, who should find a balance between familiarity and novelty, schedule and flexibility, active and quiet times, solitary and group activities, between adult- and child-initiated activities, and indoor and outdoor play.

Example: One day the housekeeping equipment was replaced with many large blocks. At first the children avoided the area because "someone had ruined our house." When the equipment had not been returned the second day, but the blocks still remained, the children began making their own table, stove, and other equipment with the large blocks. This play went on for several days. Then the housekeeping equipment suddenly reappeared! The children were actually disappointed and preferred their own innovations.

Degrees of Curiosity

Bradbard and Endsley find a difference in the degree and manner in which same-aged children satisfy their curiosity: some by touching, verbalizing, and exploring; others by quietly and independently examining objects; still others by not exhibiting any curiosity, "perhaps because they have been punished for past exploratory behavior." Bradbard and Endsley also report that

Children enjoy a variety of materials and activities.

this variability among same-aged children may be linked to genetics or the ways in which children learn to relate to other people and situations. Teachers need to be aware of these individual differences and be skilled in providing experiences to enhance the curiosity development of each child. Most young children satisfy their curiosity by manipulating concrete objects. Perhaps this experience could be enhanced through conversation and spontaneous question asking and answering in a small group or with the teacher. It would be beneficial and productive for the teacher to explain clearly to the children that curiosity behaviors, within limits, are valued and sanctioned in the classroom. When children use materials in different ways than the teacher planned, within acceptable and reasonable limits, the teacher should let the children know

that their ideas are wonderful! (''That is a different way to make a picture.'' ''You found another way to . . . .'' ''Robert used his blocks to make a road instead of a tower. What a good idea, Robert.'')

Further, classroom teachers should help reduce the children's anxiety by providing a nonthreatening environment. Children who feel anxious may prefer to work on simple and familiar tasks with children who are similarly quiet. Complexity and novelty of tasks can be added to the curriculum as these children gain confidence in themselves and in the environment. Children who are afraid to risk working with materials or children may need additional help to increase their self-esteem. Children who feel successful are more likely to try new things and to relate to different people.

Self-Esteem and Curiosity

According to research, children who exhibit a high level of curiosity have better self-esteem and show less anxiety than children who exhibit a low level of curiosity (Bradbard and Endsley, 1980).

The signs of curiosity in preschool children increase as "children gradually become confident that wondering, trying out, and discussing help them find out why things happen. Children who have explored together to reach new understandings come to believe in themselves as learners and in curiosity as a valid tool for learning" (Harlan, 1975, p. 255).

Charlesworth and Lind report that curiosity is a valuable asset to encourage the children to take a new perspective, question believed truths, and take a careful look at exceptions. This basic approach to science is natural for young children, as they use their senses and energies to learn about their environment. The outlook of curious children has freshness of approach, and their exploration and questioning have not been squelched through years of formalized experiences in school. Charlesworth and Lind write,

> Children need to be encouraged to question, wonder, ask, 'why,' and be cautious about accepting things at face value. Experiences designed around direct observation of phenomena and gathering data naturally encourage children to explore new situations in any objective and open-minded fashion. This type of experience can do much toward developing confidence and a healthy skepticism. (1990, p. 52)

Role of Parents in Child's Curiosity

Parents are important influences on how their children respond to various stimuli. Research shows that parents who are supportive, attentive, and sensitive to their children's needs—knowing when to hold on and when to let their children move toward independence and exploration—tend to have highly curious children (Bradbard and Endsley, 1980; Endsley, Hutcherson, Garner, and Martin, 1979; Saxe and Stollack, 1971). Parents of highly curious children model curiosity behavior (Johns and Endsley, 1977) and reinforce their children for being curious (Endsley, Hutcherson, Garner, and Martin, 1979). Bradbard, Halperin, and Endsley write, "Both theorists and practitioners agree that curiosity is highly related to early mother-child attachment behaviors (Ainsworth, 1980) and is a prerequisite to later learning, problem solving, reasoning, and social-intellectual competency" (1988, p. 92).

Intelligence and Curiosity

Intelligence and curiosity may sometimes be connected. However, it should not be quickly assumed that more curious children are also more intelligent children, and vice versa (Coie, 1974; Day, 1968; and White, 1959). White notes that highly curious children possess attributes that are generally associated with a broader concept of social and intellectual competence, such as creativity, flexibility, security, and a good self-image. Bradbard and Endsley recall that, "Curious children are interested in new, complex, ambiguous, and incongruous objects, people, and places" (1980). Eliason and Jenkins encourage rich surroundings, concrete experiences, sensory and manipulative experiences, with repeated exposures for children to learn and explore. They state: "A single experience is not enough to build reliable intellectual concepts; the same idea must be approached from many different angles" (Eliason and Jenkins, 1990, p. 41).

Learning opportunities can be set up for children so they learn through trial and error. But, as Gagné points out, "Discovery without guidance makes the learning of concepts a terribly slow process" (1966).

Mukherjee and Preeti report some interesting relationships between concept formation and curiosity development in preschool children. First, concept formation and curiosity are positively and significantly correlated to mental age; therefore, a child with a higher mental age develops concepts faster than a child with a lower mental age, and children of high intelligence learn concepts more readily than children of low intelligence because of transfer of learning. Second, "The correlation between 'what' questions and mental age was also significant indicating that a child with a higher mental age is more curious and therefore, asks more questions." Third, "The correlation between 'why' questions and mental age indicates that the curiosity of a child to know reasons of things and events is not significantly dependent on mental age." Mukherjee and Preeti warn that the findings of this sampling should not be hastily generalized, but that there should be sample representations from different socio-economic groups (1987, p. 30–32).

Differences between Programs

Since the early 1960s there has been research, competition, and difference of opinion about the best **teaching model** for young children. Head Start, for example, tried to identify models that made lasting differences in children's learning with their Follow-Through program. Educators still have their own favorite, eclectic, and doubted models.

Bradbard and Endsley review the different educational models—**Montessori, DARCEE, Bereiter-Englemann,** and **traditional**—and their effects on curiosity. Montessori stresses carefully sequenced tasks, manipulation of objects, and highly academic content. The child is seen as naturally curious and eager to learn. DARCEE also suggests carefully sequenced tasks, manipulation of objects, and highly academic content, but it differs from Montessori in other ways. Bereiter-Englemann is a high-performance, teacher-centered program. Traditional has many descriptions, from the early days of nursery schools (1920s) as a social non-academic program, to a more modern concept of teachers "setting the stage" for children's development in *all* areas without putting undue pressure on academics. "The *DARCEE*, *Bereiter-Englemann*, and the *traditional* programs see the child with a lack of curiosity or persistence" (Bradbard and Endsley, 1980, p. 27).

In the Bradbard and Endsley study, a "curiosity box" was used to determine levels of curiosity in the four educational models. The greatest gains in curiosity development found in children from prekindergarten through second grade were made in Montessori and DARCEE programs. "However, overall gains in curiosity were found among children in Bereiter-Englemann and traditional programs. Thus, it appears more likely that a stimulating, well-planned preschool experience, coupled with sensitive interactions with teachers and peers, rather than the specific program philosophy, contributes to curiosity development in young children" (Bradbard and Endsley, 1980, p. 27).

Curiosity and Play

Curiosity is distinct from play in several ways. Berlyne (1960), Hutt (1970), Nunnally and Lemond (1973), and others, hypothesize about these differences. Bradbard and Endsley report:

Curiosity

Seen as seeking specific information in a stimulus-rich environment. Viewed as following a sequence (looking, approaching, touching, inquiring).

Play

Seen as seeking a diversion or stimulation in a familiar environment. Viewed as following an unpredictable sequence.

Follows curiosity in temporal order (look, approach, touch, inquire). As the stimulus becomes familiar, children play with it. (1980, p. 24)

Many educators agree that intellectual curiosity is essential for learning, especially in science and mathematics.

Albert Einstein states in his autobiography:

It is in fact nothing short of a miracle that the modern methods of instruction have not yet entirely strangled the *holy*

curiosity of inquiry. . . . It is a very grave mistake to think that the enjoyment of seeing and searching can be promoted by means of coercion and a sense of duty. (1949, p. 17)

Einstein makes two important points. First, in order for children to be productive thinkers, they need to be curious about their world and how it works. Second, the way children are currently being instructed is destroying curiosity because it is frequently uninteresting, unmotivating and unsuccessful. A suggested alternative is to involve the children in play because it has the potential to encourage curiosity at all levels of development.

Ways to Foster and Acknowledge Curiosity

Adults who are attentive, sensitive, and supportive of children's needs to explore, who answer children's questions informatively, and who display positive characteristics of curious people can foster and maintain the curiosity in children (Bradbard and Endsley, 1980, pp. 29–39). Further, if children explore objects and ask questions for the intrinsic value they obtain from these activities, other external modes of reinforcement may be unnecessary. However, curiosity behavior can be facilitated in severely mentally retarded children, hyperactive children, or other unusual cases by using a token reward system. The teacher can bring up wondering about things, but should *never tell a child something he can discover for himself.* Ziemer states, "Instruction is inappropriate. We do not 'teach' science; *joyfully we investigate it together.* . . . We don't have to know all the answers. We may not be teaching facts, but we are teaching curiosity" (1987, p. 44).

There is strong support for helping young children build and value curiosity, as a few early childhood educators share here:

> Curiosity, another important element in early cognitive development, impels a child to reach out to the environment. . . . The teacher's interest and curiosity will often kindle the child's interest in exploring and finding out. (Eliason and Jenkins 1990, p. 41)

> Children's curiosity leads them to experience and the more they experiment, the more they learn science. (Holt, Ives, Levdei, and von Hippel, 1983, p. 6)

> When the teacher's own sense of wonder is alive and active, curiosity behavior is modeled for the children. (Harlan, 1988, p. 19)

> The importance of working toward science concepts in the preschool years is most strongly evidenced in the signs of quickened curiosity in the children. These signs increase as children gradually become confident that wondering, trying out, and discussing help them find out why things happen. Children who have explored together to reach new understandings come to believe in themselves as learners and in curiosity as a valid tool for learning. (Harlan, 1975, 255)

> If I had influence with the good fairy who is supposed to preside over the christening of all children, I should ask that her gift to each child in the world be a sense of wonder so indestructible that it would last throughout life, as an unfailing antidote against the boredom and disenchantments of later years, the sterile preoccupation with things that are artificial, the alienation from the sources of our strength. (Carson, 1956, pp. 42–43)

Curiosity and the Environment

Two teacher functions appear to be necessary in guiding science discovery learning for young children: nurturing the children's curiosity; and providing active learning experiences which help children extend and clarify common events (Harlan, 1975, p. 250). If the children's curiosity has been dulled from boredom or has been devalued, the teacher has an additional role: to model a personal sense of wonder through vividly expressing curiosity behavior for the children (Harlan, 1975). Glenn Blough, a noted science educator, emphasizes, "There are no records of children being inspired by teachers who themselves are not inspired" (1971).

Teachers have many opportunities to call attention to the environment in spontaneous ways.

> Example: The teacher could take the children on a) an outdoor walk to a nearby location, on a timed schedule, to see something specific, or b) an outdoor walk to enjoy the surroundings and to familiarize themselves with their school setting. Both situations have merit and should be utilized. Walk (b) allows for stopping along the way to see spontaneous and interesting things (leaves, birds, construction equipment, and so on), to go according to interests of the children, and it can be terminated at any time.

Curiosity is common in young children.

With regard to the research on children's curiosity, three issues still need to be addressed. One factor is that most of the research has occurred outside the child's natural home or school environment. It is difficult to predict if their behavior would be consistent between a laboratory and a home or school setting. A second factor is that some conclusions have been drawn on one or few observations, and it is likely that a child may respond differently under different circumstances, for example touching and manipulating in one setting, questioning in another, and no response in still other situations (Bradbard and Endsley, 1980, p. 30). A third factor is that "most researchers have examined only one specific class of curiosity behavior rather than comparing several curiosity behaviors in a given situation" (Henderson and Moore, 1979).

Some children have strong preferences for certain playthings. Relatively few children see new possibilities in materials that have become too familiar. "Routinely available play equipment does not stimulate curiosity in all children in a constant way" (Harlan, 1975, p. 250).

Frequently the teacher can suggest different ways to use playthings, encourage children to invent new ways, or add props which encourage different combinations. The teacher should avoid having expectations that are too high, such as children rapidly generating new ideas, advanced physical and mental skills, or a perfect product.

Example: A teacher tries to determine the knowledge of children by asking for abstract information. "Let's pretend we are going on a safari in Africa. What would you do if (a lion jumped on you,

you were crossing the desert and had no water, you fell in a swamp, and so on)? This situation is too removed from the child. A more realistic situation for young children would be thinking and talking about things that are happening at school or home.

Curiosity and Abused Children or Those from Different Backgrounds

An **abused child** "has been characterized as one who is anxious, shy, fearful, and self-disparaging, and who shows little interest in toys and situations that would be of interest to his nonabused agemates" (Martin, 1976; Williams and Money, 1980). Clinical literature portrays **abusive parents** as "aloof, critical, unrealistically demanding of their children, and punitive when their children (particularly those who may be intellectually more capable than their parents) display inquisitive behavior" (Friedman, cited in Freidrich and Boriskin, 1980). Also, typically abusive parents "are ambivalent about allowing their children to become autonomous, and they inconsistently push and pull their children to be both dependent and independent" (Bradbard, Halperin, and Endsley, 1988, p. 93).

In a study of abused preschool children with their mothers, a teacher, and a female stranger, Bradbard, Halperin, and Endsley report that "regardless of the social situation, the children and the adults explored the familiar objects more than the novel objects. The children explored the novel objects significantly less in the stranger-present situation than in the other situations. Finally, the pattern of adult findings indicated that abusive mothers were less likely to encourage curiosity in their

children than were teachers or strangers. These results were related to past research with white, middle-class, nonabused children" (1988, p. 91). In the sample, younger children and girls spent more time exploring familiar toys than novel ones, and the "typical child in the sample asked virtually no questions about any of the play materials. . . . Nonabused children exhibited more curiosity in the presence of their mothers compared with a stranger" (p. 101).

In a follow-up study of curiosity and exploratory behavior with disadvantaged inner-city black children, Minuchin's findings indicate "that the most curious and exploratory children at four years old are, for the most part, among the most vigorous, searching and adaptive at age six" (1971, abstract).

It appears that early childhood teachers would do well to not only encourage parents of abused children and those with diverse backgrounds to provide stimulating experiences for their children, but also to show (rather than tell) them how to go about this. This could be done over a period of time, first by letting the parents have personal hands-on experiences and then by coaching the parents as they interact with their own children or with other children. It should be a very enlightening experience for whole families.

SUMMARY

Curious children react differently than children who are not curious.

Questioning by children may or may not be a sign of curiosity. Adults need to listen carefully to the content and purpose before answering children's questions.

There are different degrees of curiosity; some children explore through different mediums.

Children who exhibit a high level of curiosity have better self-esteem and show less anxiety than children who exhibit a low level of curiosity.

Intelligence and curiosity may sometimes be connected.

Different teaching models view curiosity in different ways.

Curiosity should be fostered in young children.

The child's environment can encourage or discourage curiosity.

EXERCISES
study/discussion questions

1. Set up a situation for young children where new or stimulating materials are used. Watch the children over a ten-minute period, observing their behavior and recording conversations of the children involved. Are some of the children aggressive in using the materials or exploring the situation, while others withdraw?

2. Interview several parents regarding the curiosity behavior of their children. Does each parent look at this behavior as desirable or undesirable? Do they encourage or discourage their child in unique situations?

3. On a table in an obvious part of the classroom (one that is frequented often by the children), set out four to six different and unusual objects. Station yourself nearby so you can watch the children and hear their comments, but do not participate. After several minutes, join in the activity. Were they more interested when they could explore the objects on their own or when an adult was there to encourage, offer comments, and answer questions?

4. Over a period of days or weeks, note the activities and toys that are favorites of the children. Contemplate why the children like these toys and activities. Is it because the toys and materials are familiar (comfort), because the children have the skills to be successful in their use (power), because the children can avoid other children (seclusion), or other reasons?

5. Do some reading on hyperactivity. How can you tell the difference between a child who is curious and one who is hyperactive? Discuss this with a knowledgeable person (teacher, medical person, counselor, and so on).

6. Read one of the children's stories about *Curious George* (by H. A. Rey, published by Houghton Mifflin in Boston). With your peers, decide if George is really curious.

7. Make your own quotable about curiosity (see page 63).

8. Prepare a "think box" (where children or adults try to guess what is inside by asking questions of the teacher) or a "feel box" (where contents cannot be seen but must be

identified by feeling them). Are children interested in these activities or does an adult need to give encouragement? (see Chapter 11.)

9. Be curious yourself! Find out about something new.

7

Discovery Learning and Play

Older children and adults may observe young children at play and wonder why they are using their time so freely, so haphazardly, so inconsistently, and sometimes so seriously. As a person gets older, she may fail to remember fantasizing about things that were important, bothersome, desired, or out of reach. The play of young children helps them discover and resolve problems, create new problems, and begin to have a better understanding of their immediate environment. Both discovery and play are important in the lives of young children.

DISCOVERY LEARNING

Seeking a way to find answers and to determine what is and can be learned is called **discovery learning.** It directs thinking and emphasizes how to find answers.

Discovery learning makes it possible for children to find out things for themselves or to construct their own knowledge rather than having information imposed upon them. Constructing this knowledge does not mean that the children reinvent the wheel. When certain situations, materials, or information are available, the children determine what is done, when it is done, and how it is done, all within appropri-

ate limits. Two forms of discovery learning that Victor mentions are: **free learning,** where the child explores freely, paces himself, and makes decisions about what to do; and **guided learning,** where the teacher is a resource, assumes the controlling role and helps the child to correct decisions (1985, p. 34).

Discovery makes a situation seem vivid, important, and useful as children explore, experiment, and try and retry. Their minds work differently than those of adults. They see different possibilities; they may overlook some limitations so they need to be protected from harm or danger, while experiencing freedom and satisfaction. In a carefully planned environment, children can explore its contents.

Rather than following the typical public school model of separate times for separate subjects ("now it's time for math," "now get ready for physical education"), the curriculum for the young child is inclusive, overlapping, spontaneous, supportive, interesting, integrated, and natural. When this occurs, learning for one subject reinforces and enhances learning for another subject. However, for clarity, *science is a legitimate subject by itself.* It can enhance other curriculum areas and other curriculum areas can enhance science—combining can be strengthening and broadening. Wisdom needs to be used to determine when and how (whether individual or integrated) a topic is best presented.

In seeking information at any age or level (preschool through higher learning) four steps are involved, according to Harlan (1988, p. 25):

1. being aware of a problem (noticing)

2. hypothesizing, or proposing an explanation (wondering why)

3. experimenting (finding out)

4. communicating the results (talking about it)

When procedures and terms are understood, simplified, and related to the child's knowledge and experiences, constructing knowledge for himself can be easy and gratifying.

> Example: Micah quietly sits and watches as Walter struggles to get his wagon, heavily loaded with blocks, back on his road. Finally Micah approaches Walter and asks about the problem. Walter relates his predicament and the two boys take a closer look at the problem. Walter is near to tears and very frustrated when Micah offers several suggestions (unloading the wagon, getting adult help, or moving to another activity). Each suggestion is tried and rejected (time and effort to unload, admitting defeat, ignoring the problem) when Walter exclaims, "I know! I know!" He takes one of the long slender blocks from the wagon, backs up the wagon until he gets the front wheel on the block, and carefully pulls the wagon out of the rut and onto the road. He chants, "I did it! I did it!" As other children and adults are attracted by his joyous shouts, he relates the problem, his attempts to solve it, and finally his idea and success. He actually "constructed" a solution.

Several researchers (Piaget, 1929, 1954, 1973; Kamii and DeVries, 1978; Forman and Kuschner, 1983; Howe, 1974; and Smith, 1981) discuss the theoretical significance of **constructivism** and the role it plays in early childhood education. Piagetian theory has implications for teaching *science* to young children. Smith states,

> For Piaget, the foundation upon which all intellectual development takes place is physical knowledge, knowledge that comes from objects. This includes information about the properties of objects (their shape, size, textures, color, odor), as well as knowledge about how objects react to different actions on them (they roll, bounce, sink, slide, dry up). Children construct physical knowledge by acting on objects—feeling, tasting, smelling, seeing, and hearing them. They cause objects to move—throwing, banging, blowing, pushing, and pulling them, and they observe changes that take place in objects when they are heated, cooled, mixed together, or changed in some other way. As physical knowledge develops, children become better able to establish relationships (comparing, classifying, ordering) between and among the objects they act upon. Such relationships (logicomathematical knowledge according to Piaget) are essential for the emergence of logical, flexible thought processes. (1987, p. 35)

Carin and Sund (1985) prefer **guided discovery** over **expository** or **inquiry** because they believe it incorporates the best research and knowledge about teaching science, how young children learn, the goals and objectives of science, and the relationship among science, humanism, values, and concern for the environment.

Young children are fascinated by animals.

Benefits for Children

Being able to discover on their own is important to children. An added bonus is that it requires the same intellectual skills as later academic learning (reading, language development, coordination, and problem solving). ''You have to present a *variety* of activities so the children build a storehouse of sensory observations from which verbal (and eventually written) symbols are 'invented' by the teacher'' (Carin and Sund, 1985).

If science and educational experiences are going to have value for young children, they must be motivated to think and have time to digest what is happening to them and their environment. Piaget believes that in true learning, the children have to have time to assimilate and accommodate their experiences. Without this happening, stu-

dents are involved in what Piaget calls **pseudolearning,** parroting an explanation without a real change in mental awareness about a subject.

Role of the Adult

In spite of the term, discovery science requires much planning on the part of the teacher. It is not just a happenstance. To have meaning, there must be consideration as to where it will occur, when it would be most appropriate or of interest, when it can take precedence over other activities, what will be required, and how long a time period can be allotted. The teacher should take the following ideas individually and collectively into thoughtful consideration:

- Where is the activity more naturally suited (indoors or outside)?

- When would the children be the most

CHILD BENEFITS IN DISCOVERY LEARNING

Through discovery science, children can benefit in many ways:

- Curiosity can be valued and rewarded.

- Individuality and creativity in problem solving are encouraged.

- A pattern for problem solving and later learning can be established.

- Concept retention is increased.

- Learning occurs from an original experience through the use of the senses.

- Communication is increased by learning concepts and terms upon which to build.

- The self-concept is enhanced.

- There is an attempt to distinguish between realistic and unrealistic ideas—a better understanding of one's world.

- Children are channeled into interesting, meaningful, and acceptable activities.

- It can reduce or eliminate behavior problems through meeting the needs and interests of children.

- It can challenge and stimulate children according to their skills, interests, and abilities.

- It develops intellectual potential because the manipulation of interesting materials is highly motivating to the children (Harlan, 1988, p. 26).

- It can be a solitary (private) or cooperative (group) activity; a short (one-time) or an on-going (repeated) activity; a physical or a social activity.

- It has an atmosphere of freedom (play) where children feel less pressure to perform. It can be terminated or enhanced at the will and desire of the child.

- The children can see the activity as a whole rather than a segmented activity–gathering, making, using, cleaning, and storing materials.

interested (at the beginning, middle, or end of the day)?

- Are the children more refreshed early in the day or do they need a change during the day?

- When could the activity be most flexible and sustained?

- Will it require a lot of preparation or could items be obtained easily from shelves or bins by the children?

- How much supervision is needed?

- Are the children familiar with the activity so they could carry it on from a prior period, or do they need some verbal or physical assistance to initiate it?

- Could the activity be set up upon the request of a child?

There needs to be enough structure so the children can proceed, but not so it directs or limits the children's ability to discover on their own. The teacher should have some broad objectives or concepts in mind and the activity should be set up to help the children reach these objects or concepts on their own. Teachers should not *tell* the children what or how to proceed, nor should they attempt to have children memorize material to be repeated later.

Teacher roles in discovery science might include a **facilitator,** creating an environment for child growth; an **enabler,** helping children become thinkers and problem-solvers; or a **consultant,** listening, observing, and responding (Harlan, 1988, p. 20). Sometimes teachers combine these different roles.

PLAY

Play is a four-letter word that adds zest, variety, confidence, and excite-ment to the world of the young child. Its values are extolled frequently and widely. Science requires thinking and doing; play and science are natural companions.

Through peer interaction in both play and discovery learning, children construct many of the same attributes: imitating roles, building positive attitudes, persevering, solving problems in flexible ways, becoming more confident and independent, improving concentration and motivation skills, becoming leaders and followers, reducing frustration, developing diversity in thinking, and many other useful and desirable traits.

Books, articles, studies, films, videos, filmstrips, and other media about play are available in abundance. It is the intent of this book to show what a valuable tool play is, how important it is in the child's development, and how easily and understandable science can be when introduced in a positive, developmental, unrushed, and secure environment. Through play, the child can learn about her environment and can practice the concepts in a warm and accepting atmosphere.

Adult Control
Greenberg feels that a child who is under the control of others is frustrated, resentful, and thwarted. If this is a consistent pattern for the child, he may retaliate later in the form of **passive resistance** ("dawdling, refusing to eat, being disruptive, failing to learn later in school"), or in **direct anger** ("tantrums, hitting, biting, scratching, being balky and negative") (1989). Being controlled, Greenberg continues, a child "has no opportunity to learn to negotiate, how to take turns, how to verbally rather than physically solve

ADULT VALUES IN DISCOVERY LEARNING

Some advantages of discovery learning include, but are not limited to the following:

- Personal interests can be pursued.
- Learning patterns can be formed.
- Learning becomes intrinsic.
- Learning can be transferred.
- Divergent thinking is encouraged.
- Senses are stimulated through first-hand experiences.
- Opportunities are available for testing and reacting.
- One can note and correct discrepancies, omissions, and so on.
- Time periods can be fluid.
- Thinking rather than performance is encouraged.
- Raw materials can be used in many ways.
- Experiences can be individual or with others.
- Activities can be completed or on-going.
- Problems can be posed and freedom is permitted.
- Follow-through is possible for the child, or child and adult working together.
- Adults learn about children and activities through observing and listening.

problems, how to become a leader rather than a follower, the feeling of self-esteem, or the joy of being with others.'' (1989) Beaty states, ''Nevertheless, if the child does not have the opportunity to explore his environment—if his environment is uninteresting or sterile, or if his caregivers are harsh, controlling, or neglectful—he may not develop his intellect to the same extent as children without these handicaps'' (1990, p. 205).

In extreme cases, adult intervention has shown positive results.

Example: Dr. J. V. Hunt and other American psychologists visited orphanages in Iran. With an infant-caregiver ratio of 40 to three, many two-year-olds could not sit up, and most four-year-olds could not walk unassisted. When the caregivers were trained to use vocal play with newly arrived infants, these youngsters learned to walk and talk on schedule, and their appearance and facial features changed for the better (Pines, 1979, p. 63).

Play, Interest, and Work

Adults can learn a lot about children by watching them at play, enacting things that are of interest to them. But **play** and **interest** both worry adults. As Carini states,

Play is contraposed to work and reality, and the interesting is contraposed to the serious and the demanding—while both imply frivolity and trivia. Interest originally meant 'to be in and among things, at the center of things,' and what we call play is the child's world, his or her reality. We know that the absence of either play or interest suggests pathology in the child. Through play the child's innermost themes and world are represented and completed. (1977, p. 16)

Elkind expresses frustration in conveying the importance of play in children's learning when he writes,

When we recite the formula: 'Play is the child's work,' what we mean is that the child learns through play as well as through work. But that is not the way we are heard. Rather, our uninformed listeners hear the familiar contrast between work and play. And this perpetuates the intuitive association of learning with work, and play with fun.

While what we call children's activities may be a small issue in the grand

scheme of things, it seems to be contributing to the academic pressure on preschool education. At this point we need to do everything we can to reverse the trend. And this means belaboring the point that young children are expending a great deal of effort in learning both from their work and from their play. (1988, p. 2)

Elkind further suggests that we start talking about the "work" of preschool children—dressing, using utensils, being polite, sharing, and so on, and that we be more specific about what children learn from play. Perhaps with a better understanding of the values of play, parents and educators will "back off from the rigid curricula now being imposed at ever younger age levels" (p. 2).

Play and Knowledge

Young children are instrumental in creating ideas and in putting concepts together for present and future use by interacting with their environment (things, people, their senses, and ideas) in a way that makes sense to them. "The fact of the matter is that child's play is practice in learning to think," writes Beaty. She continues:

All of the information extracted through this playful exploration of the environment is filed away in predetermined patterns in the brain, to be used to direct or adjust the child's behavior as he continues to respond to the stimuli around him. We now know that this knowledge is organized by the brain in predictable patterns from a very early age. Some of these patterns may even be inherited. (1990, p. 203)

With meaningful materials and playful exploration, children begin to build important conceptual understandings, respond to challenging issues, learn key concepts, and develop positive attitudes toward learning (Henniger, 1987, p. 167). The value of play in science learning should be acknowledged and utilized.

SUMMARY

Children learn in different ways, at different speeds, and under different conditions. They have different amounts of interest and motivation; however, it appears that the discovery method closely approximates the developmental approach to learning and has a great deal of appeal to young children.

Discovery learning is a more personal way of learning than is presented in many school systems. In discovery learning, the children are more the focus than the material to be learned.

There are many values for adults and benefits for children in the discovery method of learning science.

Play has many positive aspects, some major and some minor. A discussion of the topic could be extensive and the list of contributors would be impressive. Play is one of the most important ways for the child to learn, and adults can learn much about the child and her environmental reactions by having an optimistic attitude, planning carefully, and observing what is said and done.

EXERCISES
study/discussion questions

1. Define **discovery learning** and give an example of its use with young children.

2. Give an example of a learning experience other than discovery learning.

3. Describe the process by which a child constructs his own knowledge.

4. Using an experience based on one of the senses, generate ideas to help young children learn through participating in the preparation of a food item for snack or lunch.

5. Provide a water experience for young children. Note their comments as they explore the medium. What discoveries did they make?

6. Identify and expand upon benefits that young children can gain from discovery learning opportunities.

7. Discuss the role of the teacher in discovery learning. Is there a difference in preparation and outcomes from other methods?

8. Divide students into two groups. One group observes children in a structured learning experience and one group observes children in a discovery learning experience. Compare participation of the children in the different groups. Also compare the teacher involvement and the success of the experience.

9. Define "play" and outline how it can aid young children in acquiring science concepts.

10. What are the role and responsibilities of the teacher in providing play experiences for young children?

11. Propose a situation where an adult (teacher or parent) says, "There will be no more *play* in this classroom. The children need *academic* preparation." What responses would be appropriate?

8

Self-Esteem and Motivation

How children feel about themselves and how freely or reluctantly they enter into activities and relationships are important considerations in learning. Both of these issues will be discussed in this chapter.

SELF-ESTEEM

While **self-concept** and **self-esteem** are frequently used interchangeably, some educators see a difference between the two terms. Dictionary definitions refer to "concept" as an idea, a thought, or a notion and to "esteem" as respect or approval. In this text the term to define how a child feels about herself will be self-esteem.

Characteristics

Healthy self-esteem is important to an individual at any age, and vital to learning. But what does a person look like who has high self-esteem? Carin and Sund describe such people as feeling "psychologically secure . . . open to new experiences . . . willing to take chances and explore, tolerate minor failures relatively well . . . more creative . . . generally in good mental health, and eventually . . . fully functioning individuals" (1985, p. 106). The opposite are children with **low self-esteem** who are highly anxious, lack self-confidence, curiosity, and adventurousness (Shymansky, 1978).

Teachers can help children develop positive characteristics by the kinds of experiences that are planned and by the way they treat the children. Secure and happy children are more likely to live up to their developmental potential. When teachers and parents take time to explain things to children and allow them to explore at their skill levels with sufficient time, the adults are setting the stage for children to gain insights into themselves and their environment—aspects of sound self-esteem. Children with low expectancy levels develop feelings of high anxiety which lead to further lowering of expectancy levels. It is a vicious cycle. The weight of research indicates that a high anxiety level generally accompanies poor student performance. (Carin and Sund, 1985, p. 107).

The descriptions on page 80 provide sketchy information but call for quick conclusions about whether these children have high or low self-esteem.

Competence and Self-Esteem

A common current term in early childhood education is **competence.** Hendrick defines it as,

> The wonder feeling of assurance exemplified by the statements: 'I can do it,' 'I am able,' 'I know how,' and 'I am an effective person.' These reveal a security and belief in oneself that are the fundamental cornerstones of self-esteem. The

CHILD	SITUATION
Annette	Annette stands on the periphery sucking one thumb and twisting her hair with her other hand.
Russell	Russell bursts enthusiastically into the room, recruits three other boys, and begins a mass block building project.
Elizabeth	Elizabeth sings happily while rocking her doll.
Leslie	Leslie hangs his head and withdraws every time a child or adult comes near him.
Peter and Peggy	Peter begs the teacher to get out the woodworking tools so he can make an airplane to fly outside. Peggy joins in the request, adding, "The wind is just right for flying planes."
Stephen and Jeff	The teacher brings in some new pets. While telling the children about caring for the pets, Stephen and Jeff sit silently, withdraw each time the teacher puts the pets near them, and are relieved when the situation is changed.
Mary and Jenny	Mary begins rolling the clay. She invites Jenny to join her. Happily they roll balls, snakes, and pancakes. Both girls are verbal, look for round objects to use to smooth the clay, and challenge each other to make different shapes.
Michael	Michael is pushing a truck across the floor. May and Henry join him, much to his dislike. But rather than say anything to them, Michael leaves the truck and the area.

fortunate possessors of such confidence are willing to risk and to explore for the sake of learning because they believe themselves to be worthwhile, competent people. (1990, p. 4)

A competent person expects to handle the demands he meets and to find joy in the encounter (Bronson, 1974, p. 243). Teachers of young children have a golden opportunity to help them move closer to competence, thereby bringing more happiness and satisfaction into their lives. Hendrick adds, "And what a powerful antidote this could be for children of the poor, whose helplessness is often a hallmark of the family's attitude toward life" (1990, p. 5).

Feelings about Oneself

In addition to competence, terms synonymous with self-esteem might include "positive self-image" and "positive self-concept." Some may make a fine distinction between these terms,

but essentially they all refer to feeling good about oneself, being happy about one's abilities, and feeling that life is good, people can be trusted, and one is respected for being oneself "including your race and ethnicity, your religion, your socioeconomic level, your behavior (even if it isn't always saintly), and your skills (even though you are 'deficient' in some of them)" (*Young Children*, May 1988, p. 57).

Positive self-esteem accompanies feelings of acceptance whether the child is within the family context or in the "outside world," at work or play, with one or more others, as a leader or follower. It is important because those who care *for* the child should also care *about* the child.

Power and Self-Esteem

A child bases at least part of his self-esteem on power, termed **locus of control** by Clark who states that the control can be either internal (making a choice based on interest) or external (making a choice because of the reward given)(1986, p. 127). The internal locus of control helps students consider their own skills and abilities as they relate to the task at hand, allowing them to make self judgments about how and whether they can complete it. Thus, when the child helps establish, through experience and cooperation, what is to be done, he learns to trust himself. Likewise, the goal of discipline is to help the child gain inner-control and understanding rather than external control (being dependent upon being told what to do, or doing solely for the reward). A strong inner locus of control helps students express themselves more freely, improve their efforts, and have feelings of joy and satisfaction. They are excited about learning. Clark adds, "This perception of responsibility for and control over one's life is the single most important condition for success, achievement, and a sense of well-being" (Also see Allen, Giat, and Cherney, 1974; Bar-tak Kfir, Bar-Zohr, and Chen, 1980; Dweck and Goetz, 1978; Lao, 1970; Morrison and Mc-Intrye, 1971; Phares, 1975).

Children need to have opportunities to ask questions, seek answers, and solve problems for themselves. Sometimes they will find direct routes to solutions and sometimes they will encounter detours and dead ends, but the learning will be theirs. They will learn to think through situations and strive for solutions. Through such learning they will build more trust and confidence in themselves and not rely so heavily upon adult direction.

Whenever possible, materials and situations should be provided so the children will experience success in a genu-ine manner. Success breeds success; teachers should plan according to the skill and development level of the children. Failure is unpleasant; sometimes children are discouraged from attempting tasks or relationships because the risk of failure or rejection is too painful.

Science and Self-Esteem

In science, it is just as important to find out what does not work as it is to find out what does. "In fact, real growth in science tends to happen when solutions do not fit what was predicted. Although students should not be constantly confronted with frustrating learning situations, a positive attitude toward failure may better serve them in developing problem-solving skills. After all, in much of science inquiry, there are no 'right' or 'wrong' answers," write Charlesworth and Lind (1990, p. 53).

The information on self-esteem in this chapter applies to teaching of any topic or curriculum area for young children. The principles are sound and success-ful. Then why such a discussion in a science book? Science is all around us; it is in all we do. Young children who are introduced to good learning opportunities can use them in any field of study.

Science is an exciting part of everyday life. When it is looked upon as something desirable, it opens many avenues.

Fostering Self-Esteem

One of the purposes of early education is to help foster competence in young children in each developmental area. Often competence is considered in a cognitive mode, but how the child feels about his total being makes up his self-confidence.

Examples of competence in the developmental areas are shown in the chart below.

Parents at home and teachers in school can help foster competence in children. The time to begin is when the children are young; the time to support the growth of competence is at every opportunity without being fake or pushy.

Adults can foster competence by first preparing themselves to know what can and should be expected of young children at different ages, realizing that while children are different they do pass through a series of growth stages. Second, they provide an atmosphere of love and caring for each and every child. Third, they plan first-hand activities and use materials that offer hierarchial levels of challenge and a variety of opportunities. They remember that preschool children learn by using play to translate experience into understanding (Piaget, 1962; Piaget and Inhelder, 1969). Fourth, they listen care-

COMPETENCE IN DEVELOPMENTAL AREAS

COGNITIVE
curiosity, using and sharing knowledge, advancing, learning new things, integrating ideas, etc.

SOCIAL
learning to live peacefully and comfortably with others, tolerance, patience, diversity, etc.

PHYSICAL
learning to use one's body effectively (solitary or team efforts), perfecting skills, enduring, advancing, integrating skills, etc.

EMOTIONAL
mastering and safely expressing one's feelings, learning to love life and welcome new experiences, empathy, sympathy, diminishing negative feelings (guilt, fear), etc.

Children enjoy the wonder of water.

tempts; they may disregard people or objects in their way; and they may even be tolerable of distractions and unwanted outcomes. Yet, they persist in their attempts. The more control the children have over experiences and the more success encountered, the more they will try new and difficult tasks.

"The nursery child has a wonderful drive and capacity to learn on her own. She finds out what she needs to know through her own effort quite as she learned to walk. It's often frustrating. At the same time, it can be an exciting challenge, a living, expanding adventure for the children," states Cartwright (1989, p. 53).

fully when children talk to them and they respect what the children say. Fifth, they know that children learn through different sensory modes and plan accordingly. Sixth, they realize the importance of language development and provide many opportunities for the children to hear and use verbal communication. Seventh, they value each child regardless of race, sex, religion, origin, or socioeconomic level. Seventh, they continually prepare themselves to better understand and meet the needs of young children and their families.

MOTIVATION

Motivation is an important factor in doing most everything. When a person is motivated, he has more commitment, more desire for success, more initiative to get started, and more satisfaction in accomplishments. Motivation in young children is no different than motivation for older children or adults. But sometimes young children do not know why they are motivated to do a thing. They may be clumsy in their at-

The desire for competence is one of the basic motivators of human behavior. Human beings have an inherent drive for mastery and competence, along with satisfying hunger, thirst, and other basic physiological needs. Maslow (1970) identifies a hierarchy of needs with different priorities (see page 84).

How Adults Help Motivate Children
Adults can help set the stage for motivation in children. When adults are caring, interested, and supportive, and provide appropriate activities and uninterrupted time, children can find happiness and accomplishment in exploring their environment. (Refer to the quote from Carson, 1956, p. 45 that appears on page 3 of this text. It is well worth rereading.)

Young Children and Motivation
Henniger describes preschool children as naturally inquisitive and eager to learn about themselves and their environment. Disagreeing with the popular belief that young children spend little time on a task, he states that their concentration on individual interests can

be for relatively long periods of time. Motivation can decrease or disappear completely for such reasons as a task being too tedious or difficult; decreased enthusiasm; competition with other activities; lack of appropriate materials, time, and encouragement; fear of the unknown; impoverished skills; or boredom from repetition or simplicity.

Piaget reports:

The principle goal of education is to create men who are capable of doing new things, not simply repeating what other generations have done . . . men who are creative, inventive and discoverers. The second goal of education is to form minds which can be critical, can verify,

MASLOW'S HIERARCHY OF NEEDS _____

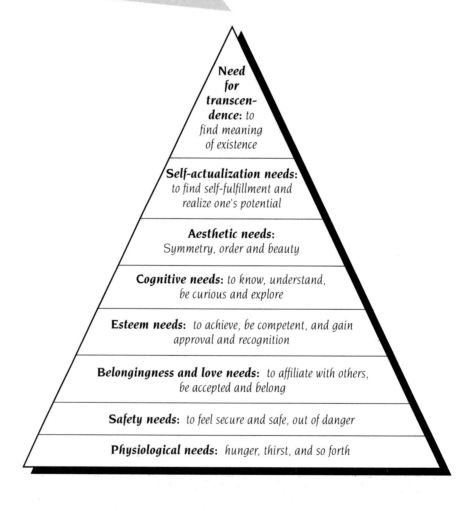

Need for transcendence: to find meaning of existence

Self-actualization needs: to find self-fulfillment and realize one's potential

Aesthetic needs: Symmetry, order and beauty

Cognitive needs: to know, understand, be curious and explore

Esteem needs: to achieve, be competent, and gain approval and recognition

Belongingness and love needs: to affiliate with others, be accepted and belong

Safety needs: to feel secure and safe, out of danger

Physiological needs: hunger, thirst, and so forth

and not accept everything they are offered. The great danger today is of slogans, collective opinions, ready-made trends of thought. We have to be able to resist individually, to criticize, to distinguish between what is proven and what is not. So we need pupils who are active, who learn early to find out by themselves, partly by their own spontaneous activity and partly through materials we set up for them. We learn early to tell what is verifiable and what is simply the first idea to come to them. (Reported in Elkind, 1981a, p. 20)

People who spend time with two-year-olds will readily agree that they are fast-movers and that they hardly ever sit still long enough to dust the chair with the seat of their pants.

Example: One teacher decided to sequence an activity so the children would remain for several minutes—quite an accomplishment! She gave the children balls of soft clay and watched them explore. Sure enough, the children lost interest within a couple of minutes. The teacher moved from chair to chair and quietly put a small pile of flour near each child. The children started sprinkling the flour on the clay, rolling the ball in the flour, and tasting both the flour and the clay. So they stayed a while longer, but then began to lose interest. Then the teacher moved from chair to chair and quietly placed a small rolling pin near each child. The experience grew in intensity with rolling pins tapping on the clay as one child would try something, another would see and repeat it, or try something different. The children stayed with the activity. But again the children began to lose interest, so the teacher quietly placed a large, colored cookie-cutter near each

child. Then the *real* activity began. There was rolling, tasting, pounding, cutting, talking, and interacting. All in all, the majority of the children stayed about twenty minutes—a real record! By adding new props, the children were re-interested, wanted to try the additions, and had great fun.

Discouraging Motivation

At times, adults need to discourage young children from looking, touching, tasting, moving, and disturbing things. Generally, a child is more satisfied with a substitution than with removal or denial of objects. Adults need to arrange the environment so that the children can use, touch, or interact with the visible items. The children are encouraged (motivated) to examine, explore, and inquire. When adults continually remove things *after* children see or touch them, the children lose their instincts to investigate. When children continually hear, "don't," "can't," "stop," and other inhibiting words, they become disinterested in their environment, and motivation is short-lived.

SUMMARY

Healthy self-esteem is important for individuals at all ages and developmental stages.

Highly anxious children tend to lack self-confidence, curiosity, and adventurousness.

Adults can help children feel worthwhile by the opportunities offered and the way children are treated.

One's locus of control can be internal (making choices and doing things for inner satisfaction) or external (doing things to avoid punishment, to gain rewards, or to conform).

Feeling responsible for and in control over one's own life builds success, well-being, and happiness.

There are many ways adults can help foster competence in young children.

Motivation is important in the development of a child's self-esteem. Positive encouragement is essential; negative experiences are detrimental.

Highly motivated people tend to be creative problem-solvers.

EXERCISES
study/discussion questions

1. Describe a person with high self-esteem. How does this person appear to himself and to others?

2. Based on the seven ways adults can foster competence in young children noted on pages 82–83, evaluate the following episodes. Indicate whether or not they will help the children build self-esteem, and if not, recommend a better substitute.

   a. On Susan's third birthday her grandparents had a trampoline delivered.

   b. To keep four-year-old Frank occupied during a vacation period, his parents bought him a chemistry set.

   c. In the springtime the three-year-old twins were given garden tools.

   d. Juan was invited to play a game with his four older siblings. Which game should they play?

      1. Fish (simple card game)

      2. Monopoly

      3. marbles

      4. tag (a running game)

      5. ring toss

   e. Heather is learning to ride a bike with training wheels.

   f. Three preschool children are helping prepare a treat for Dad's birthday.

   g. Sylvia's older brother wants her to play football with him.

   h. The parents of a four-year-old boy are planning a birthday party for him.

3. Recall and share how others (children and adults) have helped you build feelings of self-esteem and confidence.

4. Carefully consider how you feel about yourself. Are there some ways you could strengthen your self-esteem? Outline a procedure to change some of your weaknesses to strengths.

5. Select a person (adult or child) whom you feel needs encouragement in building their self-esteem. Outline a procedure for helping that person.

6. Recall what your best motivators are. Are there some conditions that would discourage or un-motivate you?

7. Assume the children in your classroom were uninterested in the following activities. Give at least three ways the children could be motivated to participate in each situation. (Remember that the children motivate themselves, but teachers can enrich the environment.)

a. the housekeeping area

b. the block area

c. the sensory table

d. a cooking experience

e. woodworking

8. List numerous ways adults discourage motivation in young children.

9. Do all children have the same motivators? Are some motivators *always* effective? (Do the same ones always work with the same children, and under different circumstances? Why or why not?)

Preparing and Disseminating Information

9

How the World Fits Together

So often in formal schooling subjects are taught independently of each other ("Now, get out your pencils for math," "We'll do that at P. E. time, not now.") In preschool, the subject matter is taught in concert with all other topics. Perhaps this integrated approach should be considered and used more often in elementary, middle, and high school classes. A more appropriate time for teaching separate subjects might be for more mature students who are preparing for jobs or advanced degrees.

It is especially appropriate when teaching young children to have science combined with and supported by other curriculum areas (play, music, physical development, and so on). Combining science with other subjects in a natural and unforced way enhances children's learning in *both science and the other subjects* (Carin and Sund, 1985, summary). In curriculum recommended by Schools Council, "Science in the infant (early childhood) classroom is very much interwoven into the activities that normally go on there, it is indistinguishable as a separate entity" (1972).

When research and curriculum are combined into a theoretical framework, both new and experienced teachers of young children can provide appropriate environments and science experiences to help children learn about their world. It also provides a criterion for evaluating activities provided for the children.

EDUCATIONAL CHANGES OVER TIME

Horace Mann's educational grade level curriculum approach in the early 1900s outlined curriculum that he believed would help students learn basic information and skills. Since that time, many changes have taken place in the educational setting. Longitudinal and current research aid in planning for the students of today. New information and methods help provide "continuous progress, challenge, and optimal learning" (Clark, 1986, p. 6) in today's classrooms as teachers recognize unique individuals and personal learning patterns.

Reporting on a study by Science for All Americans (AAAS), Worthy recommends two sharp departures from the traditional teaching of science. "First, science teaching should focus on connections rather than boundaries between traditional academic disciplines. . . . Second, science teaching should emphasize ideas and thinking rather than specialized vocabularies and memorized procedures. 'Schools do not need to be asked to teach more and more,' the report says, 'but to teach less so that it can be taught better'." (1989, p. 4)

Many researchers suggest a major challenge for the field of early childhood education, pointing out that many children experience failure in kindergarten because of the *programs*, not the *children*! Educators too often have expected children to conform to schools rather than vice versa. Early childhood educators are now becoming committed to plan for the developmental needs of young children. Some progress has been made with children of ages two through five, but more must be done to provide developmentally appropriate curriculum and success for kindergarten children and those in the primary grades. One article asks. "What are you doing in your community to educate others about kindergarten curriculum that (1) meets young children's social, emotional, physical, and intellectual needs, and (2) is based on play through hands-on activities?" ("Editor's Note: Viewpoint", *Young Children*, Jan 1986, p. 9)

Within the same school building, different types of kindergarten programs exist—some play-oriented, some academic-oriented, and some unidentified as to their goals.

> Example: *Kindergarten A* has a housekeeping area, blocks, "learn centers" (including a science table), creative materials, a piano, a tape player, and a shelf of miscellaneous toys. As the children enter, they know where they can play, where the needed items are, where they are to be replaced, and about how long the period will last. The children are free to move between activities and to stay until their interests are satisfied.

> *Kindergarten B* has the same equipment; however, when the children enter, they immediately sit in their chairs, begin scuffling and taunting, and wait for the

teacher to give the begin signal. The children are divided into small groups and told which station is for which group. Only some of the children are pleased with their assignment, but locate themselves and begin the task. The teacher determines the number of children per activity, the amount of time allowed, and how many activities the children will participate in during one period. Some children are bored quickly and others complain when they are told to rotate to another activity.

Kindergartens A and B can be found in most schools. It appears that children in group A are encouraged to explore and satisfy their needs more than those in group B. It also appears that children in group A are more likely to see a relationship between activities than would those in group B. And it is admitted that some children do better in one type of group than another.

DEFINITION AND DESCRIPTIONS

In this text **integration** is defined as combining two or more ideas or components in ways that enhance learning for young children. (Webster's *New Universal Unabridged Dictionary* defines "integration" simply as "to unite or become whole.") Integration can be accomplished in a number of ways and combinations. Some possibilities are outlined graphically on page 93.

Areas of Development
A further breakdown reveals the following:

SOCIAL/EMOTIONAL To enhance a science curriculum through the social/emotional area of development, a teacher might show the children pictures of common emotions (happy,

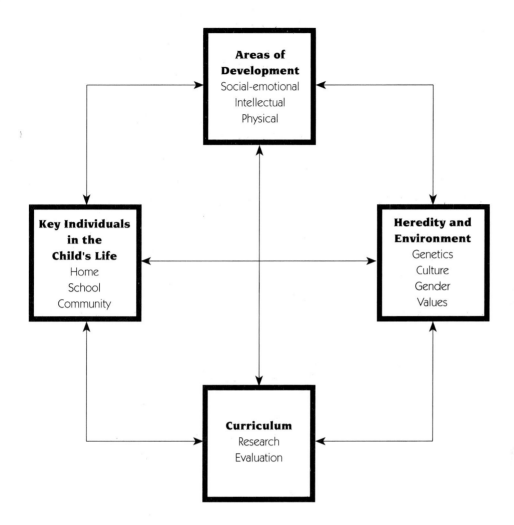

Areas of Development
Social-emotional
Intellectual
Physical

Key Individuals in the Child's Life
Home
School
Community

Heredity and Environment
Genetics
Culture
Gender
Values

Curriculum
Research
Evaluation

sad, crying, frustration). She talks with the children about how the individuals in the pictures could be feeling and why they might have those feelings. Then the teacher brings out a large hand-held mirror and shows each picture separately and asks each child to show how he would facially express that feeling while looking in the mirror.

Through observation, the teacher notes which children can easily express themselves, those who most often play in groups, what situations or condi-

tions cause children to get emotional, and what helps the children release their feelings.

Through the use of stories, poems, dress-up clothes, or other props, the teacher could introduce some science concepts, and encourage the children to reproduce or act out their interpretation or solutions to situations.

For self awareness, the teacher could provide items and activities that encourage the children to do things for themselves, such as dressing up (manipulating the fasteners on garments or trying new roles), trying new things (cutting with scissors or spreading with a knife), approaching another child for a turn, and so on. These activities give the children experiences in social science and help the child in both social and emotional awareness. Science activities should decrease rather than increase stress in the child's life. Too difficult or unreasonable situations or high expectations increase stress, while time and opportunities to use materials at their own developmental and interest level decreases stress (see Chapter 8).

Situations where children learn about and practice expected behavior, etiquette, manners, and cultural awareness can increase their own knowledge and relationships with others. Such situations include sharing toys in the sand, recognizing and appreciating the feelings of others, noting customs, and valuing others. This also helps children solidify their own values and worth.

Social: solitary/cooperative play, creating/reproducing ideas

Emotional: self esteem, stress, reduction, etiquette, manners and customs

INTELLECTUAL Language is one of the most important ways to communicate scientific concepts to children. But using language mainly to give instructions to young children is not an efficient use of the teacher's or children's efforts. The children have a limited vocabulary and sometimes their understanding is incomplete or confused. They need opportunities to initiate conversations, respond to requests and inquiries, and practice what they have heard. Adults need to consider carefully what they are saying

and how the children are responding to make sure that messages are clearly sent and received.

Some young children are interested in writing—about their pictures or experiences, about symbols they observe, and about modeling others. Because they are unskilled in writing, a teacher could write as the child dictates and then read the information back to the child. Young children will want to practice their writing skills with or without adult encouragement. They could look at large, properly written words (upper and lower case letters) and try to reproduce them using appropriately sized utensils.

Verbal and non-verbal communication give certain messages to children. Careful attention should be paid to both the giving and receiving of verbal and non-verbal cues so that messages are clear and accurate. A teacher could communicate misinformation, fear, or even disgust about a science concept merely through non-verbal response—or even no response.

Reading is, for the most part, beyond the ability of the young child; however, a teacher should attend to the child who is ready and interested in print. Together, they could obtain science concepts and experience from books, but for the most part the teacher will be doing the reading. When children inquire about a science concept or when teachers are giving information about science concepts, books can be an invaluable source. Teachers who say, "I'm not sure, let's look that up in a book," are giving children additional resources for information. Books are a valuable procedure for learning about science.

For children to comprehend scientific concepts, they will combine language and experiences. See the table on pages 28–29, regarding the right and left hemispheres of the brain for a reminder about the importance of each hemisphere supporting and enhancing the other hemisphere—another integrating technique. Better use of the brain can help every child become a more successful and effective learner.

Language: speaking/listening, spoken/written, verbal/non-verbal, reading/writing

Cognition: right/left/total brain hemispheres

PHYSICAL Young children have less control over their small muscles than they do over their large muscles. Their attention and efforts are on perfecting their large muscles. Holding a paint brush or marker in the hand and marking large strokes on a surface would be an example of a fine and gross motor combination. An activity involving development within a motor skill could be using hands and fingers together (manipulating objects or doing a science fingerplay) or using arms and legs cooperatively, as in exercising (doing jumping-jacks, lifting, or climbing).

Fine motor: fingers, hands, hand-eye coordination

Gross motor: arms, legs, body, and combinations

Key Individuals in the Child's Life

HOME Young children learn science concepts in and outside the home. They need to practice these concepts where the influence is the most natural—frequently a combination of environments. But for the first few years of life, the home (parents, siblings, and care-givers) is where children learn to love or learn to hate science. Some children spend time in child care outside the home and are influenced by the people and activities there. Science is everywhere if adults can tap into it to benefit the children.

SCHOOL In many states, five-year-old children are expected to be in school classrooms. Attention needs to be paid to the settings to which these children are exposed. Teachers, aides, and substitutes should be well prepared to deal with the children on their science developmental level and to provide understandable, accurate, and appropriate concepts. In addition to the teachers, other spokespersons have a great deal to say about the amounts and kinds of science experiences that will be presented to the children. Teachers in all grades (preschool through higher education) should have a strong knowledge of science, how to

Activities requiring children to use their hands help to develop their motor skills.

teach it, and how to make it exciting and vibrant for students. Some school administrators, over-anxious parents, and lazy teachers fail to consider the special way children learn science principles; they want the experiences from other grades to be diluted enough so that it can be taught to younger children. Children can show a life-time interest in science or they can have a life-time dread of it, depending on how it is introduced to them. Lawmakers and taxpayers should be concerned that the money spent on science programs for young children is used for classes based on how the children learn and how they build concepts.

COMMUNITY The kinds of opportunities offered in a community can call a child's attention to scientific concepts. Cities and towns that have parks, museums, playgrounds, special exhibits or displays, and natural phenomena encourage children to explore the offerings and to integrate the community into their lives. The availability of water (fishing, boating, irrigating, aesthetics) attracts certain kinds of people and activities. Children living around these settings know more about them than children who live in more arid sections of the country.

The types of employment in the community help young children understand more about the people. Most communities have the typical "community helper" occupations, and some communities have specialized kinds of occupations, such as mining, agriculture, energy, and services. Children need to know about the industry and individuals in their communities in order to expand their field of social science and their job possibilities for the future.

Home: immediate and extended family, outside care

School: personnel, curriculum developers

Community: church, helpers, legislators, tax payers

Hereditary and Environment

GENETICS Genetic inheritance determines the potential of each child; however, many individuals do not perform up to their potential. Perhaps if they were more stimulated and encouraged in their early years, they would more closely perform to their abilities. Some individuals inherit characteristics which are desirable— talents in the creating and performing arts, for example—while others inherit undesired characteristics—tendencies toward disease, learning disabilities, and so on.

CULTURE While there are many cultures and subcultures in the world today, cultural majorities are no longer limited to one place. Mobility means that people bring their own ways of life to their new locations. Prejudice need not be a problem if young children are taught about different cultures and about valuing others as they would like to be valued. Learning about other cultures should be more comprehensive than just studying dress and food preferences.

Teaching young children erroneous and abstract concepts about pilgrims, pioneers, native Americans, and others can only confuse and prejudice the children.

Example: One well-meaning teacher had been teaching about native Americans, calling them "Indians." She invited a native American to come into the classroom dressed in typical reservation costume. Many of the children were frightened and related the name, the appearance, and the concepts to their only acquaintance of Indians—television. Within her own classroom were children from this culture, but even they did not recognize any resemblance between the presentation and their own lives!

The same can hold true of people from other cultures and from other parts of the world. To understand others, the children must be able to relate concepts to their own abilities and to practice what they see and hear. Talking about people from some far away place, without tasting their food, trying on their costumes, and learning about their customs and habitat in a first-hand way (practicing the information) does little to increase the child's knowledge of our vast world.

GENDER In some countries, even our own, there have been great strides to bring equality to both males and females. No longer should we tolerate or practice gender-linking to occupations, privileges, and other areas of life. In our classrooms we should show, demonstrate, and encourage the children to participate in activities and actions that enhance and build their thinking—males do play a valuable role in home life; women do contribute to industry and the labor market.

Over the years books and stories for young children have favored males in the number of appearances, in versatility, and in activity. Fortunately, some of these gaps have begun to close. There is more media (books, movies, pictures, and so on) showing the interest and employment of both males and females in what were previously considered one-gender jobs.

VALUES A science curriculum that takes into consideration the diversity of people's backgrounds, beliefs, values, and customs will help young children adopt a broader view of social science.

Genetics: inherited potential and characteristics

Culture: perpetuation and understanding of a particular way of thinking or living

Gender: accepting one's own sex while valuing people of both sexes related to occupation, worth and individuality

Values: understanding and promoting ideas that are important to a person, family or society

Curriculum

RESEARCH Research and experience can be valuable assets when designing or planning curriculum for young children that will help them learn about their environment. Along with general findings, teachers must consider the age of the children plus individual needs and characteristics.

Research supports the following principles for teaching young children:

- First-hand experiences are preferred over demonstrations.

- Activities should be within the abilities and understanding of the children, but should be slightly challenging (slightly increasing their knowledge or integrating it with other knowledge).

- There should be provisions for (mostly) implicit and (some) explicit science experiences, which ''help children develop certain character traits or personal attributes, in addition to learning skills and subjects" (Myers and Maurer, 1987, p. 27).

- **Implicit** means spontaneous; taught through the arrangement of time, space, materials; interpersonal relationships and interactions.

Example: asking the children to find all the ways they can use a certain object.

- **Explicit** means planned; often academic and subject oriented.

    Example: showing or telling the children how they could use a certain object, then have them imitate the example.

- Most activities should be child-initiated.

- After preassessing the children, the teacher can introduce new, isolated concepts; build upon or enhance prior concepts; or show how concepts integrate into other concepts. This involves both horizontal, or **breadth** and vertical, or **depth** learning.

EVALUATION If the teacher decides on a topic, then preassess the children's present knowledge before establishing the concepts to be taught, how can he be sure that the information will be pertinent and appealing to young children? What constitutes good teaching practices, and how can the teacher know for sure the interpretation abilities of the children?

The teacher needs some method of determining the success of the materials and activities presented to the children. He needs to ask himself: Did the children actually learn what was intended? Which activities helped them best to understand the concepts? What were some of the comments of the children, and did the comments reflect true concepts? If the teacher were to teach the same topic again to these children or to other ones, what changes would be needed? How can the teacher build upon the concepts presented? What supporting ideas or materials could be placed in the classroom to remind the children of the concepts?

Research: systematic study from which facts are drawn

Evaluation: means of determining worth or whether desired objectives have been achieved

SUMMARY

Science is a vital part of our everyday lives. It is a legitimate subject, and has more meaning when it is taught in concert with any other subject matter and other experiences. This way, the children have opportunities to practice what they have learned and make it part of their lives.

Traditionally, teachers of young children have used an integrated curriculum. Subjects may be taught indoors or outdoors, through song, manipulation of body and objects, through literature, or as a social experience. The child's world really does have cohesiveness.

In this text, integration is used in a holistic manner—to combine parts (curriculum, activities, developmental areas, and so on) into a whole. It is using past experiences and knowledge with present experiences and knowledge in preparation for future experiences and knowledge. It is a means of building bridges between components rather than isolating them from each other. However, a word of caution: If things don't go together in a natural way, don't integrate them!

Besides combining and overlapping curriculum areas, science learning can be enhanced by combining areas of development, key individuals in the child's life, and heredity and environmental factors.

EXERCISES
study/discussion questions

1. Contrast the way subjects are taught in elementary schools and in a preschool or kindergarten.

2. Using story books, songs, or other media, indicate how you would integrate the following:

   a. math (numbers) with physical development

   b. language arts and outdoor play

   c. small muscle development and cooking

   d. different cultures with clothing worn

   e. social science and stories

   f. community people with school needs

3. Explain how the four language components help children with written and oral expression.

4. Give examples of implicit and explicit science experiences for young children.

5. Write a brief paragraph on how you would teach young children about a foreign culture. Get someone to respond to the soundness of your ideas (concrete or abstract).

6. How would you prepare an experience for adults and children regarding a science topic? How can you make it appealing and interesting to both groups?

10

What Children Already Know

A difficult concept for many adults is **preassessment,** or finding out what the children already know. Instead of finding out the knowledge and thinking of the children, some teachers start teaching where they have interests or materials. These adults may think that using commercial teaching products, last year's notes, or something off the top of their heads would save them time and be appropriate for all children at all times. Some teachers even use the same lesson plans year after year without considering the needs of different children, more current information, or new teaching methods. But they are wrong.

Preassessment can save time and embarrassment for teachers.

Example: Once there was a kindergarten student teacher. She decided it would be fun to teach the numbers one through ten to the children. On the day of her presentation, she said, "You will really like what we are going to do today. I am going to teach you how to count to ten!" Before she had the words out of her mouth, the children excitedly and quickly counted, "one, two, three, four, five, six, seven, eight, nine, ten!" She said, "Wait. Maybe you didn't hear what I said. I am going to teach you to count to ten!" The children counted to ten faster and louder, assuming that the teacher had not heard *them*! In her frustration, the student teacher said, "Wait.

I have spent a lot of time and money preparing for this lesson and I am going to teach you to count to ten whether you want it or not!" With this, she proceeded with her lesson. It was no wonder the children were disinterested, aggressive, disruptive, and bored.

Another student teacher, wanting to teach the numbers one to ten, approached it differently. She made individual numbers on four-by-six cards and casually handed the cards to different children. Some merely counted the cards (regardless of the written number), some put them in numerical order, and some said, "Oh, these are the A B C's," and handed them back. Immediately the teacher had knowledge about the differences of the children's understanding regarding number symbols. The teacher began planning the number experiences for the children. On the day of the presentation, she began by using fingerplays with numbers, then counting objects, counting *without* objects, looking at number symbols, matching symbols with objects, singing number songs, and following up by providing number opportunities in creative art, blocks, books, and manipulative toys. Throughout the day the children showed interest, excitement, use, and understanding of numbers.

There are ways to lose or gain the attention of an audience. Because gaining attention is more desirable than losing it, our focus will be the following:

- presenting familiar knowledge with some additional twist that will help the children incorporate the new with the already known or slightly increase their knowledge of the topic or idea

- presenting information that is of interest

- seeing to their comfort—physical environment (temperature, sound, seating, and so on)

- avoiding competition with something far more interesting (weather, sounds, smells)

- delivering complex information (jargon, concepts, sequencing) in an understandable way, such as relating it to other topics or defining terms

- speaking with tone inflection without being overly dramatic

- using eye contact and visual aids (when appropriate)

Some individuals use negative approaches with children and then wonder why they don't listen or follow instructions.

> Example: The *Science Guide* says that young children should be taught about how food grows. A diligent new teacher decides to teach about food and then check this requirement off the list because it is not a comfortable topic. She begins talking about food that is unfamiliar to the children and they lose interest. They are unresponsive. The teaching time goes on and on as the children wiggle on the cold, hard floor. They hear happy voices outside as other children play on a warm spring morning. The teacher tries to hurry the presentation only to find herself using advanced

words and presenting concepts out of sequence, making backtracking and repetition necessary. She becomes frustrated with poor classroom management and feels disgust for wasting preparation time.

Could a teacher ever be that unperceptive? The following is a closer look at what is happening and some proposed solutions.

1. **Uninteresting information.** Teachers who do not know the background and interests of the children often present repetitive or simplified information. They also have a tendency to talk down to the children. Some teachers prepare lessons and then are determined to teach them even if the children are disinterested.

2. **Lack of interest.** The teacher in the previous Example should have noted the interests of the children about plants and food. If there is interest, build upon it; if there is no visible interest, she should begin to enhance the environment with plants, pictures, a science food table, conversation at snack or lunchtime, observation of growing things, and general observations related to plants and food.

After an interest appears, she should select a narrow topic, conduct a preassessment to gain information for presentation, and plan a lesson.

Teachers can often regain the interest of the children if they change to something more active (a fingerplay, a song, a movement exercise) for a short diversion and then return to the task.

Art activities encourage problem solving.

3. **Physical environment.** If children are comfortably situated, they are more attentive. Perhaps sitting on the floor is the best way, but do they have to sit on a cold, hard floor with legs crossed for an extended time?

4. **Competition.** The teacher should see that distractions are kept to a minimum. Toys and other materials should be kept out of sight; the children should put their backs to windows; and a time should be chosen when there is less disturbance from within and without the classroom. Also group time should be avoided just before food is to be served—hungry children heed more to the food than the teacher.

5. **Complex information.** The teacher should avoid using unfamiliar jargon, especially without fully defining words, giving examples, and letting the children find out for themselves. (A teacher may define terms in a group setting provided there is opportunity soon after for the children to test the concepts.)

6. **Familiar references.** Presentations should include information that is familiar to the children and ways that the information could be of value to the children. For example, the teacher should show a plant that had been served previously or that would be served for snack following group time. Or the teacher could refer to the landscaping around the school and reiterate that some plants are helpful (food, beauty) and some harmful (stickers or thorns, poisonous, stain clothing, and so on).

7. **Delivery.** Eye contact, pleasant facial expressions, a pleasing voice, positive responses, and good body language can hold the interest of the children. If the teacher is more interested in presenting the material than meeting the needs of the children, the children feel their lack of importance.

Teachers should exercise caution to use the right amount and the right kinds of visuals. An over-abundance of visuals, those that are poorly done or abstract, or those that are hard to see or manipulate will distract from the information and will often give erroneous concepts to children.

Example: A student teacher wanted to plan a topic for discussion with the children. She knew that preassessing was a prerequisite for her teaching. Superficially she asked pointed questions and decided that the children knew little about her topic. She planned and presented the lesson. Throughout the day there was chaos, disinterest, aggression, and frustration. At the evaluation period at the end of the day, she was totally discouraged with the topic and teaching. Quickly the good things of the day were pointed out, but she heard none of them. Finally, one teacher said, ''Why did you think it went so poorly today?'' The student teacher replied, ''I worked so hard on the plan and the children just ignored all my efforts.'' A careful and thoughtful discussion followed, beginning with how superficially she had preassessed the knowledge and experience of the children and how many of the activities were teacher-directed. She admitted that she had preconceived ideas about what she wanted to teach and disregarded the preassessment. Her final comment was, ''Well, that's over! I don't want to lead the group ever again.'' But she was encouraged to heed her prior preassessment, do some additional preassessing, and re-plan the day. Her resistance was strong, but not unwavering. She rewrote her plan beginning with things that had gone well, integrated her ideas together better, and provided activities that had more direct connection with the topic and better acceptance by the children. At the end of the second teaching, she was excited about the response of the children and how smoothly the day had proceeded. She was a strong believer in preassessment and first-hand teaching.

Preassessment methods should not be used to *drill* or *grill* the children for knowledge learned. They can be used as a refresher or basis from which to expand.

Preassessing is a point from which the teacher plans. It should be done with care and precision. If it has been done well, it can lay the foundation for present and future teaching. It also can be used to determine if the children were able to grasp the concepts presented and if they could incorporate them into their world and lives.

SELECTING TOPICS FOR CHILDREN

If we help children develop a sense of curiosity and interest when they are young, we can build upon these characteristics. The chart on pages 106–107 can help adults evaluate appropriate science concepts that will foster this curiosity and interest. Children will be excited about the new and the unknown as well as confirming held ideas.

THE STEPS IN PREASSESSMENT _____

O*bserve*
Observe the interests and actions of the children. Be aware of things of interest in the school, neighborhood, TV, holidays, and so on.

D*ecide*
Decide on a topic that would be appropriate for the particular children, environment, and activities. Ask yourself if the topic has value and interest for the children. Is it appropriate for the time and situation?

D*iscover*
Set out to discover what the children already know.
- Rather than asking specific "yes" or "no" questions, ask open ended questions to gain information. (See Chapter 11 on questioning.)
- Set out activities that the children can use. Observe what they say and how they proceed.
- Preassess in a variety of ways, not just questioning. For example, sing songs about the intended topic and then discuss it, display pictures around the room, provide related props, place books in the language area, watch for interest, and listen to the children's comments.
- During outside play, introduce some ideas related to the intended topic.
- During a casual conversation (perhaps snack or lunch), introduce the topic. Ask for ideas.
- Decide on the best way to handle misinformation. Present accurate information clearly and simply.
- Think of creative ways to introduce your personality and ideas to the children; look for ways to enhance their personalities and ideas.

U*se*
Use the information gained from the preassessment in planning topics, materials, activities, and so on. If you want to teach certain concepts, make sure some of these ideas are used in the preassessment. Avoid preassessing about one thing and teaching about another, for example, preassessing about how some birds fly and then trying to tie that into kite flying. Teachers who preassess and then ignore the information in planning usually feel unsuccessful.

I*ntegrate*
Try to integrate curriculum topics and prior knowledge into the new topic, such as water with color. How can science be taught through music or physical activity?

B*roaden*
Plan to broaden or reintroduce prior topics. Maybe you taught about ducks one day. Now consider how additional information can be presented about ducks without being boring or redundant.

P*lan*
Plan a broad scope of activities and information so that both the better informed and less informed children benefit from them. Use the knowledgeable child to help others gain information and experience.

R*ecall*
Frequently recall that children learn through their senses. They need activity rather than lectures.

V*erbalize*
Remember that young children lack the necessary vocabulary and experiences to put their ideas into meaningful terms. "Children's verbal statements can either overstate or understate their knowledge. If children repeat comments they have heard but not understood, their comments give falsely favorable impressions. If children understand a concept but are too inarticulate to explain it, their statements can give an overly negative impression of their competence" (Siegler, 1986, pp. 13–14).

E*valuate*
Once the topic has been preassessed, planned, and presented, be sure to evaluate each activity. What went well? How could the activities or materials be presented in a better format? How did the children respond to the information and activities? How could this lesson be used as a preassessment for a future lesson on the same topic? Make notes on the written plan for future use.

EVALUATING SCIENCE CONCEPTS FOR YOUNG CHILDREN

Put a check by each topic as to whether it is appropriate or inappropriate for each

Number	Topic	Approp.	Inapprop.	2 Year Olds Note Why
1.	Seeds grow into plants.			
2.	Thunder is a bowling game in the sky.			
3.	Machines burn fuel.			
4.	Materials sink or float.			
5.	Milk comes from cartons in the store.			
6.	The rotation of the earth causes day and night.			
7.	Our bodies help us do many things.			
8.	Some materials absorb water.			
9.	Magnets pick up some metals.			
10.	Airplanes have wings like birds.			
11.	Evaporation and condensation are part of the water cycle.			
12.	Wheels are helpful to us.			
13.	Some colors make us feel happy.			
14.	Cacti are special kinds of plants.			
15.	Birds are animals with feathers.			
16.	Apples are a tree fruit.			
17.	Monsters are real.			
18.	Electric current travels in a circuit.			
19.	A hippopotamus is a large animal.			
20.	Pumpkins grow on vines.			
21.	Men are stronger than women.			
22.	There can be an eclipse.			
23.	Pollution is a major problem today.			
24.	Insects are animals with 6 legs.			
25.	The weather changes.			

age group listed, noting why you checked the one column over the other.

Approp.	Inapprop.	3 Year Olds Note Why	Approp.	Inapprop.	4 Year Olds Note Why	Approp.	Inapprop.	5 Year Olds Note Why

They will seek new knowledge like an unquenched thirst. They can cultivate feelings of empathy, sympathy, love, and understanding.

The younger the child, the more the topics need to be related to her present environment (home and family). As the child grows in age, skills, and experience, she will be more interested in specifics related to the home and family, and at the same time will express more interests in her ever expanding world.

Science concepts are involved with all aspects of living; thus, many topics will be of interest and value to young children. It is a prudent teacher who knows when and what topics to introduce, and just how much information to give at one time.

Reviewing the chart on pages 106–107 will help the teacher evaluate which of the 25 topics would or would not be appropriate for each of the four age groups. Some could be simplified for use and others would be totally inappropriate for all four age groups.

Some important facts about the table need to be recognized. Many of the concepts are vital for young children to learn, while others are too advanced, misleading, or abstract. Children also need to discover relationships between concepts and not just be taught facts. The topics are general, but good evaluations can be made based on knowledge about how young children learn.

Topic numbers 1, 4, 7, 8, 9, 12, 15, 16, 19, 20, and 25 are probably the easiest to teach young children; however, each one has special conditions or concepts to consider. For example, number 9 may cause some problems because young children might not know the definition of either "magnets" or "metals," and might even envision something actually "picking up" something else. Other topics may pose similar problems with definitions and familiarity of words and concepts. The teacher would need to carefully prepare methods of preassessment to determine the thinking of the children, who may need many opportunities to hear the words, practice the concepts, and relate them to something familiar or useful.

Further, topic numbers 2, 10, and 21 teach incorrect or undesirable concepts. Number 5 is also tricky—most children would agree that "milk comes from cartons in the store." Teachers need to decide the best and most accurate ways to teach concepts. Perhaps this topic needs to be taught sequentially: a visit to a dairy farm to see cows being milked, some simple experience about processing milk, delivery to the store, and then purchasing and using the milk. Available opportunities and policies help determine if a topic will be beneficial to the children.

Once a teacher determines what would or would not work for the children, he should have a discussion with other teachers to see how valid both reasonings are. After he teaches some of these concepts, he should have a reevaluation.

BUILDING ON PREVIOUS TOPICS

Some adults resent having to repeat information or experiences, especially if the experiences were not too exciting the first time. Perhaps they could learn something from young children, who seem to thrive on repetition. The newness and the excitement are relived with repetition. Of course, it can be overdone and redundant, but when teachers use prior teaching as a preassessment for additional learning, the children's memories are refreshed and additional information helps integrate prior knowledge with new knowledge or with other topics.

Example: A bird's nest is found in the play yard. The teacher listens to the comments of the children and observes their behavior with the nest. She carefully preassesses the kind of bird that could live in the nest, how the nest was built, what the bird would eat, and how it would take care of eggs and baby birds. Then she plans a simple lesson. They use the nest and a variety of birds, finally deciding that a robin was the most likely occupant of the nest. They talk about the characteristics of the bird—color, size, eating habits, and so on. They carefully examine the nest and determine that it was made with string, twigs and some mud. There surely were eggs laid in the nest because of the fragments of blue shell still remaining. The teacher reads a story to the children about a nest outside a child's bedroom window and how eggs were laid and baby birds were hatched. The story re-

lates about the mother feeding the baby birds and how they grew and learned to fly. At a later date, the teacher and children talk about other nest-building birds, how to identify them, different ways they care for their young, and what they like to eat. At still another time and before the topic gets too complex, they compare the first bird (robin) with the second bird (duck), noting similarities and differences. Eventually information can be taught about coverings of animals (scales, feathers, shells) as different kinds of animals are studied.

Through the process of reusing and integrating prior topics, both **horizontal** and **vertical learning** takes place. Horizontal learning occurs through teaching a topic in breadth (many kinds of animals), while vertical learning deals with the depth of a topic (the many attributes of one animal). Thus, learning is expanded and enhanced.

SUMMARY

Many adults do not realize the importance of preassessing present knowledge of children before planning experiences for them.

There are ways to lose or gain the attention of an audience. Gaining their attention makes teaching and learning easier.

Inappropriate teacher preparation contributes to the frustration of teachers and children.

Following simple steps in preassessment can help assure a teacher of proper topics, materials, and activities for young children.

Many science topics are of interest and value to young children. Teachers need to observe the children, remember how they process information, and plan opportunities for them to learn about their immediate world.

Unlike many adults, children like and appreciate experiences and concepts that are repeated, added upon, and integrated with other concepts.

EXERCISES

study/discussion questions

1. Discuss ways adults (speakers, teachers) can keep the interest of their audiences. What ways keep your attention when you are in a group setting?

2. Observe young children in a group setting. Select one child and determine if the child is interested or disinterested during your observation period. Suggest ways you would hold the interest of young children when they are participating as a group.

3. By watching children in spontaneous play, how can you determine if they are acting on their own interests or if they are responding to instructions from others?

4. Identify a topic you feel would be appropriate for a specific age group (knowing that children have different interests and abilities). Suggest three ways you could preassess the knowledge of the children on your selected topic. Use the table on page 105. If possible, try out your ideas.

5. Using the table on pages 106–107, Evaluating Science Concepts for Young Children, or creating five science concepts on your own, tell why they would be appropriate for three-year-olds and list several ways of preassessing current knowledge of the children.

6. Take a category of learning, and diagram how you would teach con-

cepts in a horizontal (broad) manner. Diagram how you would teach concepts in a vertical (depth) manner. Is one manner better than the other when teaching young children? Why or why not?

11

When Questions Are Effective

Questioning is one form of preassessing. Questions may be asked spontaneously or deliberately by either children or adults. It is the form of the questions and the reasons for the questions that are of concern when dealing with young children. Two-year-olds usually ask "what" questions and their replies to adult questions probably result in pointing to the object or in a physical demonstration. Three-year-olds usually ask "why" questions and usually seem unsatisfied with answers received, as if the verbalization is more important than the information. Four- and five-year-olds usually ask information or "how-to" types of questions. Their answers to adult questions may or may not indicate understanding. At any of these young ages, the answers to questions may seem incomplete, disjointed, or off-track according to adult standards. Remembering these general and basic statements about children and questioning, and the *limitations of experience and language*, adults must carefully think through what they (and young children) are asking, what the intended purpose is, and how to interpret what is verbalized.

GENERAL QUESTION ASKING

The Socratic method, successful for use with young children, is defined by Wolfinger as "a way of asking questions designed to draw information out of the students rather than pouring it into them. The Socratic method is purely verbal" (1984, p. 217). The teacher uses this method to develop content information and considers (Wolfinger, 1984, p. 219):

1. knowing the children being taught ("reading children")

2. prior experience of the children with the concept (preassessment for progress and follow-up)

3. well planned and sequenced questions (easy at first, narrowed and focused, reviewed, and then concluded)

4. back-up *questions* (alternates, if necessary)

5. back-up *procedures* (alternate approach, if necessary)

6. a method for discussion to flow smoothly

7. final points (if not reached by the children)

"Thought provoking questions, whether they come from you or the children, can do much to expand an ordinary experience. If the children are in the midst of an activity and simply want information, a straightforward answer is the best response. At other times, helping them arrive at the answer themselves may be most satisfying" (Williams, Rockwell, and Sherwood, 1987, p. 11).

QUESTION ASKING BY CHILDREN

Teachers are not the only ones who ask questions. Children ask questions as a means of finding out information or getting responses from adults. They may pose questions or they may struggle to find answers for themselves. When a child asks a question that the teacher cannot answer for whatever reason, it is acceptable to say, "I just don't know the answer to that. Perhaps we can find out together," or "I'll try to find the answer to that and we can talk about it later" *if* the teacher does make an effort (with the child, alone, or with other assistance) and then reports back to the child. Another alternative is to throw the question back to the child saying, "What do you think about it?" or "How do you think we could find out?" Just to say, "I don't know," is unacceptable.

In order to answer a child's question, the adult must listen carefully to the wording and any emotional connotation. Adults can help children become good listeners when the adults become role models, taking time and showing interest in what the child is saying and doing. The child then feels the adult's interest and will use these techniques when talking with others. Some simple but effective listening behaviors include:

1. being on the child's level (with the adult's eyes not exceeding 12 inches *above* the child's eyes)

2. having eye contact with the child

3. giving the child uninterrupted time and attention until the message has been completed

4. accepting the message and trying not to control, evaluate, or guide the conversation

5. avoiding asking too many questions so the child is distracted from the intended message

6. using facial expressions and body language to note responses to the words (smiles, nods, squeezes of the hand, postures)

7. concentrating not only on the words, but also the meaning of the conversation

8. paying attention to children who are more quiet or who seldom initiate conversations

9. using verbal communication to facilitate the asking of questions to find out information and to build good relationships

QUESTIONS FOR YOUNG CHILDREN

In designing good questions for young children, it is unreasonable for the teacher to:

- expect children to wait their turn to talk

- insist that children raise their hands and remain silent until called upon

- change subjects abruptly

- put children down for interrupting or making off-topic comments

- act bored or impatient with children's answer time or responses

The teacher should ask good questions—ones that prompt the kind of information desired, are sequenced to lead the student to the desired ideas, and allow the student time to consider a response (Wolfinger, 1984, p. 180).

Teachers also need to identify different kinds of questions for different responses: those that are evaluative, those that have limited or specific responses, those that generate many responses, those that require observation, those that require definitions or classifications, those that require a demonstration, those that require a hypothesis, and those that call for a comparison (Carin and Sund, 1985, p. 116).

The following are codes of teacher responses to questions.

CODE   TEACHER RESPONSES

A	asking only one question at a time
B	beginning with a phrase or information and then turning it into a question
C	giving a command rather than a choice or response
D	asking a broad, over-generalized question
E	designating a respondent before asking a question
F	asking questions that call for many and varied answers
G	asking questions that lead to an objective or discussion
H	asking questions that are sequential—easy to harder
I	asking questions for clarification
J	reprimanding child responses
K	rejecting answers other than expected ones
L	making a request rather than asking for a response
M	each child thinks she is supposed to respond

In general, the teacher using these codes can evaluate questions for use with children between the ages of two and five.

For example:

Question	Code(s)
Teacher: What do I have here? What color is this? Who likes this color? Jeff, why aren't you paying attention?	
Teacher: This is something I picked up on my vacation, and what do you think I could do with it?	
Teacher: What day is this?	
Teacher: Who can tell me the differences between these two objects?	
Teacher: What do you know about worms?	
Teacher: Helen, can you tie your shoe?	
Teacher: Who has been to the zoo? Now, be quiet because I have something to say. Pete, I said for you to listen. Ann, it isn't nice to sit in front of someone. Who has been to the zoo?	
Teacher: Could you put the blocks in the basket?	
Teacher: What shape is this? (No quick response.) What shape is this? (Still no quick response.) I said, what shape is this? Quick, now. What shape is this?	
Teacher: Would you like to help with the snacks or go outside? (The child selects to go outside.) Well, I need a	

Question	Code(s)

helper so you place the napkins and glasses on the table.

Teacher: Who can count to
ten? I didn't tell you to count,
I just asked who could count
to ten. Sue, can you count to
ten for us?

Teacher: Someone is not here
today. Who could it be?

Teacher: Who would like to
play a game?

Teacher: I see that Mary, Kim,
Stephen, Lane, Mitzi, Nicho-
las, Mike, Louise, Betsy,
Devan, Tyler, and Blaine have
green on today, don't they?

Teacher: Remember the day
we talked about dinosaurs?

ADDITIONAL HINTS FOR TEACHERS

The teacher should listen carefully to
the children's responses—not only for
words, but for meanings.

She needs to acknowledge each answer
before moving on and avoid accepting
the first answer as the only right answer. Also, she should avoid multiple
or rapid-fire questions and ask more
thinking questions, not just those with
specific responses.

Looking for reasons why children
would give incorrect answers, the
teacher should ask the child for further
clarification before calling an answer
wrong, or saying "No." The response
may be a better one than expected by
the teacher. Or perhaps the child has
misunderstood the question or has

prior misinformation that needs to be
corrected.

Where possible, the teacher should use
hints and sequence information, questions, or visual aids to assist in the answers.

The teacher needs to be specific in
praise, telling the child why it was a
good answer or good thinking. She
should avoid saying, "OK," or "good,"
to each answer and moving on without
actually listening to the children.

When requests are made, even in the
form of a question, they should be
worded as requests rather than
choices.

Children need time to contemplate the
question, what is expected, and how
the information will be of value to
them. Each young child responds as if
the teacher is talking to him individually. Requiring these young children
to raise their hands or only speak one
at a time is very difficult and inappropriate for them.

To avoid having children blurt out information, they should be given ideas
in advance about how to respond, such
as, "I will give you time to think about
what I am asking and then we'll talk
about it," or "If you know the answer,
put your finger on your ear and then
we will talk about it," or "Tell your
neighbor what you're thinking before
we discuss it." A child could also be
identified in advance to answer the
question. (Older children can raise their
hands and wait to respond.) Rewards
or recognition should go to the children who really think about their answers. Dr. Mary Budd Rowe finds that a
three second or longer waiting time results in more *student* responses, more

unsolicited but appropriate responses, decrease in failure to respond, increase of confidence in children, increase in variety of responses, increase in speculative thinking, and decrease in discipline. For *teachers* the benefits include a more flexible attitude toward student responses, decreases in number of questions, and a change in expectations of the children, viewing "their class as having fewer academically slower students" (reported in Carin and Sund, 1985, p. 123).

GENERAL TYPES OF QUESTIONS

Do teachers or children ask most of the questions in a spontaneous or informal setting? Who asks more in a formal or planned setting? What are the values in discussing things on a one-to-one basis? A small group basis? A large group basis? Does the interaction change with the age and number of children involved?

There are two general categories of questions: **convergent,** those that seek specific answers or have limited responses; and **divergent,** those that create information and are limited only by the thoughts and experiences of the individuals involved.

How they are used and when they are used make a vast difference. Even though the types of questions differ in specific ways, they both have a place in teaching young children. For some purposes a balance between the two types of questions is desirable. Studies show that approximately 70 to 80 percent of the questions asked by teachers require only simple recall answers (Belch, 1975).

A quiet time to think.

Teachers should use questioning in a way that allows the children to find success in the process of listening and answering. To do this, simple and familiar ideas are used, moving to more complex behaviors as the children feel more confident and gain more knowledge and experience.

Convergent Questions

For convergent questions, usually considered "closed" questions, specific answers are sought, and they have limited possibilities. They are used to review or recall prior information, which can be memorized. The process goes: question, answer; question, answer; and so on. These are teacher-centered questions in what Carin and Sund call the "ping-pong pattern" (1985, p. 124).

"Convergent questions are necessary to provide children with skills and concepts to help them move to higher levels of learning, where they can benefit from divergent or open-ended questions" (Carin and Sund, 1985, p. 118).

Divergent Questions

Encouraging a broad range of responses, divergent questions are considered "open-ended." The answers are unlimited, can be based on prior knowledge or personal experiences, and may lead the thinker to responses not directly related to the particular question. They are used to problem solve, tap into imagination, stimulate language, encourage cooperation, and to brain-storm. Generally the answers are not memorized. The process goes: question, answer, answer, answer, and so on. These questions are more student-centered and are called the "basketball-game pattern" by Carin and Sund (1985, p. 124).

Gentle probing by the teacher can increase the children's creative and critical thinking, helping them generate new possibilities, increase observational awareness, and discover things for themselves. Seeing interrelationships, making hypotheses, and drawing conclusions are very important in learning science concepts (Carin and Sund, 1985, p. 121).

In the following examples, certain circumstances indicate that a convergent question would be more appropriate, while others seem more suited to a divergent question.

1. The teacher wants to determine which colors the children know.

    Convergent question: What color is this?

    Divergent question: How many colors can you see in the picture?

2. The children are asked to stack the blocks.

    Convergent question: What shape of block goes here?

    Divergent question: Where could we put the triangle blocks?

3. The teacher wants to use a planting experience.

    Convergent question: Who can plant a seed?

    Divergent question: What things would we need in order to plant a seed?

4. The teacher plans to introduce a unit on farm animals.

    Convergent question: How many legs does a dog have?

    Divergent question: What animals on the farm have four legs?

5. The teacher is preassessing written symbols.

    Convergent question: What letter (or number) is this?

    Divergent question: Who can put the letters in one pile and the numbers in another pile?

A guide to help increase the use of divergent questions by teachers is suggested by Carin and Sund (1985, p. 121), and is adapted here for use with young children.

1. Ask questions that require more than *yes* or *no* answers because they dictate the style of the answer.

2. When necessity calls for *yes* or *no* answers, ask additional things such as "Why?" "How do you know?" "How might we find out?" "What makes you think so?" "What gives you that idea?"

3. Learn to ask questions that help children generate, discover, and compare things, "Using these objects and the bowl of water, which objects do you think will sink and float?"

SUMMARY

The following suggestions may be useful when questioning young children:

1. Ask divergent questions as often as possible, remembering that both divergent and convergent questions have value.

2. Ask only one question at a time, making sure it is developmentally appropriate for the particular children. Set the stage for discussion, but avoid lecturing and expecting children to deal in abstractions.

3. Allow time for the children to think and respond. Encourage thinking more than speed. Avoid answering your own questions if there is silence.

4. Listen carefully and acknowledge each response. Continue receiving the responses of children—not just the first one or the right one. Reward the *thinking* and the *answering*, not the answers.

5. Be accepting of responses. Before saying they are off topic, get more information from the child, who may see a connection the adult had not considered. Adults often expect children to listen and follow through, but the adult who truly listens to a child will note that the child will return often for conversations or support.

6. In a caring way, ask for additional information when necessary. "Tell us more about . . ." When necessary, reiterate the topic and direction without cutting off responses or being critical. "It is fun to talk about frogs and the song we sang the other day was about frogs, but now we are talking about the weather. What kind of weather do we have today?"

7. Begin with simple questions and move to more complex ones as the children show readiness.

8. Handle misconceptions carefully. Find out the thinking of the child. Then decide the best way to present correct information.

9. Plan to integrate questions into various areas of curriculum.

10. Periodically give answers and help the children make up the questions. Example: "I am thinking of a fruit that is round, has a bumpy peeling, is orange, has sections inside, is juicy, and grows on a tree. What is it?"

11. Play a guessing game such as "I'm thinking about . . . What do you think it is?"

12. Stimulate language and thinking through activities such as, "What would we find if we . . . (went for a walk, went to the zoo, planned a

field trip, cooked apples, and so on).''

13. Show children how to use resources (people, materials, books). ''We want to . . . and we don't know how (or what). How can we find out?''

14. Watch for children who never (or seldom) ask questions. Design some ways to help them pose and answer questions.

15. Walk the children through an activity. ''Which of these items do you think will float and which do you think will sink? (predicting) Let's make a pile for floating things and one for sinking things.'' Try the items (proceeding) and then compare then to earlier predictions (testing). ''Why do some float and others sink?''

16. Use statements such as ''John thinks the cow eats daisies; Amy saw a cow drinking water; and the picture shows the cow eating corn. What else does a cow eat?''

EXERCISES

study/discussion questions

1. Ponder the following situations and pose questions that might be asked by teachers or children:

   a. The teacher formally introduces a new toy to one child. (The teacher might ask, ''What things do you think you could do with this toy?'' rather than ''Did you ever see anything like this?'')

   b. The teacher walks with a small group of children as they spontaneously discover new flowers growing on the playground.

   c. The teacher talks with a large group of children as they spontaneously anticipate a field trip.

   d. A child sits with a new playful puppy.

2. Briefly explain the Socratic method of asking questions and give an example of its effectiveness.

3. Describe some situations and pose both convergent and divergent questions for each activity.

   a. Situation:
   Convergent question:
   Divergent question:

   b. Situation:
   Convergent question:
   Divergent question:

   c. Situation:
   Convergent question:
   Divergent question:

   Continue posing situations until you can readily and easily identify the difference between the two types of questions and when each type would be appropriate for young children.

4. List some questions that would re-gain the attention of children who had become distracted from the topic of caring for baby lambs.

12

Teachers and Parents of Young Children

TEACHERS

The role of teachers in science curriculum for young children is varied, important, and encompassing. The teachers must know how children learn, develop, and construct new knowledge; must put this knowledge into constant practice; must help the children mesh new and prior information into meaningful and useful concepts; and must learn how to evaluate the progress of the children as well as the value of the activities provided. Next to parents, teachers are the most likely ones to whom the children turn for acceptance, support, nurturance, and guidance.

Guidelines for Teachers

Assuming that teachers have a desire to teach and have the stamina and the skills to do it, how can they prepare themselves to best present science concepts to young children?

Role of the Teacher

Teachers should feel challenged in offering science curriculum to young children. Smith (1987) encourages teachers to look for daily experiences that involve science, to encourage children to explore "science-related phenomena." Teachers also should provide a variety of opportunities for the children, guide the children through such experiences, and remember that "meaningful learning is an active, self-regulated process" (Foreman and Kuschner, 1983, p. 123). Teachers should note and take advantage of children's spontaneous activities without "dulling and nullifying" the original interest of the children, thereby frustrating both the teacher and the children (Carini, 1977, p. 18).

Teachers need to recognize, foster, and appreciate the curiosity in children. Teachers who have a sense of wonder and curiosity model that kind of behavior and encourage it in children (Harlan, 1965, p. 250). A noted science educator says, "There are no records of children being inspired by teachers who themselves are not inspired" (Blough, 1971).

Many teachers tremble when they think of presenting science concepts—especially to young children. Many of these teachers have had negative or frustrating experiences with science throughout their own schooling. They envision science as being important but too difficult to understand. When asked to teach some of the concepts to children, their frustration and panic are increased. There is a constant cry for better scientific and academic preparation of children in schools. This cry could be less prominent if children and teachers look at science as something pleasurable, helpful, and exciting. To increase these feelings, teachers must exhibit a positive attitude toward science and foster science-like activities in the classroom. They must appreciate the questions and exploration of the children. This is often done by building a strong personal relationship with the children and being excited with the children. Holt remarks,

Children's negative attitudes toward science may have been 'caught' from unenthusiastic teachers who rely on textbooks as the only source of gaining information. Those teachers may have been too unsure of themselves to allow children to consider alternatives to the textbook explanations, or to find out through experimentation. (1989, p. 18)

Three teaching roles in which the teacher gains growth and satisfaction while the children gain experience, in-

TEACHER RESPONSIBILITIES _____

Philosophy	They should develop a clear philosophy about learning and young children and be able to support and defend it, especially to parents, administrators, or others who scoff at science activities for such young children.
Observation	They should observe and listen to children. What do they talk about? What are their interests—individually and collectively? They should capitalize on the fact that most children are fascinated with their environment and the people in it. Teachers should acknowledge, encourage and value the interest and curiosity of the children. For children who do not show such interest, teachers should consciously look at the environment (space allotted, time restrictions, complexity or simplicity of materials, availability of playmates, and desire for socialization).
Awareness	They should be aware that some things may not go as planned. If failures occur, teachers can turn them into learning experiences for themselves and the children. Teachers are models to help the children deal with their own failures and frustrations.
Opportunities	They should provide opportunities, materials, and props in as natural a setting as possible. Isolated facts or experiences are less meaningful to children than when they see relevance or usefulness.
Variation	They should provide a variety of opportunities, but not overwhelm the children with too many different or complex experiences at once. Familiar materials help the children build confidence, but used too often may create boredom or resistance. Teachers should integrate the curriculum areas for variety, continuity, and breadth.
Individuality	They should frequently review the characteristics of young children—collectively and individually—recalling the range of physical, social, cognitive, and language abilities of young children. Teachers should believe and plan that all children (regardless of age, sex, origin, language, and background) can become interested in science concepts.

terest, and knowledge have been identified by Holt (1989, p. 20) as,

a. the **facilitator,** who provides a learning environment where the children can practice with materials and ideas

b. the **enabler,** who ''sets a positive encouraging tone by staying in touch with his or her own excitement in discovery''

c. the **consultant,** who is an observer, a listener, a supporter, and a supplier of information while the children reflect on ideas and solutions

Each of the above roles provides opportunities for the children in slightly different ways and in differing amounts of teacher involvement. Each role is important and can be effective based on the goals of the teacher for a particular experience.

Professionalism	They should keep themselves abreast of current events (especially community events or TV programs that hold the interest of young children and families); read professional literature and related research in order to implement valid ideas into their lives and classrooms; join local, state, or national organizations or attend conferences; and associate with or organize teachers who love science and teach it well. They should be willing and able to expend the time, energy, and resources it takes to make learning fun, exciting, stimulating, and worthwhile for the children.
Process	They should be more concerned with the process of science (and in helping children construct knowledge for themselves) than in creating end products or spoon-feeding the children facts they do not understand.
Environment	They should plan a classroom environment that has many opportunities for children. What areas do the children enjoy most? Least? What could the teacher do to add appeal or authenticity to the experiences?
Techniques	They should develop teaching techniques of knowing when to offer physical or verbal assistance (and when to let children resolve problems and conflicts), and how and when to talk with children (lengthy conversations and lectures discourage children from asking questions or interacting with adults).
Evaluation	Teachers need to originate or adopt ways of determining how effective their teaching and materials have been in helping children acquire knowledge. (How does the teacher know if the children have acquired the information the teacher thought was presented?)
Inform	They should be in close contact with and inform parents frequently of what the children are doing or learning. Parents can then support the learning at home and give vital feedback to the teacher.

Some philosophies may be interpreted as restricting the child's exploration and learning, such as one that advocates that learning (and specifically science learning) must be set up in a rigid pattern where strict steps are followed, teachers have verbal input, and specific goals are achieved. A contrasting view is that of Case (1985), who believes that teachers have a better ability to guide and encourage children's intellectual development when they empathize with the children in feelings of excitement and satisfaction, and that children learn by imitating and interacting with others. To him, teaching is a social facilitation of children's problem-solving abilities.

Good teachers are necessary for teaching children to love science and learning. "A good teacher knows with caring respect not only this wonderful child process of learning, but also that a child develops unevenly, in spurts, plateaus, and setbacks. Physical, social, and cognitive achievements are interdependent and inseparable for emotional development," comments Cartwright (1989, p. 52).

Preparation of the Classroom

In eagerness to provide science opportunities in the classroom, it is possible to overwhelm the children. Such circumstances often discourage rather than encourage child participation. Some cautions may be needed. Teachers should ask themselves the following questions or observe the children as various materials and concepts are presented:

1. Is it something the children could do individually or in small groups? In other words, are activities and materials presented in a child-like way or do they require constant supervision and help from an adult?

    Example: An art activity in which the children are to mix paint, make a picture, cut it out, paste it onto a pre-drawn outline to make a headband, measure their head size, and staple the band. The teacher should make a mental or written note of the many science activities here, and consider the procedure or circumstances where the above activity would be:

    1. child-centered   2. adult-centered

    Items to consider include: methods and materials with which to mix the paint, materials for painting, quality of scissors and expectations of cutting, detail of outline, purpose of the activity, skills and experience of the children, teacher expectation, time and space allotted, sequence of the activity, interest and skills of the children, and so on.

2. Does it involve any possible harm or danger to the children?

    Example: Making pudding for snack or lunch.

    Items to consider include: cooked or instant pudding; teacher or child preparation; actual preparation, making, and clean-up; sanitation; number of individuals involved; ways to reduce or eliminate harm and danger; time and space allotted; and supervision available.

3. Are the children interested in the activities and materials and will participation be meaningful to the children? "To extend the original activity and its representations is the major responsibility of the teacher in approaching education. That is, it is the major responsibility of the teacher to strengthen the 'inner connectedness of the experience'.(Carini, 1977, p. 18)

    Example: A sensory table with dirt from the playyard—complete with rocks, leaves, weeds, and small twigs. Materials consist of two small-mesh 3-inch strainers, a wooden spoon with a long handle, and two tablespoons with bent handles. For the past week, the children have been digging roads and tunnels in the sand pile and have even planted a small garden to the rear of the playyard. Today the weather does not permit outdoor play.

The teacher should consider why the children may not be interested in the sensory table; what could be done to make the activity more appealing; how a teacher could help the children to relate the previous outdoor experiences to the sensory table; and how science can be promoted in this activity.

Teachers have a great influence upon children, their parents, and their families; however, it is the close relationship between the home and school that best serves the child's needs.

PARENTS

It may seem redundant to include a separate section on the role of parents in the learning of their young children, for it has been mentioned and stressed throughout this text that parents are the foremost teachers of their children. Parents exert a strong influence on children's lives especially during the early stages of development (Anthony and Pollock, 1985; Feldman and Nash, 1986; Patterson, 1986). Spending time, creating emotional bonds, value systems, and dependency, preparing for experiences, then following through, following up, and building upon previous experiences are only a few of the interactions between parents and children. Parents have more of a continuous relationship with their children than do teachers or other significant adults in the children's lives. Parents have privileges and responsibilities that cannot be designated to others. Thus, it is only fitting that parents are singled out for recognition in this text.

Parents do influence attitudes of children toward learning. In 1986, Thomas conducted a large-scale survey of college women and minority students regarding parents' involvement with their children's science education. The results show that positive family attitudes and encouragement were significant factors in fostering the students' interest in math and science. And a strong relationship exist between the extent to which these students enjoyed working on science hobbies as children and their science achievement in high school. Another example of positive parental involvement is Crandall's classic achievement motivation studies which confirm that the child's degree of striving to learn is significantly influenced by the reactions of important others to his efforts (1965). Harlan writes that self-esteem develops as the child feels status as a learner in the parents' eyes. Teachers can assist this process by giving feedback to parents in positive, understandable ways, such as in a conversation or newsletter encouraging them to tell the child their positive opinion about science, and to also let the child know of her good thinking and learning. The role of parents in the attitudes and learning of their children, especially in science, cannot be overstated.

Some teachers feel overburdened just preparing for and teaching young children. They feel their responsibility of teaching ends there, but the teacher who keeps parents abreast of classroom activities will find increased interest, awareness, and productivity in children and their families. Teachers of young children generally have more contact with parents than do teachers of older children. It may occur casually or formally. **Casual contacts** can be as parents bring or pick up their children, as children make comments or ask questions that can be relayed to parents in an informative way, a bulletin board that depicts the direction of learning, a casual meeting of teacher and parents away from school, notification of community events or educational TV programs, or local places of interest for visiting. More **formal contact** includes a parent meeting or conference, a phone call, a newsletter, an invitation to parents to share talents or knowledge, monthly goals prepared specifically for the parents, or written requests to parents.

While some parents feel that teaching is the responsibility of the teacher, other parents are excited to know what their children are doing away from home and can be excellent resource people in supplying feedback, objects, classroom assistance, and other individual helps.

Adults learn from each other.

Parent Education

Parent education plays a vital part of the total experience for the child and the family.

Example: In our Early Childhood Education Laboratory at Brigham Young University, we have seven different ways of delivering information to our parents—selected readings and probe questions, listening to specially prepared radio drama tapes and probe questions, monthly lectures, home visits with a prepared message, classroom participation, special topics for parents who have had other children in the program, and learning centers for ideas and materials for home use. Each set of parents selects the option that best suits their needs and briefly reports every two weeks on some activity they have had

with the individual enrolled child. The most popular selections are readings and tapes. Parent reports are positive with regard to their experiences in parent education.

In addition to planned education for our parents, we send home Learning Cards each week. These cards (usually one 8½ x 11 sheet) inform the parents about what their children are experiencing at school; they are not to be used as a model for interrogation or exploitation. Frequently as parents and children pass my open door, I hear one or the other mention the theme—either before or after the school session. Children often say to teachers, "I know what we're talking about today. It's _____." The teacher will ask, "How did you know?" and the child happily replies, "Because it was on the learning card and my mommy told me." We find parents willing to share objects and ideas from home because they know the topics in the classrooms.

The learning cards contain information for parents and also simple, inexpensive, readily available suggestions for parents to follow-up on the topic. We send the information home weekly, and because we meet four days per week, the information must be concise, have meaning, show the parents we think it is important to let them know what their children are experiencing, and still fit it on one page. (Teachers may think this is an added burden to prepare such a sheet, but feedback from children and parents proves it to be another way for teachers and parents to join in the educational process.)

Some examples would be appropriate. From the section on the painter in the "Community" section in Part IV, (pages 172–173), the following information would appear on the learning card:

Topic: Painters

Today we will talk about painters and why they paint objects (beauty and protection). We will also discuss clothes worn and tools used by a painter. We will wear painter's hats and practice using wide brushes with water outside. The experience will reinforce our prior learning on primary colors and in practicing mixing primary colors to make secondary (or new) colors. Please point out to your child certain homes, buildings, or objects that may have been painted by a painter. When possible, let your child help paint something (a picture, furniture, or toy) or help decide on a color for the object.

At times teachers may select a weekly theme (knowing full well that one day per topic is not enough for young children and they will need to build on this topic at another time). Examples could be taken from any of the topics in Part IV of this text, making sure the information and topics are appropriate for the age, location, and interests of the children.

	TRANSPORTATION	FAMILY	OCCUPATIONS
Monday Theme	Trains	Self	Garbage worker
Tuesday Theme	Buses	Babies	Doctor
Wednesday Theme	Airplanes	Parents	Grocery clerk
Thursday Theme	Boats	Grandparents	Law enforcement

Learning card examples might include:

Topic: Grandparents

On this day we will talk about grandparents and their relationships to the children. We will also talk about activities that grandparents and children can do together. The children can make cards to send to their grandparents. If possible let your child take the card to their grandparents, visit or call them, or visit an elderly person.

Miscellaneous topics might include:

Animal tails: Monday we will talk about animals' tails and how they are different in shape, size, and coloring. We will talk about why it hurts an animal to have its tail pulled or stepped on, and that some animals use their tails for practical purposes. Talk with your child about familiar animals, discussing the size, shape, covering, and usefulness of their tails.

Vegetables: Today we will talk about which vegetables grow above the ground and which vegetables grow below the ground. We will also talk about the difference between raw and cooked vegetables and that we can eat them both ways. The importance of eating our vegetables relates to growing bodies. Next time you visit a produce market or serve vegetables, help the child to remember whether they grow above or below the ground.

By informing the parents about their children's school activities, we have found great success in increasing the amount of meaningful conversation between parents and young children. Children ask questions about topics, school, and things in general. Parents initiate and enjoy interaction with their child's world outside the home.

SUMMARY

As parents and teachers, we tend to follow patterns we have seen or been part of; parents often replicate the type of discipline and the values imposed by their parents; teachers tend to teach as they were taught, not as they were taught to teach.

Perhaps in teaching young children, and especially in teaching science concepts to them, we need to take a second look at past ideas and procedures. For some, minor changes may be necessary; for others the changes may be drastic. Change may be difficult for some, "But the problem can be better understood by examining a single long-held belief and how it has limited

our ability to best educate the student.'' (Hildebrand, 1991).

Teachers who want to teach science effectively will consider:

- ages and interests of the children in their classrooms and what is developmentally appropriate for them individually and collectively

- how to introduce or enhance the interests of the children related to themselves, their community, and their world

- becoming a part of a professional group that believes in the future of the children, stimulates teachers to be progressive and productive, and supports them in their teaching

- their classroom as a whole—the atmosphere, the physical arrangement, the curriculum, the opportunities, the individuals therein, and the goals of education—to make science learning exciting, challenging, and productive

While parents are the foremost teachers of their children, some of the responsibility is shared with other adults (especially teachers) outside the family.

Positive family attitudes and encouragement are significant factors in fostering children's interest in science and other academic subjects.

The casual and formal contacts between parents and teachers help build relationships which further the education of children. Keeping parents informed about activities and interests at school will result in more feed-back and cooperation between the adults who educate children in various settings.

EXERCISES
study/discussion questions

1. As a student, recall some significant teachers throughout your schooling. Identify the characteristics of these teachers and tell why you have positive feelings about them.

2. As a novice or prospective teacher, list and describe the duties of a teacher of young children. Prioritize the list and rank your preparedness to assume these responsibilities.

3. Role play the following incident with another student: Student 1: Tell as many reasons as you can why young children should be exposed to science concepts. Student 2: Counter the reasoning of student 1 with as many valid reasons as you can why science teaching should be left for later years.
After several minutes, switch roles so student 2 now defends science teaching for young children and student 1 wants to delay it. Is the exercise one sided or are there valid reasons for both positions?

4. Ask one student (the teacher) to briefly explain the daily curriculum (or schedule) to another student (a parent) who wants her child to always be involved in strictly academic activities.

5. Ask some students to pretend they are parents of young children. In an informal discussion, find out what the parents could contribute to the classroom (hobbies, time, talents). How would they present such materials in the classroom?

6. Suppose the teacher has some special activity planned for the classroom but can not carry it out without help from parent volunteers. Explain the goals, procedures, and responsibilities of the volunteers.

7. Each student is to originate a special classroom activity and prepare a means of informing the parents about it (for example, a learning card) in hopes of getting feedback from information presented, possible misinformation, interest of their child, or follow-up of parents on the experience.

Concepts and Activities

INTRODUCTION

THIS PART OF THE TEXT CONTAINS IDEAS AND suggestions for teaching twenty different topics. There are enough ideas to preassess each topic and to teach it many times, in many different ways—in more depth, or integrated with other topics, curriculum areas, and developmental areas. The topics are mere suggestions for teachers, who should "read their children" carefully, knowing each student's readiness and each activity's appropriateness.

Teachers should consider the following:

- The children have both common and individual interests.

- The topics should be well planned and *not* intended as time-fillers.

- Children need many encounters with concepts.

- Teachers should provide an introduction, learning, practicing, and broadening of each topic.

- There should be unity and continuous information, not isolated facts presented one at a time.

- Teachers can refer to printed science resources, but they cannot rely on these resources to fit all children.

- Science should be open-ended and encourage discovery.

After the children have participated in an experience, the teacher should evaluate the activity for appropriateness, value, truthfulness, and application for the children. The teacher should carefully note what changes, additions, or deletions need to be made for another time or group of children. The teacher should also design some way of building upon the current information in preparation for later teaching.

Hopefully, these suggestions and topics will encourage teachers and parents to include more science experiences for young children—and be excited about doing it!

Air

CONCEPTS AND ACTIVITIES

The concept of **air** seems so commonplace. Adults may take it for granted, but teaching concepts about air to young children is far from easy. It is an abstract concept; it is difficult to teach through the senses. Often adults do not stop to contemplate that without air life would not be possible. We breathe without considering its complexity. We fail to think about how air makes our work easier, how it cools and warms the body, how it facilitates transportation, or how it helps in many other vital ways.

If air is an abstract concept, and teachers are strongly encouraged to teach on the developmental level of the children (which is first-hand and sensory for young children), why is it important to introduce them to air? Because it is so essential to our very lives. Children can begin building a basis for learning about air through their environment and experiences. It must be combined with the familiar parts of their lives so it has a connection for them. Air is a part of health, food, growth, enjoyment, beauty, relaxation, and many other aspects of our daily lives.

In teaching about air, as with other science topics, true concepts must be taught. Partial concepts, ''magical'' ideas, and advanced principles can only confuse and mislead young children. The concepts will be very basic, but when they are true, the children can build upon them as their vocabularies, experiences, and abilities progress. Unlearning wrong information causes confusion in the children. Learning true facts, especially when they are developmentally appropriate for the children, encourages learning.

The teacher needs to preassess the children's knowledge about air through an information gathering process, not a performance or interrogation. Based on what they already know, the teacher can use some of the following basic activities to reinforce, clarify, and further their knowledge as the children show readiness. Categories of buoyancy, environment, force/pressure, inflation, movement, temperature, and water are suggested. The teacher should use appropriate suggestions or design ones to teach air concepts that are more appropriate.

BUOYANCY

a. Using a water trough or tub, provide some plastic containers with tight lids. Encourage the children to try and sink the containers. Remove the lids and try to sink the same containers. Why do they float with lids on and sink without lids?

b. Accumulate some items familiar to young children. Help the children decide which would sink and which would float. Let the children try the items in water, then revise their "float" and "sink" piles if necessary. Talk about size, shape, air contained in the objects, and so on.

ENVIRONMENT

a. With the children, note the air quality in the community. Observe possible pollutants. Ask children for suggestions about clear air and why it is important.

b. Smell some non-harmful odors. Talk with the children about how air increases or decreases the strength of the odor.

c. Discuss how air helps us avoid dangerous situations (odors, smoke, heavy winds, and so on).

FORCE/PRESSURE

a. Use a tank-type vacuum and a ping pong ball. Turn on the vacuum and hold the ball near the end of the tube. Note the strong force to suck and hold the ball. Then attach the tube to the opposite end of the vacuum and note how the ball can be juggled in the air. Talk about the force of air.

b. Using the same size of glass pop bottles, fill the bottles with varying amounts of water. Gently blow across the top of each bottle and note the different sounds made. Bottles can be tuned.

c. Take a pop bottle filled with water, a straw, and some modeling clay. First ask the children to drink through the straw. Then seal the top of the bottle around the straw. Ask the children to drink through the straw again. "In order to drink through a straw, you must have air pushing on the surface of

the water. When the top of the bottle is sealed, air cannot get in to push, so drinking is impossible. Soda cans have either two holes or one hole shaped in such a way that air can get in as the liquid pours out; narrow-necked bottles 'gurgle' because they don't" (Tolman & Morton, 1986, p. 42).

d. Give each child a straw and place some objects on a surface. Tell the children to see how many of the objects can be blown off. Why can some be blown off and others can't?

e. Assist the children to inflate an inner tube. Note how the tube responds to increased inflation. Can the tube be rolled when it is not completely inflated? How does the air get into the tube?

f. Help the children to make small parachutes from square pieces of fabric by tying the corners with string and then threading the string through a bead or washer. "Drop the parachute from various heights and predict what will happen. Cut a hole in the top of the parachute and observe any differences. Make parachutes out of different materials, such as plastic or cupcake liners, and compare their flight" (Charlesworth and Lind, 1990).

g. During an art period, let the children experiment with eye droppers and diluted food coloring dropped onto absorbent paper or mixed in cups of a foam egg carton. Talk about how the color gets into the tube and how it is released.

h. Provide semi-thick paint, straws and paper. Encourage the children to slightly suck on the straw until paint enters the tube. Then release the paint onto the paper and blow it to make interesting shapes and color combinations.

i. Predict with the children how different objects will react when dropped or blown (feather, block, seed, paper, scarf, pencil, toys, balloons, and so on).

j. Help the children make simple sail boats or provide some commercial ones. In a water trough encourage the children to sail their boats and to change the speed by fanning the boats.

k. Invite a guest to show the children how woodwind instruments are played.

l. Prepare an item for snack where air is an important process (whipped cream, angel food cake, beaten eggs, and so on).

m. Take a can with one end removed (and edges smoothed) and try to push the open end straight down in the water. Note the force. Tip the can slightly and push it into the water. Note that the water replaces the air.

INFLATION

A. Bubbles

1. Give the children large frames (made from pipe cleaners, string, metal jar rings, plastic circles, and so on) and let them enjoy making, chasing, and popping bubbles. Solutions can be made from 1 cup of liquid dishwashing detergent, 1 gallon of warm water, and 3 tablespoons of glycerine (to make the bubbles stronger), or commercial products can be purchased. Help the children to note the size, shape, color, and weight of the bubbles.

2. In a low container place a soapy mixture. Provide straws and encourage the children to blow into the

mixture. Talk about how the air blown into the water escapes through the bubbles.

3. At the eye level of the children, have an aquarium or fish bowl. Talk with the children about how the fish breathe and watch for the bubbles.

4. In a bowl about five or six inches across and three inches deep, place a soapy solution. Using a straw, encourage the children to blow bubbles until they overflow. Carefully place a paper towel or other paper over the top so the bubbles break and make a design on the paper. Colored solutions make colored designs.

B. Balls

Procure some inflatable balls. Have the children notice the shape of the uninflated ball and the ball's lack of response when thrown or bounced. Using a tire pump, inflate the balls to varying amounts of fullness. Try throwing or bouncing the balls. Completely inflate the balls and repeat the throwing and bouncing. Discuss the usefulness of the balls when they are fully inflated. Show the children how the pump inflates the balls.

C. Balloons

NOTE: *Balloons can be good teaching tools or they can be dangerous. Do not let the children keep the balloons or any broken pieces. Uninflated and popped balloons can get caught in a child's throat and prevent air passage. Make sure balloons are gathered up and properly stored after each activity.*

1. Inflate some sturdy balloons. Practice throwing and catching the balloons. Talk about the differences between throwing and catching balloons and balls. Which is easier? Why?

2. Inflate a large balloon. Talk to the children about blowing air into the balloon and about the air escaping by using the following examples.

a. Let go of the unsecured end and watch the balloon move through the air and deflate.

b. Place the unsecured end inside a plastic bag. Note how the deflating of the balloon inflates the plastic bag.

c. Place the unsecured end under water and note the bubbles made by the released air.

MOVEMENT

a. Ask the children if they can feel air when they move their hands in the air. Then have them dampen their hands and again move them in the air. Can they feel a change?

b. Show pictures of activities involving air or wind (for example, a child running or riding a bicycle, clouds, non-movement of leaves, sail boats, or kites). Ask the children how they can tell if the wind is blowing. (Remember, some young children prefer to show rather than tell their thoughts.)

c. Give each child a scarf and play a participation record that involves wind or air (for example, *My Playful Scarf*, Children's Record Guild #1019, or *My Playmate the Wind*, Young People's Records #4501). After children participate with the record, talk about how the scarves moved as the children used them in different ways or how the wind moved things.

d. Outdoors or in a large open area, give each child a crepe paper or fabric streamer, a piece of fabric, or a scarf. Encourage movement of the streamer while the child is stationary (waving or shaking) and then when the child is in motion (running, skipping, or twirling).

e. Bring some ready-made kites or help the children make their own kites. Take the kites outside and fly them. Is it easier to fly a kite when the wind is blowing? Will the kite fly while the child is stationary?

f. Attach a streamer to a fan where the blades are well protected. Using alternate speeds, note how the streamer responds. Have the child dip his hand into water and place it near the fan. Note how the hand dries. Talk about the use of air driers in some restrooms or hair dryers at home.

g. On a warm day when children are overheated, show them how the use of a hand-held fan can make them feel cooler.

h. For an art activity, provide paper and coloring utensils. Encourage the children to decorate the paper and then show them how to fold it and use it as a fan.

i. Assist the children to make pinwheels from typing paper or wallpaper. Attach them to a stick or pencil and watch them turn with varying amounts of wind.

j. Assist the children to make and fly simple paper gliders. How does the glider respond when wings are folded differently?

TEMPERATURE

a. Use a thermometer to check the temperature in the classroom, outdoors, during cooking, and other activities.

b. Involve the children in determining how heat changes things (food, temperature, enjoyment, expansion, and contraction).

WATER

a. Provide a water trough or tubs. Give the children doll clothes (or fabric items) to wash and hang up to dry. Periodically remind them to check on how their ''wash'' is doing. Note which fabrics dry fastest. How does the temperature of the air aid the drying process?

b. With a moist sponge wipe a section of a chalkboard. Note that the color has darkened. Fan the moist section and note how it dries.

REFERENCES

Althouse, R. (1988). **Investigating science with young children.** New York: Teachers College Press.

Althouse, R., and Main, C. (1975). **Science experiences for young children: Air.** New York: Teachers College Press.

Brown, S. E. (1981). **Bubbles, rainbows and worms.** Mt. Rainer, Md: Gryphon House.

Carin, A. A., and Sund, R. B. (1980). **Discovery activities for elementary science.** Columbus, OH: Merrill Publishing.

Charlesworth, R., and Lind, K. K. (1990). **Math and science for young children.** Albany, NY: Delmar Publishers, Inc.

Rice, K. (1986). Soap films and bubbles. **Science and children.** May, 5–9.

Tolman, M. N., and Morton, J. D. (1986). **Earth science activities for grades 2–8.** West Nyack, NY: Parker Publishing Co., Inc.

Ziemer, M. (1987). Science and the early childhood curriculum: One thing leads to another. **Young Children,** 42(6), 44–51.

BOOKS FOR CHILDREN

Brandt, K. (1985). **Air.** Mahwah, NJ: Troll Associates.

Branley, F. (1986). **Air is all around us.** New York: Scribner's.

Ets, M. H. (1963). **Gilberto and the wind.** New York: Viking.

Friskey, M. (1953). **The true book of air around us.** Chicago: Childrens Press.

Galleant, K. (1958). **Jonathan plays with the wind.** New York: Coward-McCann.

Keats, E. J. (1964). **Whistle for Willy.** New York: Viking.

Lamorisse, A. (1957). **The red balloon.** New York: Doubleday.

Lowery, L. F. (1969). **How does the wind blow?** New York: Holt, Rinehart & Winston.

Nodset, J. L. (1970). **Who took the farmer's hat?** New York: Scholastic Book Services.

Podendorf, I. (1972). **The true book of science experiments.** Chicago: Childrens Press.

Rey, M. (1958). **Curious George flies a kite.** Boston: Houghton Mifflin.

Scarry, R. (1971). **Great big air book.** New York: Random House.

Selsam, M. (1960). **Plenty of fish.** New York: Harper & Bros.

Stevenson, R. L. (1951). **A child's garden of verses.** New York: Golden Press.

Tresselt, A. R. (1950). **Follow the wind.**
New York: Lothrop, Lee & Shepard.

Weise, K. (1948). **Fish in the air.** New York:
Viking.

RECORD SOURCES

(See Appendix C on pages 285–286, or preschool educational catalogs.)

My Playmate the Wind. Young People's
Records, #4501.

My Playful Scarf. Children's Record Guild,
#1019.

Animals

CONCEPTS AND ACTIVITIES

From birth young children enjoy animals of many kinds. They cuddle, tote, and jabber to the stuffed ones; they point to and mimic the pictures; and they imitate the movements and pretend to be various real animals whether large or small, friendly or frightening. Children learn much about various animals as they have contact with them. It would be easy for adults to teach children stereotyped information about animals, or perhaps over-emphasize some ideas and overlook others.

Sometimes the contact children have with animals at home is limited to media without any clear understanding of size, covering, habitat, living patterns, usefulness, availability, protection, reproduction, or other interesting characteristics. Sometimes pets can be included in the classroom—at least for limited periods. Teachers need to make sure that pets or animals in the classroom are well cared for and that the children also have a good experience.

Example: One teacher kept a tarantula in her classroom for many years. Class after class tended it, watched it, and enjoyed it. One day the tarantula died. It surprised the teacher. She could have just bought a new spider and hoped the children would not realize the difference, but she thought she needed to explain to the children what had happened. At a convenient time she gathered the children around and showed them the dead spider. Some of the children expressed sorrow. One child said, "We better bury him!" Another one said, "We can pick some flowers, too." The situation quickly turned to a child-centered one. The teacher quietly talked about the spider, and told the children that she had brought a new tarantula for the classroom, and then it was over. Without such a thoughtful teacher (keeping the tarantula in the classroom, and then replacing it), many of the children would have thought that you stomp on every spider you see.

Pets in the classroom may cause joy for some and problems for others.

Example: One teacher brought a rabbit into the classroom, then a hamster, and then a cat. Finally she gave up on furry animals when she discovered that one child had severe allergies and others had mild allergies.

Children need to have pleasant experiences with animals of all kinds—whether it is caring for and handling them, looking at them in books, taking field trips to see them, or having activities in the classroom related to them.

Because experiences with animals will be varied and sometimes determined by school policies, some suggested activities are proposed here. The teacher should modify them, use them, or create new ones for the enjoyment and benefit of the children within the classroom. The categories provided include general animals and experiences, birds, dinosaurs/other, domestic, insects, water/land, and wild.

GENERAL ANIMALS AND EXPERIENCES

a. Depending on the children's ages, introduce animals that would be familiar to them. Then introduce other animals as the children are ready (pets, farm, zoo, and ones within the community).

b. Talk to children about pets (love, proper care, exercise, behavior, sounds they make, and so on). If possible, have a pet in the classroom. Teach the children how to care for it. If an animal is kept too long, the children may get tired of it and neglect it (Pratt, 1965; Eliason and Jenkins, 1990, pp. 652–655).

c. Have a variety of pets in the classroom. A child or teacher could bring a pet for classroom enjoyment for a period of time. Some pet shops will loan or rent pets.

d. If feasible, have a pet day at school, but be wise. Some animals are compatible and others are not.

e. As a preassessment for teaching about animals (or after an introduction to various animals) play this game:

  1. As the teacher or a child

    a. makes animal sounds

    b. imitates the behavior of an animal (walking, flying, swimming)

    c. shows or names some foods

    d. shows or describes the covering (fur/hair, shell, feathers, smooth, scales)

    e. describes the appearance of the animal (movement, tail, nose)

    f. shows foot prints of animals

  2. the others try to guess the proper animal.

f. A large picture of an outdoor scene is displayed. Together the children and teacher locate the many places an animal could make a home (tree, pond, hole, and so on). Introduce words such as nest, burrow, lodge, den, hive, anthill, and so on.

g. Take the children on a nature walk and look for possible homes for animals.

h. Using replicas of animals and of animal homes, help the children match the animals to where they live (underground, tree, water, cave, and so on). Have some examples that help the children to think and discuss rather than just place the animals easily. Could the animal live in different places?

i. Compare the animal to the children (locomotion, body parts, abilities, and so on).

j. Make or purchase some animal cards. Help the children sort the cards into groups (animals, birds, insects, fish).

k. Use animal puzzles. If the children see the completed puzzle before they disassemble it, they know what the animal will be. If they first see a disassembled puzzle, they will be curious to find out what the animal will be. Use fewer puzzle pieces for inexperienced children and more pieces for more experienced children. Floor puzzles are fun and interesting for young children.

Puzzles can easily be made by mounting a large picture on poster board or cardboard and then cutting it into pieces.

l. On a large bulletin board, have an outline of an animal. Using precut pieces, put each piece in while talking with the children about what animal you are making. Encourage discussion and child participation.

m. Using a particular animal take the children through its life cycle by having the animal in the classroom in varying cycles of development, for example, tadpole to frog, caterpillar to chrysalis to butterfly, or egg to chick.

n. Use appropriate terms for animals to help the children increase their knowledge and vocabulary. Use such terms as paws, claws, beak, and hibernate to give the children opportunities to use and practice these words.

o. Talk about how animals live during different seasons of the year (hibernate, migrate, heavier covering, camouflage).

p. On separate small cards, paste a picture of various animals. On a sheet of paper or light cardboard, draw the outline of the same animals. The child is to take the picture and place it over the outline.

q. Using animals that are familiar to young children, talk about the colors of each animal. Have the children sort the animals by color. Some animals are a specific color while others may vary in color or be multicolored.

r. Help the children learn the names of baby animals and their parents, for example, horse—stallion, mare, foal; rabbit— buck, doe, baby rabbit; goat—billy, nanny, kid; or duck—drake, duck, duckling. Have pictures of parents and babies so children can match them and practice their names. Some animals resemble their parents from birth (horses, rabbits, pigs, deer, and so on), while some look different from the parents at birth (frogs, insects).

s. On a science table, have samples of the different coverings of animals (fur, hide, feathers, shells, skin, and so on). Have pictures of different kinds of animals. Talk with the children and help them separate the kinds of coverings and then match them to the appropriate animals. Talk about the smoothness or roughness of the coverings and whether they belong to animals on land, sea, or water.

t. During an art period, assist the children to make animals, for example, a ladybug from an empty walnut shell, a hippopotamus from a square tissue box, a turtle from small paper plates, a lizard from a paper towel roll, a rabbit with cotton balls, a pig from a toilet paper roll, an insect with pipe cleaners for legs and an egg carton for the body, sack puppets of any animal, or clay snakes. Supply necessary scraps of paper or fabric and let the children create their own animals. Take caution to see that the activity is child-centered and not difficult or discouraging.

u. Cut animal foot prints in potato halves. Provide thickened paint and let the children make design prints on absorbent paper or make large, heavy patterns for the children to trace and then color.

v. Invite a guest, such as a trainer, fisherman, veterinarian, or beekeeper into the classroom who can demonstrate experiences with animals. Help the guest participate at the level of the children.

w. Provide scissors, paste, and magazines that have animal pictures in them. Assist the children to make an animal collage.

x. Place a board (flannel with flannel cut-outs, or magnetic with magnetic figures) where children can manipulate the objects (animals in this case) and talk about their actions.

y. Have books, pictures, and replicas available in the classroom for the children to explore and enjoy. Make animals a part of daily teaching even when it is not the main topic.

z. Encourage the children to reenact stories, such as *Ask Mr. Bear* (Flack), or experiences they have had with animals. A story such as *Go Away Dog* (Nodset) can help children reduce their fears of dogs.

aa. Make a poster or bulletin board with clusters of food that animals eat. Have cut-outs of animals large enough to cover each cluster. The children place the picture of the animal over the type of food that animal eats.

bb. Make another poster or bulletin board, only on this one, the children are to place the picture of the animal over the type of house the animal lives in.

cc. At informal or spontaneous times, talk with the children about animal experiences they (or you) have had.

dd. Use pictures or props to show how animals clean themselves. Ask the children which animals use the different methods.

ee. Sing songs, do finger plays, and read books about animals.

ff. On a science table, place replicas of different animals and various food items eaten by animals. Help the children separate the animals and then place the food by the corresponding animal that eats it. Have some animals and also food that does not match so the children will have some non-examples as well. (More mature children could look at animal and food pictures on a paper and then draw a line between those that belong together.)

BIRDS

a. Bring a bird into the classroom. Watch how it preens and fluffs its feathers. Put a drop of water on a feather and see what happens. Let the children examine feathers under a magnifying glass. Listen to the sounds the bird makes. Make a picture using feathers (Carin and Sund, 1980, pp. 294–298).

b. If possible, hatch eggs in the classroom. To shorten the incubation period, get eggs near the time of hatching. Use a calendar to count when the eggs will hatch. Talk about some animals that hatch from eggs, keeping it simple.

c. During an art activity, make a collage using birdseed, feathers, leaves and twigs.

d. If possible, get an abandoned bird's nest. Let the children examine how it is made. Discuss the size and number of eggs that might be laid in the nest. Compare different birds' nests if they are available.

e. Make a bird feeder and hang it where the children can observe it often. Note which seeds the birds eat and which ones they leave.

f. Wash and dry empty egg shells. Leaving them in large pieces, put them into various colors of food coloring and water. Dry them on paper towels. The children can make colorful collages with glue and construction paper.

Contributions of Animals

Explain to the children how some animals are useful to people. Avoid saying that animals *give* things to people (for example, "Cows *give* us milk") because young children visualize the animals actually handing things to people. Some suggestions:

a. transportation—horses, camels

b. food—butter, whipped cream, ice cream, cheese, meat, honey-butter

c. clothing—wool, yarn, feathers

d. protection—dogs

e. companionship—birds, cats, dogs, pets

Tie the ideas together for the children—animal to product or service—in a useful and understandable way. Have follow-up experiences.

DINOSAURS/OTHER

a. Occasionally introduce an unfamiliar animal. Most children are fascinated with dinosaurs. At this time talk about dinosaurs living a long time ago, what they ate, where they lived, and what they looked like (only use one species at a time). Support the learning by showing replicas, pictures, and other items that accurately depict the dinosaurs. Further enhance the experience through reading, using the blocks, or doing an art activity. The children could make dinosaurs using paper-maché; eggs from balloons, heavy paper or light cardboard; dinosaur stencils; or cut-out pictures.

b. Sing songs, do fingerplays, role play, and use records (for example, "Our Dinosaur Friends." ATA #3225. American Teaching Aids, P. O. Box 1406, Covina, CA 91722).

c. Make puzzles out of dinosaur pictures mounted on cardboard.

d. Use dinosaur stencils for the children to trace around, color, or cut out, depending on individual skills and preferences.

e. Canvass the community for opportunities to teach the children about different reptiles.

f. Discuss with the children that some animals, such as dragons, are make-believe. (This may be hard for some of them to accept.)

DOMESTIC

a. Sing animal songs, for example, "Old MacDonald's Farm." The teacher supplies a nose mask for each child imitating an animal (pig, duck, cat, and so on). Or sing "Gray Squirrel," for which the children use their hands at their backs to represent the tail, and their hands to hold the nut, and so on.

b. Children may have pets at home who have given birth. Arrange with the parents to bring the mother and babies into the classroom when the babies are mature enough.

c. Plan learning experiences about a single type of domestic animal at a time. Use books, pictures, replicas, and so on.

INSECTS

a. Introduce insects to the children. Hunt for insects on the playground. "Spiders are not insects. They have eight legs and are classified as arachnids. Caterpillars are insects. Although they appear to have more than six legs, only six are true, joined ones," writes Harlan (1988, p. 66). Where necessary, talk about precautions but avoid transmitting unnecessary fear. There are some stinging creatures the children should be aware of, such as mosquitos, ants, spiders, bees and wasps, scorpions, and some caterpillars (Blackwelder, 1980, pp. 261–265).

b. The children could help make a terrarium in a glass gallon jar. Add some soil, branches, leaves, moisture, and small animals such as snails, earthworms, or lizards (Carin and Sund, 1980, p. 82). Care for the animals in the classroom.

c. Display ant farms or bug jars in the classroom. Children enjoy watching animals or catching bugs (Carin and Sund, 1980, pp. 293–304; Charlesworth and Lind, 1990, pp. 584–586).

d. Sing songs or do fingerplays about insects ("Eency, Weency, Spider," bees, butterflies, and so on). Move around as the insects would move.

e. Make caterpillars or insects out of egg cartons, using pipe cleaners for legs/antennae, foil, fabric, or cotton balls.

f. With some supervision, let the children look at insects through a microscope or magnifying glass.

g. Describe how insects are similar and different. Help the children role play some of the actions and movements of insects.

WATER/LAND

a. Bring in some hermit crabs. Talk with the children about the number of legs, the different shapes of the body, shell living, parts of the body, and so on.

b. Bring in a fish (preferably a live one). Watch it in its natural setting, water. A goldfish or tropical fish may add to the atmosphere of the classroom. A large fish may be displayed or cooked and eaten.

c. Make fishing poles out of dowels, string, and a magnet. Cut fish out of colored poster board and attach one or two paper clips on the face of the fish. Children catch the fish as the magnet attracts the paper clips.

d. If fishing is common in your area for recreation or occupation, talking about it will be interesting and timely.

e. Stuff newspaper into small brown-paper sacks to look like fish. The children can paint or decorate the fish.

f. Provide materials that resemble a fish bowl or aquarium, such as rocks, weeds, and fish. Let the children paste or draw an underwater picture. Cover the picture with light blue cellophane.

g. Draw land, water, and air scenes on individual pieces of paper. Give the children plastic replicas of animals to place on the paper representing the animals' habitat, or let the children glue or put stickers of animals on the color of paper that represents the animals' homes. (For a more advanced exercise, provide sheets of colored paper to represent land, water, and air and give replicas, pictures, or stickers of different kinds of animals. Have some familiar animals and some that are less well known. Note how the children place the animals.)

h. Discuss with the children the distinguishing characteristics of some water and land animals, such as their type of tail, length of neck, method of protection, or design or coloring. Discover with the children how characteristics differ between water animals, land animals, and animals that live in both water and land.

i. If possible get some polywog eggs and watch them grow and change into mature frogs.

j. Talk about water and land animals that are near your vicinity and how they feed, live, and add to the environment.

WILD

a. When possible visit a museum or have a visitor bring appropriate learning materials to the classroom. Seeing life-sized animals brings them into perspective.

b. Plan experiences that will give the children opportunities to learn about wild animals. If possible, visit a zoo or provide play with replicas, costumes, props, or suggestions.

c. Plan a day around a circus theme, making sure the children are ready for the concepts. Recall that circus animals behave differently than similar ones in the wild.

d. Read books about wild animals.

REFERENCES

Althouse, R. (1988). **Investigating science with young children.** New York: Teachers College Press.

Althouse, R. (1975). **Science experiences for young children: Pets.** New York: Teachers College.

Blackwelder, S. K. (1980). **Science for all seasons.** Englewood Cliffs, NJ: Prentice-Hall.

Bowden, M. (1989). **Nature for the very young.** New York: John Wiley & Sons.

Brown, S. E. (1981). **Bubbles, rainbows, and worms.** Mt. Rainer, Md.: Gryphon House, Inc.

Carin, A. A., and Sund, R. B. (1980). **Discovery activities for elementary science.** Columbus, OH: Merrill Publishing.

Cartwright, S. (1989). Kids and science—Magic in the mix. **Exchange,** June 51–54.

Charlesworth, R., and Lind, K. K. (1990). **Math and science for young children.** Albany, NY: Delmar Publishers.

Eliason, C., and Jenkins, L. (1990). **A practical guide to early childhood curriculum.** Columbus, OH: Merrill Publishing.

Fehrenbach, C. R., Greer, F. S., and Karnes, B. (1989). Dinosaurs—Back in the classroom. **Science and children,** January, 12–14.

Harlan, J. (1988). **Science experiences for the early childhood years.** 4th ed. Columbus: OH: Merrill Publishing.

Hampton, Hampton, Kammer. (1988). **Classroom creature culture.** Washington, D.C.: National Science Teachers Assoc.

James, S. (1989). Introducing horseshoe crabs! **Science and children,** April, 12–14.

Kramer, D. (1985). The classroom animal: Mealworms. **Science and children,** 22(4), 25–26.

McGlathery, G. (1989). Mealworms in the classroom. **Science and children,** March, 29–31.

Moore, J. E. and Evans, J. (1987). **Learning about animals: Resource book.** Monterey, CA: Evan-Moor Corp.

Pratt, G. K. (1965). How to care for living things in the classroom. **Science and children.**

Puppet Enrichment Program 6510 (animal and insect characters), Oaklawn, IL: Westinghouse Learning Corp., 5005 W. 10th Street, 60453.

Scott, L. B., and Thompson, J. J. (1985). **Rhymes for fingers and flannelboards.** New York: McGraw-Hill.

Seeger, R. (1950). **Animal folk songs for children.** Garden City, NY: Doubleday.

BOOKS FOR CHILDREN

Aliki. (1988). **Dinosaur bones.** New York: Crowell.

Anderson, C. W. (1952). **A pony for Linda.** New York: Macmillan.

Arnosky, J. (1987). **Raccoons and ripe corn.** New York: Lothrop, Lee & Shepard.

Ayres, P. (1987). **Guess who?** New York: Alfred A. Knopf.

Banks, M. (1990). **Animals of the night.** New York: Scribner.

Bare, C. S. (1987). **To love a dog.** New York: Dodd.

Barton, B. (1990). **Bones, bones, dinosaur bones.** HarperCollins.

Bason, L. (1974). **Spiders.** Washington, D.C.: National Geographic Society, Books for Young Explorers.

Blos, J. W. (1989). **Lottie's circus.** New York: Morrow Junior Books.

Brandt, K. (1985). **Insects.** Mahwah, NJ: Troll Associates.

Berg, J. H. (1951). **Baby Susan's chicken.** New York: Wonder Books.

Blough, G. O. (1957). **Who lives in this house? A story of animal families.** New York: McGraw-Hill.

Branley, F. M. (1982). **Dinosaurs, asteroids, and superstars: Why the dinosaurs disappeared.** New York: Thomas Y. Crowell.

Brett, J. (1988). **The first dog.** New York: Harcourt Brace Jovanovich.

Brown, M. W. (1980). **Christmas in the barn.** New York: Harper & Row.

Burton, J. (1988). **How your pet grows! Caper; dubble; gipper.** New York: Random House.

Burton, M. R. (1988). **Tail, toes, eyes, ears, nose.** New York: Harper.

Carle, E. (1987). **1, 2, 3, to the zoo: A counting book.** New York: Philomel (Putnam).

Carle, E. (1988). **A house for hermit crab.** Saxonville, MA: Picture Book Studios.

Carle, E. (1979). **The very hungry caterpillar.** New York: Wm. Collins and World.

Carson, R. (1956). **A sense of wonder.** New York: Harper & Row.

Caudill, R. (1964). **A Pocketful of Cricket.** New York: Holt, Rinehart & Winston.

Coats, L.J. (1987). **The oak tree.** New York: Macmillan.

Cohn, D. (1987). **Dinosaurs.** New York: Doubleday.

Cole, J. (1985). **Large as life: Daytime animals.** New York: Alfred A. Knopf.

Cole, J. (1985). **Large as life: Nighttime animals.** New York: Alfred A. Knopf.

Conklin, G. (1958). **I like caterpillars.** New York: Holiday House.

Conklin, G. (1960). **I like butterflies.** New York: Holiday House.

Conklin, G. (1962). **We like bugs.** New York: Holiday House.

Conklin, G. (1967). **I caught a lizard.** New York: Holiday House.

Cole, S. (1985). **When the tide is low.** New York: Lothrop, Lee & Shepard.

Cook, B. (1956). **The curious little kitten.** New York: Young Scott Books.

Cristini, E., and Puricelli, L. (1985). **In my garden.** Natick, MA: Picture Book Studio USA.

Cristini, E., and Puricelli, L. (1984). **In the pond.** Saxonville, MA: Picture Book Studio USA.

Curran, E. (1985). **Life in the pond. Life in the forest. Life in the sea.** Mahwah, NJ: Troll Associates.

Dunn, J. (1981). **The animals of buttercup farm.** New York: Random House.

Ehlert, L. (1990). **Color farm.** HarperCollins.

Ets, M. H. (1955). **Play with me.** New York: Viking Press.

Ets, M. H. (1958). **Cow's party.** New York: Viking Press.

Facklam, M. (1987). **I eat dinner.** Boston: Little, Brown.

Facklam, M. (1988). **But not like mine.** New York: Gulliver/HBJ.

Facklam, M. (1988). **So can I.** New York: Gulliver/HBJ.

Fischer-Nagel, H. (1986). **Life of the ladybug.** Minneapolis: Carolrhoda Books.

Fisher, A. (1962). **Like nothing at all.** New York: Thomas Y. Crowell.

Fisher, A. (1966). **Best little house.** New York: Thomas Y. Crowell.

Fisher, R. M. (1982). **Animals in winter,** in **Books for young explorers** (Set 9). Washington, D.C.: National Geographic.

Fitzsimmons, C. (1987). **My first fishes and other water life: A pop-up field guide.** New York: Harper.

Fitzsimmons, C. (1987). **My first insects: Spiders and crawlers.** New York: Harper.

Flack, M. (1960). **Ask Mr. Bear.** New York: Collier Books.

Flack, M. (1961). **Angus and the cat.** New York: Doubleday.

Flack, M., and Wiese, K. (1961). **The story of Ping.** New York: Viking Press.

Florian, D. (1986). **Discovering butterflies.** New York: Charles Scribner's.

Florian, D. (1986). **Discovering frogs.** New York: Charles Scribner's.

Florian, D. (1986). **Discovering seashells.** New York: Charles Scribner's.

Freeman, D. (1961). **Come again, pelican.** New York: Viking.

Friskey, M. (1961). **Johnny and the monarch.** Chicago: Childrens Press.

Gag, W. (1952). **Millions of cats.** New York: Putnam.

Gans, R. (1980). **When birds change their feathers.** New York: Thomas Y. Crowell.

Gardner, B. (1985). **Guess what.** New York: Lothrop.

Gibbons, G. (1988). **Dinosaurs, dragonflies and diamonds: All about natural history museums.** New York: Four Winds.

Gibbons, G. (1987). **Zoo.** New York: Crowell.

Ginsburg, M. (1980). **Good morning, chick.** New York: Greenwillow.

Goudey, A. (1964). **Butterfly time.** New York: Scribner's Sons.

Graham, M. B. (1967). **Be nice to spiders.** New York: Harper & Row.

Hall, D. (1985). **Elephant bathes. Gorilla builds. Polar bear leaps.** New York: Alfred A. Knopf.

Heller, R. (1985). **How to hide a butterfly and other insects.** New York: Grosset & Dunlap.

Hewett, J. (1987). **Rosalie.** New York: Macmillan.

Hide and seek. (Oxford Scientific Films). (1986). New York: Putnam.

Hirschi, R. (1987). **What is a bird?** New York: Walker.

Hirschi, R. (1987). **Who lives in . . . the forest?** New York: Dodd.

Hoban, T. (1985). **A children's zoo.** New York: Greenwillow Books.

Hoban, T. (1986). **Panda, panda.** New York: Greenwillow.

Hoban, T. (1987). **Dots, spots, speckles, and stripes.** New York: Greenwillow.

Imershem, B. (1988). **Animal doctor.** Englewood Cliffs, NJ: Messner.

Isenbart, H. (1984). **Baby animals on the farm.** New York: Putnam.

Kalas, S. (1986). **The goose family book.** Saxonville, MA: Picture Book Studio.

Kanao, K. (1987). **Kitten up a tree.** New York: Knopf.

Kalan, R. (1981). **Jump, frog, jump.** New York: Greenwillow.

Keats, E. J. (1971). **Over in the meadow.** Soquel, CA: Four Winds Press. (Imprint Macmillan)

Keats, E. J. (1974). **Pet show.** New York: Macmillan.

Kellogg, S. (1971). **Can I keep him?** New York: Dial.

Kitchen, B. (1987). **Animal numbers.** New York: Dial.

Kuklin, S. (1988). **Taking my cat to the vet. Taking my dog to the vet.** New York: Bradbury.

Lavies, B. (1990). **Backyard hunter: The praying mantis.** New York: Dutton.

Lemieux, M. (1985). **What's that noise?** New York: Morrow.

Lesser, C. (1984). **The goodnight circle.** New York: Harcourt Brace Jovanovich.

Lillegard, D. (1989). **Sitting in my box.** New York: Dutton.

Lilly, K. (1984). **Animal builders.** (Others in the series: **Animal climbers, Animal jumpers, Animal runners,** and **Animal swimmers**) New York: Random House.

Martin, B., Jr. (1983). **Brown bear, brown bear, what do you see?** New York: Henry Holt.

Matsuoka, K. (1989). **There's a hippo in my bath!** New York: Doubleday.

McCloskey, R. (1941). **Make way for ducklings.** New York: Viking.

McCloskey, R. (1952). **One morning in Maine.** New York: Viking.

McCloskey, R. (1982). **Blueberries for Sal.** New York: Penguin.

McPhail, D. (1988). **Animals A to Z.** New York: Scholastic.

Munsinger, L. (1986). **A porcupine named Fluffy.** Boston: Houghton Mifflin.

National Geographic Society. (1974). **Books for young explorers** (series). Washington, D.C.: Author.

National Wildlife Federation. **Ranger Rick's wildlife magazine.** Washington, D.C.: Author.

National Wildlife Federation. **Your big backyard magazine.** Washington, D.C.: Author.

Nodset, J. (1963). **Go away dog.** New York: Harper.

Oppenheim, J. (1987). **Have you seen birds?** New York: Scholastic.

Patterson, F. (1985). **Koko's kitten.** New York: Scholastic.

Podendorf, I. (1981). **The new true book about insects.** Chicago: Childrens Press.

Podendorf, I. (1954). **The true book of pets.** Chicago: Childrens Press.

Prelutsky, J. (1988). **Tyrannosaurus was a beast.** New York: Greenwillow.

Provensen, A., and Provensen, M. (1978). **The year at Maple Hill Farm.** New York: Atheneum.

Richter, Mischa. (1978). **Quack.** New York: Harper.

Rinard, J. E. (1984). **What happens at the zoo?** Washington, DC: National Geographic Society.

Rinard, J. (1985). **Helping our animal friends.** Washington, DC: National Geographic Society.

Rowe, E. (1973). **Giant dinosaurs.** New York: Scholastic.

Ryden, H. (1989). **Wild animals of Africa ABC.** New York: Dutton.

Sabin, F. (1982). **Amazing world of ants. Wonders of the forest.** Mahwah, NJ: Troll Associates.

Sabin, F. (1985). **Wonders of the pond. Wonders of the desert. Wonders of the sea.** Mahway, NJ: Troll Associates.

Sattler, H. R. (1984). **Baby dinosaurs.** New York: Lothrop, Lee & Shepard.

Selsam, M. E. (1962). **Terry and the caterpillars.** New York: Harper & Row.

Selsam, M. (1967). **Questions and answers about ants.** New York: Scholastic Book Services.

Selsam, M. (1971). **All kinds of babies and how they grow.** New York: Scholastic Book Services.

Selsam, M. E., and Goor, R. (1981). **Backyard insects.** New York: Scholastic, Inc.

Selsam, M., and Hunt, J. (1987). **A first look at caterpillars.** New York: Walker.

Selsam, J., and Hunt, J. (1989). **Keep looking.** New York: Macmillan.

Shaw, C. G. (1947). **It looked like spilled milk.** New York: Harper & Row.

Shaw, E. (1972). **Alligator.** New York: Scholastic Book Services.

Simon, S. (1982). **The smallest dinosaurs.** New York: Crown.

Sisson, E. A. (1987). **Nature with children of all ages.** Englewood Cliffs, NJ: Prentice-Hall.

Skaar, G. (1950). **Nothing but cats, cats, cats** and **What do they say?** Eau Claire, WI: E. M. Hale.

Skaar, G. (1947). **All about dogs, dogs, dogs** and **The very little dog.** Eau Claire, WI: E. M. Hale.

Slobodkina, E. (1968). **Caps for sale.** Reading, MA: Addison-Wesley.

Spier, P. (1979). **Gobble, growl, and grunt.** New York: Doubleday.

Tafuri, N. (1987). **Do not disturb.** New York: Greenwillow.

Tafuri, N. (1988). **Spots, feathers, and curly tails.**

Ungerer, T. (1958). **Crictor.** New York: Harper.

Walker, H. B. (1967). **A moth is born.** Chicago: Rand McNally.

Ward, L. (1952). **The biggest bear.** Boston: Houghton Mifflin.

Watson, J. W. (1983). **Dinosaurs and other prehistoric reptiles.** New York: Golden.

Watts, B. (1990). **Hours in a forest.** New York: Watts.

Wexler, J. (1990). **Pet gerbils.** Niles, IL: Whitman & Co.

Wildsmith, B. (1967). **Wild animals.** Oxford, England: Oxford University Press.

Wildsmith, B. (1968). **Birds.** New York: Franklin Watts.

Wildsmith, B. (1982). **Fishes.** New York: Oxford University Press.

Wildsmith, B. (1982). **Pelican.** New York: Pantheon.

Wolff, A. (1986). **A year of beasts.** New York: E. P. Dutton.

Udry, J. (1956). **A tree is nice.** New York: Harper & Row.

Zion, G. (1958). **No roses for Harry!** New York: Harper & Row.

Zion, G. (1956). **Harry, the dirty dog.** New York: Harper & Row.

POETRY SOURCES

Brown, M. W. (1959). **Nibble nibble.** New York: Young Scott Books.

deRegniers, B. S., Moore, E., and White, M. M. (1973). **Poems children will sit still for.** New York: Scholastic Book Services.

Milne, A. A. (1961). **Now we are six.** New York: E. P. Dutton.

Ryder, J. (1985). **Inside turtle's shell, and other poems of the field.** New York: Macmillan.

Stevenson, R. L. (1969). **A child's garden of verses.** New York: Airmont.

Thompson, J. M. (1957). **Poems to grow on.** Boston: Beacon Press.

RECORD SOURCES

(See Resources Section on pages 285–286 or check educational catalogues.)

The Animal Fair. January Productions. Fair Lawn, NJ.

Mills, A. **Fourteen numbers, letters and animal songs.** Folkways Records.

Our dinosaur friends. American Teaching Aids, #3225.

Palmer, H. **Folk song carnival.** Activity Records, Inc.

FILMSTRIPS

Check the National Geographic Educational Services Catalog, Educational Services, Washington, D.C. 20036.

Some filmstrips listed for Pre-K-2 children are:

''Ready, Set, Go: How Animals Move''	#30527
''Alike and Different''	#30074
''Amazing Animals A–Z''	#30316
''Who Lives Here?''	
''Animals in Backyards''	#30698
''Animals In and Around People''	#30698
''Animals of the Sea''	#30705
''Animals of the Desert''	#30705
''Animal Games''	#30060
''What Can You See and Hear''	#30081
''Animals, Animals!''	#30619
''Fins, Feathers, Fur: Animal Groups''	
''A Gaggle of Geese: Social Animals''	
''Insects Are Amazing''	#30249

Body
CONCEPTS AND ACTIVITIES

Young children are so enamored with their bodies. Babies look at their hands and nibble on their toes. Toddlers are proud of their ability to walk, pull, push, carry, and climb. Each advancement is a great milestone in their lives. Once they start getting autonomous, they never slow down. Children should be proud of their bodies and their abilities; a healthy self-concept is a great asset in getting along in this world.

Adults should be careful not to expect too much of young children or that all children of the same chronological age have the same skills, interests, and abilities.

For purposes of grouping body activities, the following areas are covered in this chapter: body awareness, sensory learning, and small muscle and large muscle development.

BODY AWARENESS

a. Two-year-olds need practice in naming and pointing to their body parts. They may need to be reminded that they have two of some parts (''Where is your other eye?''). Young children can comprehend language much earlier than they can speak it; therefore, the adult will need to initiate this type of activity. Later the children can point to a body part *and* name it.

b. As the child is being dressed or undressed, the adult can name the article of clothing and the body part upon which it goes. The child soon identifies that the sock goes on the foot, and so on.

c. When the children become more familiar with the labels for body parts, they can learn more about their particular characteristics (for example, hair is on the head; fingers are part of the hand; the eyes, nose, and mouth are part of the face, which is part of the head). They can also learn less familiar parts such as eyebrows, eyelids, and fingernails.

d. Young children are quite agile and like to play body games (touch your toes; touch your nose; put your nose on your knee). Exercises should be simple and not last too long. The adults may tire before the children do.

e. Use the names of the body parts when there is interaction between adult and child (''Now we'll wash your back and then your arms.'').

f. Young children know when they have been injured (and usually refer to the injury as an ''ow-w-w-ie''). Have a first-aid kit available and know how to use it. Post emergency phone numbers in visible places.

g. Young children are generally interested in looking at a skeleton (when you are talking about bones), but trying to understand that their bodies also have a skeletal structure is difficult for them. Likewise, trying to relate chicken (or other animals') bones to the human body is equally difficult. Talking about someone with a broken bone and a cast may be more realistic, but still advanced.

h. Display a photograph of each child on the eye level of the children. This gives them a sense of belonging and helps them get acquainted with other children. Having a name tag for each child also gives the child a sense of belonging and is often a sign of symbol recognition.

i. When possible, keep a camera close so that pictures can be taken of children in different activities and then posted for the children to enjoy and recall the circumstances.

> Example: One teacher had taken photographs of the children in her class and had posted each child's picture on the outside hall door so the children would feel that was their room and they belonged there. The only picture the teacher had of Courtney was one in which she was crying. Frequently Courtney requested the teacher to open the door so she could see if "my's still crying"!

j. To help the children gain a perspective of their size, have each child (who wants to) lie down on a piece of white paper that is longer than the child is tall. An adult traces the body outline. The child then colors in the outline (perhaps representing the clothing the child is presently wearing). When the children hang up their outlines, they are quite surprised they are so large.

k. Strategically place mirrors (large and small) around the classroom. Periodically call the child's attention to his appearance (perhaps in dress-up clothing), facial expression, or activity.

l. Weigh and measure each child over a period of time. Show each one how she has grown. This is an individual activity and not one of competition ("I grew 2 inches and 3 pounds," rather than "I am bigger than you!"). These concepts are fairly new to children and they may use them in child-like ways: "I weigh 35 inches," or "I am seventy-eleven inches tall!"

m. Talk about physical characteristics of the children in general. How many are blond? What is special about red hair? How many have lost baby teeth?

n. On an informal or planned occasion, talk with the children about the body needing rest, food, exercise, and sunshine to stay healthy. Plan some simple learning experiences to support each one of these needs.

o. In the dramatic play area, put some doctor's kits, some bandages, dolls, and other props. Watch the children and listen to their comments. If necessary, suggest some ways of using the equipment, but leave the play to the children.

p. Take time to show the children where the rest rooms are and how to use them (flush the toilet, wash hands, dispose of paper, and so on). Especially encourage the children to wash their hands before handling food or after using messy materials.

q. Provide a tooth brush for each child. Individually or in small groups tell the children why it is important to keep their teeth and mouth clean, and show them the proper way to brush their teeth.

r. Casually work with the children on personal grooming (face washing, hair combing or brushing, clean clothes, and so on).

s. Invite the children to do finger painting (or foot painting). Point out the print made by fingers, hands, toes, feet.

t. Stress safety in the classroom (where to play, how to climb, rights of others, and so on). Together make some guidelines for the classroom and playground and help the children to maintain them. Children who help formulate rules usually follow them better than when rules are imposed upon them; however, always step in and assist if a person is being harmed or property is being destroyed.

u. Ask which children have been sick. How did they feel? What did someone do to help them feel better? Have any of them had common diseases? How many of them are immunized against common diseases? Check their health records and remind parents of the recent measles epidemic because of lack of proper immunization.

v. Play games using the body parts, such as ''Do As I'm Doing,'' ''Simon Says,'' ''Mother May I,'' ''Lobby Loo,'' or ''Head, Shoulders, Knees, and Toes.'' Play group games such as ''London Bridge,'' ''The Farmer In the Dell,'' ''Freeze,'' or ''Duck, Duck, Goose.''

w. Talk with the children about their feelings, remembering that the children may be better able to demonstrate rather than verbalize how they feel. How do you feel when you are happy (the children may just smile)? What do you do when you are tired (the children may close their eyes or lie down on the floor)? Show pictures of different but common emotions. Let the children tell you about the pictures, then decide how the situations could be made more positive.

x. Using a flannel board and felt cutouts, watch and listen as the children dress and undress the characters.

y. Play the sponge game. Each child has a sponge about three by five inches. Color is unimportant. The teacher gives directions and the child follows them (''Put the sponge on your head . . . on your foot . . . under your chin . . . on your back or tummy when on the floor . . . between your elbows,'' and so on).

z. On a bulletin board, have pictures of things which help us stay healthy and things which promote weakness or illness (example of foods, cleanliness, exercise, and so on). Talk about good health practices, such as staying away from someone who is ill, covering the mouth and nose when sneezing, and not sharing things that are placed in the mouth.

aa. Talk about the children growing up. Display pictures of babies playing and preschoolers playing. Remind them how they can do more things now than when they were babies. Use *The Growing Story* (Krauss), or the record, ''When I was very young.'' (See further resources at end of chapter.)

bb. Play a game where a certain body part is exercised:

1. fingers—pinching, tickling, touching, rolling, holding, pointing, tracing, squeezing, scratching, pulling, rubbing, patting, lacing, winding, tapping, folding, tying, cutting, intertwining, snapping

2. hands and arms—swinging, clapping, reaching, stretching, drooping, swimming, punching, pulling, lifting, carrying, waving, sweeping, picking up, shaking, grasping, throwing, patting, pounding

3. feet and legs—kicking, tapping, stamping, wiggling, bending, shaking, galloping, lifting, sliding

4. two or more body parts combined

cc. Let the children help make nourishing foods for snack (yogurt, fresh fruit, vegetables, dairy products, grains).

dd. On a sunny day, or using a lamp, encourage the children to make shadows with their bodies. Note how the body size changes depending on the distance from the light source. Make animal or other designs using the hands and arms.

ee. In a simple and generalized way, talk about muscles and how they help the body move in work and play. This may be a difficult concept for young minds to comprehend.

ff. Adults in home and school settings need to learn how to detect and reduce stress in the lives of young children through appropriate and acceptable releases (music, art, physical activity, dramatic play, verbalization or whatever helps the child cope with the situation).

gg. When the children first begin a group experience, the teacher can talk with them about what will happen (activities, toys, eating, safety, and so on). During an early group experience, center the period on picking up toys, where they go, role playing, puppets demonstrating, and so on.

hh. Make up a story (or sequences of events) where a child expresses a number of emotions. As the emotions are discussed, have a large hand-held mirror where the children can see their faces as they express the emotions. Most of the time the children smile rather than imitate the emotions proposed.

SENSORY LEARNING

(See also Senses Chapter, pp. 233–241.)

A. Sight

1. There may be some children within the group who have some special needs (such as glasses, crutches, or hearing aids). On a relaxed and positive basis, plan experiences where all the children can more fully understand the children with special needs.

> Example: Using a magnifying glass one teacher helped the children see how items can be made larger— thereby easier to see. One group of children talked about eyes during a sensory theme and then made glasses using pipe cleaners. The glasses were then prized possessions.

2. Looking at pictures or picture books, ask the children to locate certain items—a lady bug, a worm, an apple, and so on.

3. Using different sizes or shapes, ask the children to identify large and small items. (Older children may be able to talk about "medium" or "middle," but this is difficult for very young children.)

4. Providing a group of objects, help the children to put like objects together. Young children will group them by a single characteristic— color *or* shape, for example. Older children can handle more complex situations—color *and* shape.

B. Sound

1. Use records or tapes that have instructions or instrumental music. Encourage the children to listen and follow the instructions. Note the body movements of the children.

2. Help the children listen for loud and soft sounds. When are loud sounds used? When are soft sounds used?

C. Touch

1. Select a group of objects of different textures. Talk with the children and help them put names with the different textures.

2. Talk with and show the children how we protect our hands (gloves, lotion, and so on).

SMALL MUSCLE DEVELOPMENT

a. In the housekeeping area, provide medium-sized dolls and clothing to fit them. Have a variety of clothes fasteners (zippers, snaps, buttons, and so on) for children's practice.

b. Usually children ages two through five are unable to tie things; however, opportunities for practice can be provided. Use lacing frames, dress-up clothing, and other items so the children become familiar with the tying process.

c. Have puzzles of people and animals for the children to develop an understanding of relationships between body parts.

d. Provide pegs and peg boards, but do not expect the children to use them for long periods of time.

e. For children who are ready, help them learn to cut with scissors. (The type of scissors, the materials to be cut, and the complexity of the design will influence the success rate of the children.)

f. Using a string or yarn with a tip (needle, shoe lace, paste, or tape), encourage the children to thread objects (spools, cereal with hole, cut straws, or noodles).

LARGE MUSCLE DEVELOPMENT

a. Give the children opportunities to develop body skills, such as balance, coordination, and cooperation. Informally practice locomotion skills (march, hop, jump, gallop, and so on), nonlocomotion skills (bending, twisting, reaching, and so on), and manipulative skills (sliding, climbing, swinging, catching, and so on).

b. Provide materials and activities for the children to practice perceptual-motor awareness, that is, discrimination, eye-hand coordination, control, finger dexterity, and flexibility. Such activities include pegs and boards, puzzles, art, finger plays, manipulative toys, and so on.

c. Be aware of and provide activities for spatial awareness. Rather than teaching prepositions through lecture or using objects, encourage the children to use their bodies (stand *by* the chair, climb *under* the table, step *over* the rope). For an extension of positioning, ask each child to put his hand on body parts as you call them out (back, ankle, neck, and so on).

d. Set up a bowling game in an area that will be undisturbed. Show the children how to set up the pins and roll the balls.

e. Toss bean bags into large containers.

f. Move to music using body parts or props, such as scarves, balloons (with caution), streamers, and so on.

g. In the play yard, make a simple obstacle course using boxes, boards, tunnels, short ladders, paper streamers, barrels, and other available items. As the children become more proficient, lengthen the course or make some activities more challenging. The course should always be successful for children of varying strengths and skills.

h. Using body cards, encourage the children to make their body shapes with the cards (can be a body outline or stick-person form). Rotate the position of the cards for a different experience.

i. As a beginning balance activity, put a piece of yarn, string, or paper on the floor. Ask the children to walk only on the line. As they become more successful, use a walking board directly on the floor, then raise it gradually for those who are ready. Ways to use the balance beam creatively include: changing the position of the arms; walking forward, backwards, or sideways; or carring a small object, such as a bean bag. Plastic stilts also help develop good balance.

j. Encourage outdoor play daily. Provide opportunities to exercise large muscles (digging, pedalling, climbing, running, and other available activities). Rather than expecting the children to generate their own activities, have a focus item (planting, parachute, movement and music, stick horses, and so on) whether or not the children use it. See that outdoor equipment is the correct size for the children and that it is kept in good repair.

k. Use a small parachute with the children. They can help move it, run under it, bounce a ball or small toy on it, or other easy activities.

l. Hoola hoops are fun for children outdoors (and indoors, if the area permits). Children can lay the hoops on the ground and jump into and out of them, they can stand them up and walk through them, they can roll them, they can be safe within them, they can toss

bean bags in them, they can use them in an obstacle course, and other ways limited only by the imagination of the children. Hoops are light-weight, can be stored on a hook, are often colorful, and can be purchased or made inexpensively.

m. Some young children like to do gymnastics, but are unskilled and tire easily. If a tumbling mat or pad is available, the children can use their bodies in a variety of ways.

n. Ask the children to pretend they are different animals or objects and to move around the room in an appropriate manner—''Be an elephant, now a giraffe, now an airplane, and now a baby.''

o. Name some situations (''be very small, be very big,'' and so on), and ask the children to imitate them with their whole bodies.

REFERENCES

Althouse, R. (1988). **Investigating science with young children.** New York: Teachers College, Columbia University, pp. 163–173.

Althouse, R., and Main, C. (1975). **Science experiences for young children: How we grow.** New York: Teachers College Press.

Elkind, D. (1981). **The hurried child.** Reading, MA: Addison-Wesley.

Elting, M. (1986). **The Macmillan book of the human body.** New York: Macmillan.

Hackett, J. K., Moyer, R. H., and Adams, D. K. (1989). **Merrill science: A natural in your classroom.** Columbus, OH: Merrill.

Honig, A. S. (1986a). Stress and coping in children, Part I **Young Children,** 41(4), 50–63.

Honig, A. S. (1986b). Stress and coping in children, Part II **Young Children,** 41(5), 47–59.

Kostelnik, M. J., Stein, L. C., and Whiren, A. P. (1988). Children's self-esteem: The verbal environment. **Childhood education,** 65(1), 29–32.

Lind, K. K. (1983). Apples, oranges, baseballs and me. **Understanding the healthy body,** pp. 123–125. Columbus, OH: SMEAC Information Reference Center.

Lind, K. K. (1985). The inside story. **Science and children,** 22 (4),122–123.

Mancure, J. B. (1980). **Love, and Kindness, and Caring.** Chicago: Childrens Press.

Margolis, H. (1987). Self-induced relaxation: A practical strategy to improve self-concepts, reduce anxiety, and prevent behavioral problems. **Clearing House,** 60(8), 355–358.

O'Brien, S. J. (1988). Childhood stress: A creeping phenomenon. **Childhood education,** 65(2), 105–106.

BOOKS FOR CHILDREN

Adelson, L. (1957). **All ready for school.** New York: McKay.

Alili. (1990). **My feet.** New York: Harper-Collins.

Aliki. (1984). **Feelings.** New York: Greenwillow.

Aliki. (1962). **My hands.** New York: Crowell.

Anglund, J. W. (1960). **Love is a special way of feeling.** New York: Harcourt Brace Jovanovich.

Anglund, J. W. (1983). **A friend is someone who likes you.** New York: Harcourt Brace Jovanovich.

Bains, R. (1985). **Health and hygiene.** Mahwah, NJ: Troll Associates.

Berenstain, S., and Berenstain, J. (1985). **The Berenstain bears and too much junk food.** New York: Random House.

Bonsall, C. (1964). **The Greedy Book!** New York: Harper.

Brenner, B. (1970). **Faces.** New York: Dutton.

Clothes. (1972). New York: Wonder Books.

Davis, G. (1985). **Katy's first haircut.** Boston: Houghton Mifflin.

Ets, M. H. (1965). **Just me.** New York: Viking.

Facklam, M. (1988). **But not like mine.** New York: Gulliver/HBJ.

Freeman, D. (1955). **Mop top.** New York: Viking.

Green, M. M. (1960). **Is it hard, is it easy?** Reading, MA: Addison-Wesley.

Hair. (1972). New York: Wonder Books.

Hines, A. G. (1985). **All about myself.** New York: Clarion.

Hoban, L. (1985). **Arthur's loose tooth.** New York: Harper.

Krauss, R. (1971). **The growing story.** New York: Scholastic.

Lindsay, T. (1985). **When Batistine made bread.** New York: MacMillan.

Lioni, L. (1986). **It's mine! A fable.** New York: Knopf.

Leonard, M. (1988). **What I like series: Going to bed, getting dressed, eating, taking a bath.** New York: Bantam Books.

McCloskey, R. (1952). **One morning in Maine.** New York: Viking.

Mayer, M. (1983). **All by myself.** New York: Western.

Mayer, M. (1983). **When I get bigger.** New York: Western.

Pachard, M. (1985). **From head to toe: How my body works.** New York: Messner.

Pragoff, F. (1987). **Growing.** New York: Bantam Doubleday Dell.

Raskin, E. (1969). **Spectacles.** New York: Atheneum.

Rockwell, A., and Rockwell, H. (1982). **Sick in bed.** New York: Macmillan.

Rogers, F. (1985). **Going to day care.** New York: Putnam.

Sabin, F. (1985). **Human body.** Mahwah, NJ: Troll Associates.

Schlein, M. (1968). **See me grow.** New York: Abingdon.

Showers, P. (1967). **Hear your heart.** New York: Crowell.

Showers, P. (1972). **My friend the dentist.** New York: Golden Press.

Showers, P. (1980). **No measles, no mumps for me.** New York: Crowell.

Showers, P. (1982). **You can't make a move without your muscles.** New York: Crowell.

Silverman, J. (1988). **Some time to grow.** Boston: Addison-Wesley.

Udry, J. (1969). **Let's be enemies.** New York: Harper.

Zim, H. (1969). **Bones.** New York: Wm. Morrow.

RECORD SOURCES

(See Appendix C on pages 285–286 or preschool educational catalogues.)

Getting to know myself. Hap Palmer Record Library, #AR543 or #AC543.

On learning basic skills through music. Vol. 1, Hap Palmer Record Library, #AR526 or #AC526.

When I was very young. The Children's Record Guild, #1031.

A visit to my little friend. The Children's Record Guild, #1017.

My playful scarf. The Children's Record Guild, #1019.

Hokey Pokey. (Many versions are available.)

Bean bag activities and coordination skills. Kimbo Educational, #7055.

OTHER SOURCES

(See Appendix C on pages 285–286 or preschool educational catalogues.)

''I dress for the weather,'' **Judy/Instructo Educational Materials.** Flannelboard Set #285.

''My Body,'' **Judy/Instructo Educational Materials.** Flannelboard Set #284.

Clothing

CONCEPTS AND ACTIVITIES

Articles of clothing are of interest to young children. As anyone who has watched toddlers knows, these youngsters struggle with various pieces of apparel, and are capable of undressing themselves long before they are able to dress themselves. Shoes and socks are easily taken off and on, but items of clothing that have fasteners (zippers, buttons, ties, and so on) present more of a challenge. As young children grow, they become more intent upon dressing themselves—often with mismatched socks, wrong-side-out or backwards shirts, uncoordinated color combinations, and fasteners left open. But nonetheless, the child exclaims with dignity and pride, "I dressed myself!"

What does clothing have to do with science? It relates in several important ways. First, because clothing protects the body from nature—extreme temperatures, harm, embarrassment, and so on. Second, clothing increases feelings of security, independence, and comfort. Third, clothing integrates other aspects of the environment, such as culture, color, textures, materials, designs, and variety.

Following are some ideas that can be used, adapted, or replaced according to the interests and needs of young children at home or in groups.

PROTECTION

a. Talk about how clothing protects the body from temperature—both heat and cold. Use pictures, props, role playing, and so on.

b. Show a variety of gloves (sport, dress, seasonal) and talk about their purpose and function.

c. Show a variety of gloves used to protect hands when doing different occupations. Compare them in weight, materials, and purposes.

d. Talk about how wearing clothes makes us feel (pretty or handsome, comfortable, appropriate for certain activities, and so on).

e. Talk about the kinds of clothing needed for different types of activities and weather. For example, in a small suitcase have articles of clothing and talk about a trip or situation where a change of clothing is needed. "What shall we take on our trip when it is summertime?" "Would we use the same clothing for a trip in the winter?"

f. Talk about appropriate clothing for water activities (swimming, water play, rain, and so on). Is clothing that absorbs the water more important than clothing that repels the water? Use a tub of water and various fabrics to demonstrate the points, but keep it on the children's level of understanding.

g. On a stormy day, talk about rain gear—preparing for warmth and dryness or for coolness and dryness.

h. Sing songs and do finger plays that address articles of clothing. Make up ideas and sing to the tune of "Mulberry Bush" or "This Is the Way We Wash Our Clothes."

SECURITY, INDEPENDENCE, AND COMFORT

a. As a child is dressed, name the articles of clothing and explain how they are put on ("Lift up both arms so we can put on the shirt," "First we put on the socks, and then the shoes,"). Make dressing and undressing a fun activity.

b. Name the articles of clothing as they are handled (for the laundry, for dressing, for folding, for putting away, and so on).

c. For very young children, purchase and use clothing that is easy for them to manipulate, such as pullover shirts instead of button ones, or elastic waistbands instead of snap and zipper openings.

d. As the child starts developing finger skills and independence, purchase and use clothing with easy fasteners: large (and few) buttons, zippers, velcro, and so on.

e. As independence develops, let the child select between a few choices as to what to wear (the blue shirt, or the red one; shorts or slacks; striped socks or plain ones).

f. It is easier for small fingers to learn how to manipulate fasteners when the clothing is not on the child's body (doll clothes, lacing and buttoning frames, sewing cards, and so on).

g. Over-sized zippers, buttons, and laces teach manipulation skills. Give the children opportunities to practice these.

h. The child's ability to dress and undress herself will have a definite affect on her self-confidence. Encourage her to do these things for herself, but be willing and available to either talk her through situations or offer some assistance.

i. During clean-up use rags instead of sponges or paper towels. Talk about how some rags absorb more water than others.

j. Talk with the children about their bodies growing and clothing getting too small.

k. Some young children can use sewing cards, spool knitting, regular knitting, sewing on large buttons, sewing through burlap, or stringing objects, but generally these activities are too advanced for small and experienced fingers.

l. Before using a messy or wet creative art activity, encourage the children to use a cover-up (some object to "aprons") and explain why the cover-up is important.

m. Talk about the use of pockets. Play a game where the children go around the room and see what they can place in their pockets. (For children who do not have pockets in their clothing, make a simple tie-on bag or provide a small sack.) Gather, display, and talk about the items.

n. Talk about the care of clothing (putting it away, washing or cleaning, mending, and so on).

INTEGRATION OF ENVIRONMENT

a. Fabrics that feel good to the touch encourage children's use more than those that are harsh or stiff.

b. Articles of clothing should be sturdy and of interesting colors and patterns. Children like vivid colors. The color of an outfit is so important to a young child that he usually refers to it by its color rather than its style or type.

c. Young children like clothes similar to those of their playmates—not identical, but alike in style and color.

d. Children are more free to play when their clothes fit properly and are attractive to them. If necessary, keep some extra clothing handy for children to use when the situation calls for it.

e. Heavy paper dolls and clothing can be made from cardboard and fabrics (or purchased commercially). Young children like to dress and undress the dolls by using adhering costumes (for specific activities, weather, or cultural occasions).

f. In the dramatic area, place hats that indicate different occupations or activities. Have a large mirror nearby.

g. Frequently provide dress-up clothes of family members or occupations to stimulate dramatic play and an introduction of the child to the world around. Be sure to include accessories such as purses, jewelry, ties, hats, suspenders, belts, boots, and billfolds.

h. On occasion, focus on a certain occupation, for example, use doctor kits, clothing, cots, and bandages. Are uniforms worn for some occupations? Think and talk about non-sexist occupations.

i. Display and use puzzles and pictures of articles of clothing.

j. Make a collage using pre-cut fabric swatches in different textures, colors, shapes, and patterns. (Even if the children can cut with scissors, pre-cut pieces are important because cutting fabrics can be rather difficult.)

k. Have duplicates of a variety of fabric swatches large enough for the children to visualize and manipulate. Ask the children to put like pieces together. (They may match patterns, colors, or sizes, so before you correct their activity, briefly and casually discuss it with them. They may sort differently than an adult and they may be right!)

l. Have a variety of fabric swatches. Ask the children to place them in order of softness, or ones they like to touch most.

m. Provide fabric loops and metal frames about 5 inches square. Show the children how to weave the loops to make a design.

n. Have a wide selection of one type of clothing, for example, shoes. Ask the children to put the same kind of article in one pile (shoes with laces in one pile, buckles in another pile, and so on).

> Example: One preschooler was told that he had his shoes on the wrong feet. Following a puzzled look, he responded, "But these are the only feet I have."

o. If the children are well supervised and are interested, try tie-dying some fabrics or dye some macaroni so the children can see how color is absorbed.

p. Generally, talking about the origin of fibers (plants, animals, or synthetics), weaving, dying, and characteristics of fabric (strength, use) are above and beyond the interest or understanding of young children. However, some children may be interested for a short period of time.

q. Make the children aware of certain environmental or weather conditions that pertain to your specific area and why certain clothing is worn or not worn. (Children who live in the desert have different clothing needs than ones who live near the ocean.)

RESOURCES

Herr, J., and Libby, Y. (1990). **Creative resources for the early childhood classroom.** Albany, NY: Delmar Publishers.

BOOKS FOR CHILDREN

Borden, L. (1989). **Caps, hats, socks, and mittens.** New York: Scholastic.

Cleary, B. (1987). **The growing-up feet.** New York: Dell.

Corey, D. (1985). **New shoes!** Niles, IL: Whitman & Co.

Daly, M. (1986). **No so fast, Songololo.** New York: Atheneum.

Hill, A. (1986). **The red jacket mix-up.** New York: Golden Press.

Fitz-Gerald, C. M. (1987). **I can be a textile worker.** Chicago: Childrens Press.

Flournoy, V. (1985). **The patchwork quilt.** New York: Dial Press.

Hoban, T. (1987). **Dots, spots, speckles and stripes.** New York: Greenwillow Books.

Keats, E. J. (1962). **The snowy day.** New York: Viking.

Kent, J. (1978). **Socks for supper.** New York: Parents Magazine Press.

Krauss, R. (1971). **The growing story.** New York: Scholastic.

Payne, E. (1972). **Katy no-pocket.** Boston: Houghton Mifflin.

Rubel, N. (1984). **I can get dressed.** New York: Macmillan.

Shreckhise, R. (1985). **What was it before it was a sweater?** Chicago: Childrens Press.

Tyrrel. A. (1987). **Elizabeth Jane gets dressed.** Woodbury, NY: Barron's.

Waber, B. (1975). **Ira sleeps over.** Boston: Houghton Mifflin.

Watts, M. (1981). **Hiram's red shirt.** New York: Golden Press.

Winthrop, E. (1986). **Shoes.** New York: Harper & Row.

Wells, R. (1979). **Max's new suit.** New York: Dial Press.

RECORD SOURCES

(See Appendix C on pages 285–286 or preschool educational catalogues.)

I'm dressing myself. The Children's Record Guild, #803.

Palmer, H. What are you wearing? Learning Basic Skills Through Music.

Color

CONCEPTS AND ACTIVITIES

Color gives variety and interest to the world. It stimulates different emotions. It adds warmth and coolness to our lives. Without color, the environment would be monotonous and similar. Do not neglect or expect too much from children who are vision impaired, color-blind, or cannot relate labels to colors.

Even though children have sensitivity to color and pattern from a very young age, it is not until they can put a label on a color that it becomes different from others. Some children learn color names quickly and others have difficulty. Practice in learning basic colors is essential to further discrimination.

a. Begin by introducing the children to one color at a time (and not too rapidly) using the primary colors: red, yellow, and blue. Focus on one color by highlighting it throughout the day or week through bulletin boards, toys provided, stories and finger plays, and so on. Avoid making the experience monotonous by eliminating all other colors. (The children also need experience in distinguishing between colors—what is *not* blue, for example.) Assist the children to learn *labels* or *names* for the different colors. Be patient. Name the colors as objects are handled; use repetition, but avoid monotonous drills.

b. Have a number of objects of the same shapes in the primary colors. Help the children sort the shapes by color. Name each color as it is sorted.

c. Have a number of objects of different shapes in the primary colors. Ask the children to put all like colors in one pile. After they become proficient at this, ask them to sort them another way. Note if they sort them by size, shape, or color. Young children center on one dimension and may be able to sort in only one way, such as color.

d. Talk with the children about common colors of specific things, but don't be surprised if thinking about color spills over into other topics.

e. Name and show a certain color, like yellow. With the children's help, gather or name objects in the room that are the same color. Then use a different color in the same way. Observe which color pile has the most objects.

f. Assist the children to mix paint for the easel (or other activities). In a water trough or tub place small containers, a small pitcher of water, brushes or tongue depressors for stirring, and containers of dry tempera. When the paint is mixed, encourage the children to test the paint to see if it is too thin or too thick. The paint will begin as true colors, but may quickly be combined. Talk about painting with the

new colors that emerge. Haskell (1979, p. 74) suggests that contrasting rather than complementary colors be provided for early experiences to prevent muddy results, such as yellow with blue, red, green, or brown; orange with green, purple, brown, or red; and white with blue, red, green, or purple.

g. In a small box or paper bag, put objects of one selected color, but also include a few other colors so the children have a chance to decide which are the selected color and which are not. Make sure that the colors are true so the children will be successful in grouping them.

h. Play the color song on the Hap Palmer record listed at the end of the chapter. Keep in mind that older children follow directions more quickly than younger ones.

i. Use songs, fingerplays, stories and other activities that name or use colors.

j. Focus on the color white, which is frequently neglected. Notice things in the environment (clothing, toys, nature, and so on) that are white. Assist the children to mix white dry tempera into jars of other colors. What are the new colors called? Talk about white food that we eat. Give each child a piece of black paper and white paint (or cotton balls for gluing) to make "snow" pictures.

k. Occasionally have the children work on a group mural which will hang in the classroom. Note the colors the children use and the feeling the mural gives to the children.

l. In the domestic area use plastic dishes of bright colors and ask the children to set the table so all the dishes for one person are the same color.

m. Talk with the children about safety measures as a traffic signal is introduced (green means "go," yellow means "be careful," and red means "stop").

n. Use puzzles that have vivid colors and the names of colors written by the appropriate objects.

o. Obtain some paint or color laminated chips for the children to sort, avoiding shades, hues, and tints for now.

p. Sing songs about individual children and the colors in their clothing, for example, "Mary Wore Her Red Dress," in Ruth Seeger's *American Folk Songs for Children*.

q. As some children learn the primary colors, gradually introduce and talk about secondary colors (orange, green, and purple). Let the children mix these colors by using colored cellophane, diluted food coloring and eye droppers, mixed paint, or an art project. Name the original colors, the new colors, and how they were made.

r. Of special note is the color-blind child who may never be able to recognize certain colors.

> Example: One teacher was very disturbed that a child would color the American flag brown until she discovered that the color labels were off the crayons—and the child was color blind!

s. Some objects do not have color (water, air, clear plastic, or glass). Help children to describe such things.

t. Fabrics many be a single color or multi-colored. Help children to identify specific colors among many colors.

u. Discuss how heat (and freezing) can change the color of things (food, sun bleaches or burns, and so on).

v. Observe that some colors can be seen as symbolic of such things as holidays, feelings, safety, and foods.

w. Encourage the children to finger paint on a plastic tray or heavy white paper. Begin with a colorless (or white) paint; add dry tempera of child's choice. Note the conversation and color changes as the paintings progress.

x. The children can brush a mixture of milk and food coloring in a variety of colors onto white bread. After the bread is toasted, the children enjoy it for snack, commenting on their design and color creations.

y. As a creative activity, mix dry salt and dry tempera together. The children drizzle glue on the paper in various designs or motions. Then the colored salt-tempera is applied over the glue by shaking it from a salt shaker.

z. Dilute green or blue food coloring in water in a clear jar. Insert a stalk of celery or a white carnation. Watch the color extend to the leaves and blossoms.

aa. As the seasons change, point out color changes in the child's environment (snow, drought, heat, cold, and so on).

bb. Group children (or dismiss them from a group activity) by color. "All children wearing purple can get their smock for creative time." (Do not overdo this type of behavior.)

cc. Sing a rainbow song. Note the order of the colors.

dd. Assist children to sort poker chips into colored baskets.

ee. Make or purchase games such as Color Lotto, Color Dominoes, or Color Bingo.

ff. Supply wooden beads and laces for stringing. Make different patterns for the children to duplicate.

gg. Tear or cut a variety of pieces of colored tissue paper one to two inches (easy for young fingers to handle). Provide an unwaxed paper plate and liquid starch. The children apply the liquid starch to the plate with a brush, then place the tissue paper on the starch. This is easy to do and makes a very interesting and colorful picture.

hh. On an easel place two pieces of paper and several brushes and jars of paint (or place two easels side-by-side). This provides a fun and social experience for young children.

ii. Provide materials (paint, chalk, finger paint, crayons, felt-tip markers, colored clay, paper, and so on) and *uninterrupted time* and let the children explore and experiment with colors and media. Assist the children to select, get out, and clean up their activities. Be assistive but nondirective.

jj. Help the children develop a good feeling about themselves. One way is to encourage their participation in creative art activities and give honest praise for their efforts. Let the child make the project how *she* wants it. Notice and comment on the colors used, the motion of the strokes, the color combinations, and encourage the child to discuss the project if *she* wants to.

  1. Be specific but noncritical.

  2. Display the art work frequently.

  3. Have materials available so the children can select when and what they use.

  4. Know the children in the group and provide opportunities for successful experiences and interactions.

(Scissors may be inappropriate for most of the young children; however, for those who have or are ready to develop cutting skills, have available some *good* scissors and easily cut materials.)

REFERENCES

Althouse, R., and Main, C. (1975). **Science experiences for young children: Color.** New York: Teachers College Press.

Beaty, J. J. (1990). **Observing development of the young child,** 2d ed. Columbus, OH: Merrill Publishing, pp. 208–211, 303–318.

Eliason, C., and Jenkins, L. (1990). **A practical guide to early childhood curriculum,** 4th ed. Columbus, OH: Merrill Publishing, pp. 359–371.

Haskell, L. L. (1979). **Art in the early childhood years.** Columbus, OH: Merrill Publishing.

Neuman, D. B. (1978). **Experiences in science for young children.** Albany, NY: Delmar Publishers.

Sands, N. L. (1991, March). A splash of color. **Science and Children,** 28(6), 38–39.

Smith, N. R. (1982). The visual arts in early childhood education: Development and the creation of meaning. In Bernard Spodek (ed.), **Handbook of research in early childhood education,** pp. 295–317. New York: The Free Press.

BOOKS FOR CHILDREN

Bright, R. (1959). **My red umbrella.** New York: Wm. Morrow & Co.

Bright, R. (1955). **I like red.** New York: Doubleday.

Brooks, R. (1975). **Annie's rainbow.** New York: Wm. Collins & World Publishing Co.

Carle, E. (1984). **The mixed-up chameleon.** 2d ed. New York: Harper & Row.

Carle, E. (1971). **My very first book of colors.** New York: Macmillan.

Duvoisin, R. A. (1956). **The house of four seasons.** New York: Lothrop, Lee & Shepard.

Ehlert, L. (1990). **Color farm.** New York: HarperCollins.

Ehlert, L. (1988). **Planting a rainbow.** San Diego, CA: Harcourt Brace Jovanovich.

Feczko, K. (1985). **Umbrella parade.** Mahwah, NJ: Troll Associates.

Fenton, E. (1961). **The big yellow balloon.** New York: Doubleday.

Freeman, D. (1978). **A rainbow of my own.** New York: Puffin Books.

Graham, B. (1987). **The red woolen blanket.** Boston: Little, Brown & Co.

Hoban, T. (1978). **Is it red? Is it yellow? Is it blue?** New York: Greenwillow Books.

Hoban, T. (1989). **Of colors and things.** New York: Greenwillow.

Hurd, E. T. (1982). **I dance in my red pajamas.** New York: Harper.

Johnson, C. (1955). **Harold and the purple crayon.** New York: Harper.

Kellogg, S. (1980). **The mystery of the flying orange pumpkin.** New York: Dial Press.

Kellogg, S. (1978). **The mystery of the magic green ball.** New York: Dial Press.

Kellogg, S. (1974). **The mystery of the missing red mitten.** New York: Dial Press.

Lerner, S. (1969). **Orange is a color: A book about color.** Minneapolis: Lerner Publisher.

Lionni, L. (1975). **A color of his own.** New York: Pantheon.

Lionni, L. (1959). **Little blue and little yellow.** New York: McDowell Obolensky.

MacDonald, G. (1944). **Red light, green light.** New York: Doubleday.

McGovern, A. (1969). **Black is beautiful.** Bristol, FL: Four Winds Press.

Martin, B. Jr. (1967). **Brown bear, brown bear, what do you see?** New York: Holt.

McMillan, B. (1988). **Growing colors.** New York: Lothrop, Lee & Shepard.

Petersham, M., and Petersham, M. (1949). **The box with red wheels.** New York: Macmillan.

Robinson, D. (1976). **Anthony's hat.** New York: Scholastic.

Schneider, H. and Schneider, N. (1975). **Science fun with a flashlight.** New York: McGraw-Hill.

Seuss, Dr. (1960). **One fish, two fish, red fish, blue fish.** New York: Random House. (Or 1969, New York: Beginner Books.)

Slobodkina, E. (1947). **Caps for sale.** New York: Wm. R. Scott. (Or 1968, New York: Scholastic.)

Steiner, C. (1967). **My slippers are red.** New York: Knopf.

Stinson, K. (1983). **Red is best.** Toronto, Canada: Annick Press.

Tison, A., and Taylor, T. (1979). **The adventures of the three colors.** New York: World Publishing Co.

Zolotow, C. (1963). **The sky was blue.** New York: Harper.

RECORD SOURCES

(See Appendix C or preschool educational catalogues)

Caspell, J. **Color me a rainbow.** Melody House Records, 819 Northwest 92nd Street, Oklahoma City, OK 73114.

Hoban, T. (1987). **Dots, spots, speckles, and stripes.** New York: Greenwillow.

Palmer, H. "All the colors of the rainbow," **Learning basic skills through movement,** vol. 5. New York: Educational Activities, Inc.

Palmer, H. "Colored ribbons," **Creative and rhythmic exploration.** Educational Activities, Inc., Box 392, 1937 Grand Ave., Freeport, NY 11520.

Palmer, H. "Colors," **Learning basic skills through movement,** vol. I. New York: Educational Activities.

Palmer, H. "Parade of colors," **Learning basic skills through movement,** vol. 2. New York: Educational Activities, Inc.

Pragoff, F. (1987). **What color?** New York: Doubleday.

Seeger, R. (1948). **American Folk Songs for Children.** New York: Doubleday.

There's music in the colors. Kimbo Records, P.O. Box 477, 10 North Third Avenue, Long Branch, NJ 07740.

Community
CONCEPTS AND ACTIVITIES

The young child really has three communities with which to become acquainted: the home, the school or classroom, and the area surrounding his home.

Because of the limited language and experience of young children, they will want and need to become thoroughly acquainted with their immediate environment before taking any field trips. For the present, it is better for parents rather than teachers to take the children to new places; however, if parents do not accept this responsibility, another adult can take the children to places that are fairly close and reasonably safe.

HOME

With a change in residence, children need to become familiar with the new environment. Often, parents do not realize that a change in housing, from neighborhoods to bedrooms, can be a traumatic experience for young children. The setting and rules may be different, and as the children learn to get around under their own power (crawling, walking, running, and so on), new avenues are available. They are learning to navigate and discover new territories.

To ensure safety, parents must establish some guidelines for behavior— where the child can jump, climb, and run. Forbidden places and objects must be replaced by ones where the child can explore and function. *Tell the child what he can do, where he can play, and what he can use rather than leaving him hanging in air with too many "don'ts," "can'ts," and "stops!"*

The family home and yard are the community for young children. Show them how and where to safely explore, enjoy, and learn about their environment.

SCHOOL OR CLASSROOM

When a child joins a group, she will want to locate the important physical aspects of the classroom or school, including where to put personal items, where rest rooms are, where the toys are used and stored, what activities are done inside and what are done outside, where food is served, and who the people are. It is important that each child is comfortable in the new setting.

Within the classroom, the teacher can talk about being friendly; types of activities that will occur; special limitations, routines and sequences; personal space for each child; and guidelines for safety. The teacher should introduce new children, use the names of all individuals frequently, reassure the children of their place in the group and the return of their parents, and other items related to the particular group.

As children become more secure in the classroom, the teacher may want to take the children to other parts of the building or school. They may visit with the custodian, the cook, the secretary, and so on.

The teacher can help the children feel at home by taking them on a tour of the school's physical facilities (play-rooms, kitchen, rest rooms, entrance and exit routes, and so on).

Depending upon the community, financial resources and liabilities, and the number of adults in the classroom, the teacher may invite a guest to the classroom rather than take the children to a particular site. This can be a better learning experience for the children; however, there are some cases where a guest in the classroom does not give the children a true perspective of the topic. Sometimes the people with the most ordinary jobs are your best classroom resource.

The children can take walking field trips in the playyard, the school grounds, or the area close to the school, always observing good rules of safety.

The teacher could make or purchase a large map made of plastic or canvas showing different elements of a community and provide the children with props so they can drive small cars, move small animals and people, and act out community happenings.

SURROUNDING COMMUNITY

For Parents
a. Parents frequently take their children on errands with them. Instead of thinking of the children as burdens or distracting appendages, adults should simply and verbally talk about where they are going, what they expect to see, what they will need to do, and so on. This is done casually and informatively, not a running, boring dialogue. ("We'll stop at the station and get gas so we can run our errands without running out of gas." "We need to get the clothes from the cleaners so we can wear them to the party.") Talk to the children about paying money for the goods or services. Children often think adults are the payees instead of the payors because they frequently receive change.

b. Familiar routes to certain destinations give children security, especially when parents describe as they go: "We drive (or walk) past the church, around the park, and down the lane to get to Grandma's house." Unfamiliar routes often cause children to think "you can't get there from here."

Teachers
a. Have a portable science kit ready to take out with the children on walks. It should include magnifying glass, tape measure, flashlight, string, plastic bags, clear jars or containers, small garden trowel, or other items to help fulfill the reason for the walk.

b. Young children need to exercise and sharpen their senses. Taking a hike in the playyard (or nearby), suggest something for the children to look for— shapes, colors, senses in nature; count similar objects; see how much refuse they could get into a sack; collect insects; and so on. Make a list of the things the children find. Some of the items could be brought back to class for further examination and discussion.

c. Provide props in the domestic or dramatic play area so the children can practice various roles (family members, community helpers, and so on).

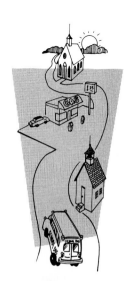

d. Have doll houses and props for the children to play with.

e. Following dramatic play about an occupation or field trip, place pictures on the bulletin board to help the children reconstruct the visit or play.

f. Encourage the children to make a picture to send to someone. Help them address, stamp, and mail the envelope.

g. Talk with the children about different kinds of buildings (stores, houses, apartments, garages, offices, and so on). Help the children make different kinds and sizes of buildings by using blocks, boards, and boxes.

h. Using paper dolls, puzzles, or props, assist the children to dress people in their occupational clothing.

i. Provide safety and street signs for children using trikes and wagons outside, and smaller signs for indoor floor play with cars, blocks, and so on.

j. Here is a suggested activity that could be done within the classroom relating to a community helper: a painter. The teacher dresses up in a pair of painter overalls and a cap. There are three large cardboard boxes sitting on a tarp or plastic cover. The teacher (painter) comes to the first box, knocks on it and then says to the occupant: "Hello, I am a painter and I have just come to town. Can I paint your house?" The occupant says, "Yes, I would like my house painted. What colors do you have?" The painter says, "I have red, yellow, and blue." The occupant says, "I would really like to have my house painted purple." The painter scratches his head and says to the children: "I only have red, yellow, and blue paint. How am I going to paint this house purple?" Some of the children might give suggestions. Or the painter

tries to make purple by painting some strips of each color, and then tries combinations. He finds that mixing red and blue make purple, so he takes his *paint brush* and paints the house purple. He goes to the next house and says, "Hello, I am a painter and I have just come to town. Can I paint your house?" The occupant says, "Yes, I would like my house painted. What colors do you have?" The painter names the three colors. The occupant says, "I would really like to have my house painted green." The painter repeats the earlier procedure to see how to make green. Finding the way, he takes his *roller* and paints the house green. He then goes to a third house and says, "Hello, I am a painter and I have just come to town. Can I paint your house?" The occupant says, "Yes, I would like my house painted. What colors do you have?" The painter names his three colors. The third occupant says, "I would like to have my house painted yellow!" The painter takes out his *spray can* and paints the house yellow. The teacher reviews with the children how the painter was dressed, about the primary colors and how the painter made different colors by mixing two of the original colors, and also the three different methods the painter used to apply the paint. (Recalled from an experience demonstrated by Lynette Robertson, head teacher, Early Childhood Education Labs, Brigham Young University, Provo, Utah.) As a follow-up activity for the children, have them put on protective clothing and choose from among the following activities:

1. Food coloring is mixed with a small amount of milk. The children take clean, small paint brushes and brush the different colors of milk on white bread. The bread is then toasted and served for snack.

2. Water colors and brushes are provided for the children to mix and paint on white paper.

3. Children are assisted to mix colors of paint for the easel and to paint pictures.

4. Old pieces of crayons are grated. One piece of waxed paper is placed on a pad of newspapers. The children sprinkle the crayon pieces over the paper and cover it with another sheet of waxed paper. The teacher helps the children to carefully iron over the sheets. The crayons melt and make an interesting design.

5. Outside or over a tarp or plastic cover, a large appliance box is placed. The children mix easel paint and then use small rollers to cover the box like the painter did. Or the children could use the rollers to make a mural on paper or sheets of cardboard.

INTO THE COMMUNITY

a. When young children are taken on a visit within the community, make sure that they are well prepared for what will occur, that all precautions for safety have been taken, that parents have given permission, and that a pre-visit has been made (Taylor, 1991, p. 193).

b. Be sure to provide some follow-up activities for the children to practice what they learned on the field trip.

c. Bring in a back-pack and have the children pack it for

  1. an overnight away from home

  2. school (pencils, books, lunch, and so on)

  3. a camp-out or vacation

The teacher should provide appropriate and inappropriate items and discuss them before the children place them in the back-pack. Discuss why items were included or excluded.

d. If possible, take the children to visit the home or apartment of one of the teachers. Have a story or snack there. Some young children think that teachers are always at school and it would be interesting for them to see where a teacher lived when away from school.

e. Before taking the children on a field trip, draw a large map of the route and some important landmarks for them to look for. After the trip talk about the route.

f. Places for young children to visit within most cities could include library, museum, fire station, police station, dairy, grocery store, farm, water plant, park, and so on.

g. Be sure to acquaint the children with the occupations most visible in your community. A visitor could be invited into the classroom or a visit could be made to the site, whichever would be more valuable.

RESOURCES

Borden, E. J. (1987). The community connection—it works! **Young Children,** 42(4), 14–23.

Eugster, K., and Janke, D. (1988). A butcher, a baker, a candlestick maker. **Science and children,** Nov/Dec, 24–25.

Jennes, M. (1987). Schoolyard hikes. **Science and children.** March, 23–25.

Nunnelly, J. C. (1990, Nov.). Beyond turkeys, santas, snowmen and hearts. **Young Children,** pp. 24–20.

Redleaf, R. (1983). **Open the door, let's explore: Neighborhood field trips for**

young children. St. Paul: Toys 'n Things.

Russell, H. R. (1973). **Ten minute field trips: A teacher's guide.** Chicago, IL: J. G. Ferguson Publishing Co.

Sunal, C. S. (1990). **Early childhood social studies.** Columbus, OH: Merrill Publishing Co.

Taylor, B. J. (1991). **A child goes forth.** New York: Macmillan.

BOOKS FOR CHILDREN

Baker, E. (1980). **Safety first—fire.** New York: Creative Press.

Barton, B. (1988). **I want to be an astronaut.** New York: Crowell.

Beim, J. (1980). **Country fireman.** New York: Wm. Morrow.

Brown, R. (1988). **100 words about working.** San Diego, CA: Gulliver.

Burton, V. L. (1974). **Katie and the big snow.** Boston: Houghton Mifflin.

Burton, V. L. (1977). **Mike Mulligan and his steam shovel.** Boston: Houghton Mifflin.

Chlad, D. (1983). **When I ride in a car.** Chicago: Childrens Press.

DeSantis, K. (1988). **A dentist's tools.** New York: Dodd, Mead/Putnam.

Durham, R. (1987). **World at work.** Chicago: Childrens Press.

Durham, R. (1987). **Around the neighborhood.** Chicago: Childrens Press.

Durham, R. (1987). **Around the house.** Chicago: Childrens Press.

Galdone, P. (1961). **The house that Jack built.** New York: McGraw-Hill.

Geis, D. (1987). **Rattle-rattle dump truck.** Los Angeles: Price/Stern/Sloan.

Gibbons, G. (1988). **Farming.** New York: Holiday House.

Gibbons, G. (1984). **Department store.** New York: Crowell.

Gibbons, G. (1985). **Fill it up! All about service stations.** New York: Crowell.

Gibbons, G. (1982). **Tool book.** New York: Holiday House.

Gibbons, G. (1982). **The post office book.** New York: Crowell.

Goldreich, G., and Goldreich, E. (1975). **What can she be? A police officer.** New York: Lothrop, Lee & Shepard.

Greene, C. (1960). **I want to be a dentist.** Chicago: Childrens Press.

Hawkesworth, J. (1980). **The lonely skyscraper.** New York: Doubleday.

Imershem, B. (1988). **Animal doctor.** Englewood Cliffs, NJ: Messner.

Johnson, J. (1988). **Sanitation workers A to Z.** New York: Walker.

Keats, E. J. (1971). **Apt. 3.** New York: Macmillan.

Kuklin, S. (1988). **Taking my cat to the vet. Taking my dog to the vet.** New York: Bradbury.

Kuklin, S. (1988). **When I see my doctor.** New York: Bradbury.

Kunhardt, E. T. (1985). **The taxi book.** New York: Golden Books.

Lillegard, D. (1987). **I can be a secretary.** Chicago: Childrens Press.

Lumley, K. W. (1985). **I can be an animal doctor.** Chicago: Childrens Press.

Maass, R. (1989). **Fire fighters.** New York: Scholastic.

McMillan, B. (1988). **Fire engine shapes.** New York: Lothrop, Lee & Shepard.

North, C. (1985). **The house book.** Racine, WI: Western Publishing.

Nims, B. L. (1989). **Where is the bear at school?** Niles, IL: Albert Whitman.

Nerlove, M. (1989). **Halloween.** Niles, IL: Albert Whitman.

Peatrie, C. (1987). **Joshua James likes trucks.** Chicago: Childrens Press.

Provensen, A., and Provensen, M. (1983). **The glorious flight.** New York: Viking Press.

Reit, S. (1984). **Jenny's in the hospital.** Racine, WI: Western Publishing Co.

Rockwell, A. (1988). **Handy Hank will fix it.** New York: Holt, Rinehart & Winston.

Rockwell, A. (1986). **Fire engines.** New York: Dutton.

Rockwell, A. (1986). **Things that go.** New York: Dutton.

Rockwell, A. (1988). **Trains.** New York: Dutton.

Rockwell, H. (1973). **My doctor.** New York: Macmillan.

Rockwell, H. (1975). **My dentist.** New York: Greenwillow Books.

Rockwell, A., and Rockwell, H. (1985). **The emergency room.** New York: Macmillan.

Rogers, F. (1986). **Going to the doctor.** New York: Putnam.

Scarry, R. (1972). **Richard Scarry's cars and trucks and things that go.** New York: Western.

Showers, P. (1962). **How many teeth.** New York: Crowell.

Snell, N. (1979). **Tom visits the dentist.** London, England: H. Hamilton Publishers.

Titherington, J. (1986). **Pumpkin, pumpkin.** New York: Greenwillow.

Watson, J. W., Switzer, R. E., and Hirschberg, J. C. (1987). **My friend the doctor.** New York: Crown.

Wandro, M. (1981). **My daddy's a nurse.** Reading, MA: Addison-Wesley.

Wolf, B. (1980). **Michael and the dentist.** New York: Four Winds Press.

RECORD SOURCES

(See Appendix C or preschool educational catalogues.)

Jenkins, E. **My street begins at my house.** (Kaplan).

Palmer, H. **Pretend.**

Rogers, F. **These are the people in my neighborhood.**

We all live together. Youngheart Records.

Ecology
CONCEPTS AND ACTIVITIES

The changes in our environment are becoming more and more of a world-wide concern. Forests are being destroyed by fire and man, water is being polluted, air is unhealthy to breathe, chemicals are being added to our food. We need to know how to reduce or eliminate the harmful influences in our environment. Teaching children how to protect the universe will help adults to be more conscious of the problems and possible solutions.

Information should be presented to inform children but not to frighten or overwhelm them!

General Activities

a. Introduce the word "litter" to children. Show them some examples inside the classroom, on the playground, and in other community places through a field trip, pictures, or role playing. Give the children litter bags to clean up their room, grounds, and other places.

> Example: One teacher placed crumpled papers, empty food boxes, and other litter around the classroom. Only one child made a comment. "This is a messy room," he said as he walked by the litter. After a group discussion about keeping things clean, the teacher gave each child a small bag and provided large garbage cans. The children quickly cleaned up the room and began talking about litter after just ignoring it before. It not only needs to be called to their attention, but the children also need to physically and verbally do something about it.

b. There may need to be daily reminders about placing waste items in containers. Where items are being recycled, there can be separate containers for those items (glass, cans, paper). Encouraging the children to place waste in proper containers can help the children become more aware of the appearance, safety, and health of their surroundings. Even very young children can participate in keeping the environment clean. In fact, some children turn it into a game and want to put everything in the containers, so check them periodically to see if anything other than waste has been discarded.

c. Many areas of the country are putting emphasis on "leaving things cleaner than you found them." This is a good practice for both young and old to follow. Role playing sometimes helps reinforce the concept.

d. Simulate a camping trip. Talk about how food would be prepared and served, camp safety, campground behavior, and other appropriate items.

e. On a nice day, take the children to a park or other public place. Take garbage sacks. Divide the children into small groups, each with an adult, and assign the groups to certain areas to pick up litter. Put the sacks into appropriate containers or take them back to class to examine the kinds of garbage collected (*if* this seems appropriate).

f. If convenient, take the children to a local garbage dump or land fill and let them watch the machinery dump, move, or cover the garbage. Back at school put similar pieces of machinery in the sand area and watch the children reproduce the sights they saw.

g. Talk with the children about the weather. Can they see the sky? If not, is it because of clouds, smoke, smog, or other pollution? Talk about the beauty of the environment when the air is clear and fresh.

h. If possible, take the children to a nearby water source (stream, lake, pond, and so on). With careful supervision, note the color of the water and any pollutants. Discuss the habitat and plants that live in the water and the difficulty they have when things are thrown into the water.

There are many kinds of conservation that can be brought to the awareness of young children: paper, energy, water, food and other materials. While other kinds of pollution are extremely important to our environment (air, sound, and soil, for example), they seem to be beyond the understanding of the age group for which this text is intended.

Paper

Young children do not understand that paper comes from trees and that our forests are being depleted. They do understand about using paper. The teacher should consider using the following:

a. smaller tissues for wiping children's noses or putting the tissue into their pockets for reuse

b. art products on surfaces other than paper—fingerpaint on trays or table tops

c. tables and easels covered with newspaper

d. group murals

e. reusable dishes for serving food

f. individual hand towel for each child

g. drinking fountains instead of individual cups

h. plastic rather than paper bags *when appropriate*

i. sponges and rags for clean-up purposes

j. saving and using scraps of paper for art projects

k. fabric of permanent backgrounds for bulletin boards

l. laminated visual aids for longer life span

m. consolidating records on the children

n. information to parents (monthly instead of weekly)

o. old magazines for cutting and pasting

p. fewer art projects taken home— more emphasis on the process rather than the finished product

q. better use of the paper—without making the children feel slighted or that the adults are stingy

r. conservation of paper at home—recycling, awareness, and so on. (Tolman and Morton, 1986, p. 191)

Energy

a. car pools and walking—trikes, bikes, and wagons for riding and hauling

b. natural light and heat when possible

c. hand-operated appliances to give children more experience and safety

than power driven ones—manual egg beaters, ice cream freezers, hand held fans, and so on

d. wind and water power—pumps, sails, and so on

e. energy conservation at home

f. efficient methods and appliances in food preparation

Water

a. bucket or container during rain or near a sprinkler to measure and use the water

b. buckets or containers for activity use rather than leaving the hose running

c. drinking from fountain without letting the water run

d. washing hands quickly and flushing toilet after use

e. watering pets and plants carefully

f. putting water into a sink when washing objects rather than letting the water run

g. container of water near messy activity for cleanup

h. filling water trough carefully to avoid causing spills

i. filling washer for amount of clothing such as cover-ups and dress-up items, to be washed

j. setting water temperature in classroom so water does not need to run to either heat or cool it

k. using dishwasher for full loads or adjusting the amount of water to the size of the load

l. talking about ways water could be conserved at home.

Food

a. encouraging the children to take the amount of food they will eat (if served family-style)

b. using food products *sparingly* for art projects, or instead using rocks, nut shells, spools, feathers, weed pods, straws, or earth clay

Holt (1985, p. 19) states, "We do not have to choose (yet) between survival and art, but we do need to examine how our teaching practices demonstrate our regard for the earth's resources and the people who rely upon them."

c. preserving and using left-over food carefully, feeding it to a pet or using it in a compost for planting flowers and vegetables

d. helping the children plant, harvest, and eat produce from a garden they assisted in; saving some of the seeds for roasting or planting

e. talking with the children about edible parts of plants—stalk, leaves, blossom, ear, pod, and so on

f. letting the children help prepare and serve food

g. serving a variety of food, including fruits and vegetables, to enrich the child's diet

h. talking about the basic food groups and how the right food helps bodies to grow strong and healthy

i. taking some simple, close field trips to a market, bakery, produce stand, or field, and talking about selecting, storing, serving, and enjoying the food

j. talking about some people in your community who help provide food

k. talking about how food could be conserved at home

Other Materials

a. using all materials sparingly

b. preparing and storing materials so there is less waste

c. using materials so that waste is reduced—crayons instead of markers, string instead of tape, and so on

d. asking for and using containers and bags that are biodegradable—paper instead of plastic bags, food containers, and so on

e. repairing items quickly to prevent further damage

REFERENCES

Altman, I., and Wohlwill, J. (eds). (1978). **Children and the environment.** New York: Plenum.

Altman, I., and Wohlwill, J. (eds.) (1983). **Behavior and the natural environment.** New York: Plenum.

Branley, F. M. (1983). **Rain and hail.** New York: Crowell.

Brighton, C. (1987). **Five secrets in a box.** New York: Dutton.

Brown, V. (1980). **The amateur naturalist's handbook.** Englewood Cliffs, NJ: Prentice-Hall.

Cole, S. (1987). **When the tide is low.** New York: Lothrop, Lee & Shepard.

Cornell, J. B. (1979). **Sharing nature with children.** Nevada City, CA: Ananda Publications.

Crase, D., and Jones, N. S. (1974). Children learn from recycling. **Young children,** 29(2), 79–82.

DiPerna, P. (1981). **Environmental hazards to children.** New York: Public Affairs Committee.

Dorsey, J. (1982). **Introducing your kids to the outdoors.** Washington, DC: Stonewall Press.

Dow Brands, P. O. Box 368, Greenville, SC 29602 (800–331–6426). (Send a postcard for pamphlet on using empty plastic containers.)

Evans, G. W. (ed.) (1982). **Environmental stress.** New York: Cambridge University Press.

Garden Club of America, 598 Madison Avenue, New York, NY 10022. (Send for pamphlet "World Around You," on water conservation.)

Gates, R. (1982). **Conservation.** Chicago: Childrens Press.

Hackett, J. K., Moyer, R. H., and Adams, D. K. (1989). **Merrill science: A natural in your classroom.** Columbus, OH: Merrill Publishing Co., pp. T84a–T85f, and 86–102.

Higdon, P. G. (1988). Getting the dirt on soil. **Science and Children.** Nov/Dec: 32–33.

Holt, B. (1989). **Science with young children.** Washington, DC: National Association for the Education of Young Children.

Holt, B. (1985). Ideas that work with young children: Food as art?'', **Young children,** 40(4), 18–19.

Langham, B. (1987). Your place is poison-proof? Look again. **Texas Child Care Quarterly,** 11(1), 3–9.

Perez, J. (1988). **Explore and experiment: Adventures in science and nature for young children.** Bridgeport, CT: First Teacher.

Postel, S. (1985). **Conserving water: The untapped resource** (Worldwatch Paper 67). Washington, DC: Worldwatch Inst.

Tolman, N. M., and Morton, J. O. (1986). **Earth science activities for grades 2– 8,** pp. 186 and 191.

BOOKS FOR CHILDREN

Brighton, C. (1987). **Five secrets in a box.** New York: Dutton.

Coats, L. J. (1987). **The oak tree.** New York: Macmillan.

Cowcher, H. (1988). **Rain forest.** Garden City, NY: Farrar.

Henkes, K. (1985). **Bailey goes camping.** New York: Greenwillow.

Hoban, T. (1990). **Shadows and reflections.** New York: Greenwillow.

Jonas, A. (1987). **Reflections.** New York: Greenwillow.

Kandoian, E. (1987). **Under the sun.** New York: Dodd.

Livingston, M. C., and Fisher, L. E. (1986). **Earth songs.** New York: Holiday House.

McMillan, B. (1990). **One sun: A book of terse verse.** New York: Holiday House.

Mitgutsch, A. (1986). **From wood to paper.** Minneapolis: Carolrhoda Books.

Rey, M., and Shalleck, A. J. (1985). **Curious George goes hiking.** Boston: Houghton Mifflin.

Skofield, J. (1984). **All wet! All wet!** New York: Harper.

Udry, J. (1956). **A tree is nice.** New York: Harper.

Welch, M. M. (1982). **Close looks in a spring woods.** New York: Dodd, Mead.

Family

CONCEPTS AND ACTIVITIES

The family is the hub of the young child's life. It is here that the child learns values and practices for later social and emotional experiences. The younger the child, the more the home setting is the main environment.

Usually by the age of two, the child has passed the "fear of stranger" period; however, the child may still be reluctant to accept outsiders and want to cling to familiar people. When the child is placed in a setting where people and the environment are unfamiliar, it is possible (even probable) that the child may be fearful, uncooperative, or aggressive. She may cling to parents or familiar people. It is inappropriate to force the child from familiarity into a strange environment. Young children entering a group should be introduced to the group gradually—over a period of hours or days if necessary. A sudden and abrupt abandonment may cause separation anxiety to last even longer or be more severe.

Some toddlers and preschoolers are ready to join a small group of unfamiliar peers and adults. Occasionally parents have difficulty "letting go." Then, it is the parents who need reassurance that the child will be looked after lovingly and thoughtfully.

One of the most important tasks of a family is to help each child develop and build confidence and self respect. In a group setting, the adults and children can be substitute family members, or can be the school family. Young children may rely on a teacher as a substitute parent and peers as substitute family members. The teacher should carefully invite the child to interact with him and possibly a few peers, but have patience in being accepted.

Ways to Introduce All Children into a New Group Family

With the origination of a new group (where the children have not had prior experience one with another), the procedure begins with inviting the child and a parent (generally) to check out the classroom, the routines, and the procedures. With this familiar adult, the child will likely feel more at home and explore the setting easier than with a new adult. After the child feels somewhat comfortable (minutes or days later), the parent and the teacher could observe from a location that is visible to the child. As the child gains confidence, the period of separation from the parent can be extended until the child is staying happily and coming into the group willingly.

Ways to Introduce a New Child into an Ongoing Group Family

Once a group is established and a new child is added to that group, it may be difficult for the child to feel comfortable and accepted. This is partly due to the fact that routines have been established, friendships have been formed, and the new child is at a loss to participate. This new child may require a parent to stay on a pattern established above in the "new group family."

Teachers can help children adjust into new situations by building the group around the new child rather than expecting the new child to break into ongoing play and friendships. For example, if children are playing in the domestic area and roles have been assumed, the teacher could give some props to the new child and a suggested role. Or the teacher could begin an interesting activity with the new child and invite others to join. Still another way is to let the new child present some new toys or activity. In that way the children are drawn to the new child.

When children spend time together, they need to learn how to cooperate and be empathetic, supportive, and cohesive—to be like a family. This can be accomplished over a period of time with opportunities for the children to practice and with the loving support of adults.

Ways to Help Children Feel They Belong in an Out-of-Home Group

a. When possible, use name tags for the children. Even if the teachers and peers know the names of the children, the children like to look for, select, and wear their name tags. This one item helps show that the child does belong. Young children like to hear and be called by their names. (Be consistent with the name the child is called at home. The exception would be if the child is called a nickname at home and adults at school feel uncomfortable about promoting it at school.)

b. Help all the children feel comfortable in the group. Greet them daily, have some conversations with them during the school time, and bid them farewell with anticipation of seeing them the next day.

c. Have activities that simulate a home environment, such as dramatic play props, eating times, child-sized equipment and utensils, and times to talk and enjoy other people.

d. Because of timidity or limited vocabulary of toddlers (and even some preschoolers), ask questions and initiate conversation about things which are important to them—their family, pets, activities, and play. Remember that two- and three-year-olds are better at showing than telling. Try to ask questions that call for a short comment or discussion; avoid questions that require "yes" or "no" answers.

e. Establish a procedure if children bring toys or objects from home. Show their treasures and then return them to their locker or cubbies so fewer toys will be lost, ownership is established and dealt with, and so on.

Suggestions for Group Teaching about the Family

a. Have pictures of families strategically placed throughout the room at the eye level of the children. Comment on the pictures occasionally and hope that the pictures will initiate ideas and activities for the children.

b. Sing songs, do fingerplays, and read stories about families.

c. Talk individually as well as in small groups about the members of each child's family. Acknowledge that families have different members and are of different sizes.

d. Ask the children (or find out otherwise) about the extended family. Does grandmother live with the family? Are pets considered as family members? Who is Uncle Bill? (Young children may use the terms for relatives, but few understand the relationships.)

e. Feature a child of the week. Have a family member come to tell about the child and family, or have someone send photographs and information so an adult can tell about the child and family.

f. Talk about the different kinds of housing for families (apartment, house, mobile home, and so on).

g. Acquire a large appliance box. Cut a door and window. Let the children help paint the outside and encourage suggestions for how to use the new house.

h. Discuss the different occupations of family members. Provide props for children to practice the different roles.

i. Have one of the adults tell the children about his family as a child and now as a grown-up.

j. Ask parents if they have any meaningful traditions that could be shared with young children.

k. Provide puzzles that show families and occupations.

l. For an art activity, provide the children with large sheets of paper, glue, scissors (for those able to cut), and magazines or pictures. Let the children browse through the magazines and use the pictures to make a replica of their family. For non-cutting children, have many pictures of individuals at all ages for the children to select as their family members and to paste on a sheet. The adult must know each family composi-tion in order to assist the children, but keep in mind that some children may want to use certain pictures, or even add to or eliminate members from their families. (Catalogues, slick paper, and other advertising are good sources for this activity.)

m. There may be different ethnic families represented in the group of children. On a basic level and with respect, talk about the similarities and differences within the group.

n. Teach about families in a positive way. Help children to build love and respect for older and younger members. Talk about sharing and helping all members, and how privileges and responsibilities change as members get older and as others come into the family (grandparents, adoptions, babies).

o. No longer is the average family one with two parents, two children, white, and American. Some children come from single-parent families (with either a male or female parent at the head); some are combined families; some have only one child while others have many children; many races, religions, and cultures are represented in our country. Teach the children to value all people regardless of their color, creed, or race. This can be initiated through conversation, through books and pictures, through encouraging the children to play one with another, through families sharing their customs, through helping each child to value her own background, through activities and concepts provided, and through being accepting yourself.

p. Promote an anti-bias curriculum related to gender so that stereotyped roles will be reduced or eliminated. This can be done through many of the suggestions in "o".

q. Help parents to be informed about the developmental characteristics of children, new research, and provocative topics related to young children and families through spontaneous conversations, newsletters or learning cards, reading materials, television and community programs, group meetings, parent conferences, telephone conversations, home visits, and referral services.

r. In the block area include wooden or plastic replicas of family members and encourage dramatic play.

s. Set up a puppet stage or box and provide hand puppets for the children to dramatize family life.

t. Provide small paper bags, scraps of paper, yarn, scissors and glue. Suggest that the children make family sack puppets. (Parts of the face and head could already be cut out for children to use who don't have scissor skills.)

u. When encouraging dramatic play, provide clothing suited for pre-teens rather than a grown-up. The clothing will still be large enough to dress-up but not too cumbersome.

v. Prepare silhouette cut-outs of various family members including both sexes and several sizes (grandparents, teens, babies). The children can manipulate them on a flannelboard and talk about family life.

w. From a sack or box the children take an article of clothing. Alone or with help they decide which member of the family would wear it and during what activity. Why do you think it is that person or that activity? Some good comments should evolve.

x. Talk about families who have members with special needs (visual or audio impairments, physical problems, and so on), but do not dwell on the negative aspects.

y. Pay careful and particular attention to the needs of the families of the children in the group. Maybe selected families are dealing with difficult problems (divorce, death, illness of a family member, handicaps, and so on). Maybe several families are dealing with the same type of problem outside their control (unemployment, disaster in the community, war, and so on). Plan carefully to reduce the stress and fears of these children and families. Perhaps a community resource person could offer suggestions and help.

z. Talk with the children about the ways they help at home. What responsibilities do other family members have? What do they do to make others happy? What could they do in the classroom to make it a good place to be?

A DAY ON THE FAMILY—PLAN

The number of activities will depend upon the number of children in the group, the length of play, and the maturity of the children involved. Also, plan for some diversions so that the children will not be bombarded by or directed exclusively to family matters.

Freeplay
a. As children enter the group, provide for dramatic play in the domestic area: dress-ups, dolls, dishes, plastic food, and so on. (When possible include native costumes and items without being too overwhelming.)

b. In a quiet but obvious place, have several mirrors (some large hand-held ones and some full-length) where the children can admire themselves as they dress up.

c. On low tables place puzzles of people in different occupations.

d. In a quiet place, have pictures, books, and flannelboard stories for the children to use.

e. In the block area set out large unit blocks, wooden or vinyl family characters, and types of vehicles.

Group Times

a. Do fingerplays, poems, and role playing about families.

b. Tell a story about a family getting ready for a vacation and the clothes they would need to take (choose your own focus).

c. Invite a guest to help the children learn about other cultures or people (very simple concepts). Include hands-on activities.

d. Sing songs, play games, and encourage record participation about family activities, occupations, and leisure.

e. Creative art could include making occupational hats (cut, design, paint); cutting and pasting pictures of family members out of magazines; drawing or painting pictures of family members; bathing, dressing, and caring for dolls.

f. Food experience could consist of making something to eat (pancakes, sandwiches, vegetable or fruit plate, butter), serving food family-style, using good manners, and cleaning up.

g. Set up a science table for the children to explore a common household product, such as flour, cornmeal, rice, or water.

Outdoor Play

a. Provide wagons, trikes, and wheel toys for dramatic play.

b. Have sand toys for making roads, sculptures, towns, and for cooking.

c. Put out dress-up clothes and large boxes for houses or stores.

d. Use tools for different occupations.

A SEGMENT ON THE FAMILY— PLAN

When you teach just a segment of the day on a precise topic, you need to decide if the segment is to be for all the children or just those who select it. If it is meant for all the children, it is best taught during a group time; if it is optional, provide the materials and information during play when children select between activities and stay or move on at their discretion.

Example: Suppose we wanted to preassess current information of the children about babies to be used later for a full day on babies. We could provide pictures of babies, dolls, clothes, furniture (cribs, strollers, high chairs), and other items used for babies. We might even bring a tub or sensory table nearby for bathing the babies. To find out the understanding and concerns of the children, we would listen to their comments and observe their actions. At a later date we may have a mother bring in a baby to bathe, dress, and feed. Supporting activities could be provided in other areas of the curriculum, like language and books, creative art, music, and so on.

REFERENCES

Allen, J., Freeman, P., and Osborne, S. (1989). Children's political knowledge and attitudes. **Young children,** 44(2), 57–61.

Derman-Sparks, L. (1989). **Anti-bias curriculum: Tools for empowering young children.** Washington, DC: National Association for the Education of Young Children.

Eliason, C., and Jenkins, L. (1990). **A practical guide to early childhood curriculum.** Columbus, OH: Merrill Publishing.

Gardner, R. (1985). **Science around the house.** New York: Julian Messner.

Herr, J., and Libby, Y. (1990). **Creative resources for the early childhood classroom.** Albany, NY: Delmar.

Kendall, F. E. (1983). **Diversity in the classroom: A multicultural approach to the education of young children.** New York: Teachers College Press.

Ramsey, P. G. (1982). Multicultural education in early childhood. **Young children,** 37, 13–14.

Rogers, D. L., and Ross, D. D. (1986). Encouraging positive social interaction among young children. **Young children,** 41(3), 12–17.

Saracho, O. M., and Spodek, B. (1983). **Understanding the multicultural experience in early childhood education.** Washington, DC: National Association for the Education of Young Children.

Smith, C. A. (1986). Nurturing kindness through storytelling. **Young children,** 41(6), 46–51.

Sprung, B. (1975). **Non-sexist education for young children: A practical guide.** New York: Citation Press.

Yawkey, T. D., Dank, H. L., and Glosenger, F. I. (1986). **Playing inside and out: How to promote social growth and** learning in young children including the developmentally delayed child. Lancaster, PA: Technomic Publishing.

BOOKS FOR CHILDREN

Adoff, A. (1982). **All the colors of the race.** New York: Lothrop, Lee & Shepard.

Barton, B. (1981). **Building a house.** New York: Greenwillow.

Berry, J. (1987). **Teach me about brothers and sisters.** Chicago: Childrens Press.

Berry, J. (1987). **Teach me about mommies and daddies.** Chicago: Childrens Press.

Berry, J. (1987). **Teach me about relatives.** Chicago: Childrens Press.

Boegehold, B. (1985). **Daddy doesn't live here anymore.** Racine, WI: Western.

Bourgeois, P., and Clark, B. (1987). **Big Sarah's little boots.** New York: Scholastic.

Buckley, H. E. (1961). **Grandmother and I.** New York: Lothrop, Lee & Shepard.

Buckley, H. E. (1959). **Grandfather and I.** New York: Lothrop, Lee & Shepard.

Burton, V. L. (1978). **The little house.** Boston: Houghton Mifflin.

Charlip, J., and Moore, L. (1975). **Hooray for me.** New York: Parents Magazine.

Christiansen, C. B. (1989). **My mother's house, my father's house.** New York: Atheneum.

Cleary, B. (1987). **The growing-up feet.** New York: Dell.

Cleary, B. (1960). **The real hole.** New York: Dell Publishers.

Dantzer-Rosenthal, M. (1986). **Some things are different, some things are the same.** Niles, IL: Whitman and Co.

Delton, J., and Tucker, D. (1986). **My grand-**

mother's in a nursing home. Niles, IL: A. Whitman.

Drescher, J. (1986). **My mother's getting married.** New York: Dial.

Durham, R. (1987). **Around the house.** Chicago: Childrens Press.

Duvoisin, R. (1956). **The house of four seasons.** New York: Lothrop, Lee & Shepard.

Flournoy, V. (1979). **The best time of day.** New York: Random House.

Goldman, S. (1978). **Cousins are special.** Niles, IL: Whitman.

Greenfield, E. (1978). **Talk about a family.** Philadelphia: Lippincott.

Griffin, L. (compiler) (1970). **Multi-ethnic books for young children.** Washington, DC: National Association for the Education of Young Children.

Hayward, L. (1982). **When you were a baby.** Racine, WI: Western.

Henkes, K. (1986). **Grandpa and Bo.** New York: Greenwillow.

Henroid, L. (1982). **Grandma's wheelchair.** Chicago: Whitman.

Hines, A. G. (1986). **Daddy makes the best spaghetti.** New York: Houghton Mifflin.

Hoyt-Goldsmith. (1990). **Totem pole.** New York: Holiday House.

Interracial books for children: Bulletin (1966 to present). Council on Interracial Books for Children. New York: Author.

Iwasaki, C. (n.d.) **Momoko's lovely day.** London, England: Bodily Head.

Iwasaki, C. (1970). **A brother for Momoko.** London, England: Bodily Head.

Iwasaki, C. (1972). **Momoko and the pretty bird.** London, England: Bodily Head.

Kalman, B. (1985). **People in my family.** New York: Crabtree.

Keats, E. A. (1971). **Apartment 3.** New York: Macmillan.

Klein, N. (1973). **Girls can be anything.** New York: Dutton.

Kraus, R. (1971). **Leo, the late bloomer.** Old Tappan, NJ: Windmill Books.

Lasker, J. (1974). **He's my brother.** Chicago: Whitman.

Lerner, M. R. (1960). **Red man, white man, African chief: The story of skin color.** Minneapolis: Lerner Co.

Merriam, E. (1973). **Mommies at work.** New York: Simon & Schuster.

North, C. (1985). **The house book.** Racine, WI: Western.

Omerod, J. (1985). **Messy baby.** New York: Lothrop, Lee & Shepard.

Phillips, T. (1989). **Day care ABC.** Niles, IL: Whitman.

Raynor. D. (1977). **This is my father and me.** Niles, IL: Whitman.

Rogers, F. (1985). **The new baby.** New York: Putnam.

Salus, N. P. (1979). **My daddy's mustache.** Garden City, NY: Doubleday.

Seuling, B. (1985). **What kind of family is this? A book about step families.** Racine, WI: Western.

Simon, N. (1976). **Why am I different?** Niles, IL: Whitman.

Simon, N. (1976). **All kinds of families.** Niles, IL: Whitman.

Udry, J. M. (1970). **Mary Jo's grandmother.** Niles, IL: Whitman.

Viorst, J. (1976). **Alexander and the terrible, horrible, no good, very bad day.** New York: Atheneum.

Ward, S. G. (1986) **Molly and grandpa.** New York: Scholastic.

Ward, S. G. (1986). **Charlie and grandma.** New York: Scholastic.

Watson, J. W., Switzer, R. E., and Hirsch-berg, J. C. (1986). **Sometimes I'm jealous.** New York: Crown Publishing.

Zindel, P. (1975). **I love my mother.** New York: Harper.

Zolotow, C. (1989). **The quiet mother and the noisy little boy.** New York: Harper & Row.

RECORD SOURCES

(See Appendix C or preschool educational catalogues.)

Sounds around us. Glenview, IL: Scott Foresman and Co.

The sleepy family. New York: Young People's Records.

Small voice, big voice with Dick, Laurie and Jed. Folkway Records and Service Corp.

When I was very young. The Children's Record Guild, #1031.

Food

CONCEPTS AND ACTIVITIES

Food and eating should be a pleasant time for the children. But when the children are ravenously hungry or emotionally upset, they may not find eating a positive experience.

Teachers introducing food as a science experience should be careful to plan activities and opportunities that will enhance the children's knowledge and skills in the preparation, consumption, enjoyment, and value of food to the body.

Many food ideas have already been introduced in other sections of this book, but because of their relevance to this topic, they will appear in this section as well.

When possible, children should be encouraged to help prepare food. Preparation may take longer, but the joy and satisfaction felt by the children are well worth the extra effort. They can also help in the cleaning up and storing of food items, a different type of learning experience than preparation.

Children should be encouraged to serve themselves, with a reminder to pour liquid up to a certain point on the glass or just dish the amount of food they will eat. Otherwise, the pouring and dishing becomes more enjoyable and important than the drinking or eating.

HELPING CHILDREN ENJOY THEIR FOOD

a. Young children are unacquainted with many different foods; however, very early they tend to form food preferences. Adults should introduce a variety of foods to the children on a gradual basis in a friendly setting. Encourage the children to taste new food without insisting that they eat a large amount of it. A good variety of nutritious foods will encourage the child to eat good foods.

b. From toddlerhood on talk about cleanliness related to food preparation and eating. Encourage the children to wash their hands carefully when involved with food. Help them to understand the importance of cleanliness and let them practice washing their own hands.

c. Use glass or plastic cups. This shows the children that you have confidence in them to use such containers and these containers can be sanitized in a dishwasher. Show (and assist when necessary) how to hold the glass with one hand while pouring from a small pitcher or covered container with the other hand. (Paper cups are unstable even though they may save on washing.)

d. Children have very sensitive taste buds so food should be lightly seasoned. Children usually dislike and resist foods that are highly seasoned or strongly flavored.

e. Young children prefer their food in separate piles, rather than mixed together as in soups and casseroles. Some children actually sort out like items before eating.

f. Young children prefer food that is slightly warm rather than hot or cold.

g. Talk with the children about people who help provide food for them (perhaps even some local individuals). Some children may have dairy products delivered to their homes; others may know about farmers or bakers.

h. Inform the parents about your food, cooking, and nutrition experiences at school and encourage them to involve their children in food shopping and preparation at home.

i. Talk about the characteristics of different foods (color, texture, taste, and so on).

j. Ask the children what they like to eat for breakfast, lunch, and dinner. Ask them what they had to eat before coming to school. How close do the items match?

k. Avoid using words and phrases which confuse young children, for example, referring to a ''lemon,'' your ''bread and butter,'' ''pie in the sky,'' being in a ''stew,'' the ''apple of your eye,'' or a person as a ''cupcake.''

Health

a. Talk with the children about the good food they should eat. Show produce, talk about where it is grown, how it is usually prepared, and how it helps the body. (Remember the age of the children will depend upon how much information is given at any one time.) Talking about food at snack time or

spontaneously will be more valuable to the children than having lengthy prepared discussions. Show and talk about some nourishing foods as well as those with empty calories to help the children distinguish between good and poor food.

b. Have a toothbrush for each child and encourage its use following meals and snacks.

c. Serve snacks that add to the health of the child and help to clean the teeth (raw fruits and vegetables). Avoid sugar, chocolate, salt, and fat. Teach good eating habits so the children will not become obese in childhood or later years.

Preparation, Serving, Storing

a. When children help prepare and serve food, they are proud of their efforts and have a tendency to eat more. There are many items they can help prepare under the supervision of an adult. Following are some examples:

1. setting the table for snack or meals—chairs, napkins, and utensils for each child

2. spreading butter or peanut butter on crackers

3. making simple pizzas—English muffins with pieces of lunch meat, tomato sauce, and cheese

4. making muffins from a mix

5. making their own sandwiches

6. preparing vegetables and fruit as finger food

7. making cookies or bread products from scratch

8. brushing vegetables, shelling peas, or snipping beans

9. making gelatin or instant pudding

10. stirring frozen juice and making popsicles

11. following a large picture recipe

12. using different kinds of utensils— egg beater, sifter, spatula, rolling pin, knife, and so on

13. making popcorn (Spread a large sheet or clean white paper on the floor. Remove the lid from the popper and let the corn pop onto the sheet or paper. Remind the children that the corn will be hot and to let it cool before they touch or eat it. Briefly talk about what makes the kernels pop. Sing a popcorn song.)

14. making ice cream in a manual freezer

15. comparing rice kernels (Let the children feel the rice and talk about its characteristics. Depending on the kind of rice, because some rice has more nutrients when it isn't pre-washed, wash and soak it. Cook the rice and serve it for snack or a meal. Compare the uncooked and cooked rice.)

16. making butter (In small baby food jars, fill the jar one-half to one-third full of whipping cream that is room temperature. Let each child have a jar to shake until it turns to butter. Pour off and taste the buttermilk. Add coloring and salt if desired. Serve on crackers.)

b. Work with the children so they can understand that certain food items can be eaten in different forms, for example, an apple can be fresh, juice, sauce, hot, cold, and so on.)

c. Involve the children in an experience with a food item, such as an egg. Show them how the egg can be used in different ways (boiled, fried, in a recipe, and so on), and can be prepared by different methods, such as heating, beating, combining, and so on.

d. Let the children wash some stalks of celery. With the adult's help or supervision let the children cut the celery into two- or three-inch lengths. Give each child a small plastic or paper container of peanut butter or softened cream cheese and a small plastic but sturdy knife. The child can put the filling into the celery and eat it.

e. Tell the parents what you will be making for snack at school and ask each one to send an ingredient (vegetables for a soup; fruit for a salad). Help the children prepare and mix the food. Eat it for snack.

f. If safe and convenient, take a few children at a time and show them where their food is prepared. Let them talk with the nutritionist, see the food in preparation, and eat the food at snack or lunch.

g. If safe and convenient, take a few children at a time to a nearby food market. Notice the produce, the baked goods, the canned goods, and so on. If practical, decide in advance what food item you will purchase. Make the purchase, return to the classroom, prepare the food, and eat it.

h. Prepare and dry fruit to make leather. Dry grapes to make raisins.

i. Place several cut fresh fruits and vegetables on a plate. Note the discoloration as they are exposed to the air, and the change in odor as the food deteriorates.

j. Let the children make a dip and use it as a snack with vegetable or fruit pieces.

Growing

a. Help the children prepare a space and then plant a garden. Water and

weed the garden. Harvest and eat the produce.

b. Soak some beans overnight. Let the children spoon dirt into five- or eight-ounce clear plastic cups. Tell the children to carefully plant their seeds so they can see them through the plastic. Have a special place to keep the cups. Remind the children to water than occasionally. Watch the roots grow down, the stems grow up, and eventually blossoms will form.

c. Start a plant in the classroom using a sweet-potato or carrot. Place the plant in a sunny, warm place and watch it grow.

d. Talk about grains (corn, wheat, rice, oats). How do they grow? In what forms do we eat the products of each?

e. Using a magnifying glass, examine the seeds from a variety of fruit (apple, pomegranate, banana, peach, and so on).

f. Provide a variety of nuts, some nut crackers, and a bowl for shells. Note the covering on the different kinds of nuts. Encourage the children to crack and eat the nuts.

g. Have pictures of fruit and vegetables. Have seeds sealed in small plastic bags. Talk with the children about how the fruit and vegetables grow and try to match the seeds with the mature fruit.

h. Show how water is taken into leaves by placing a stalk of celery in a jar of water that contains food coloring. As the stalk takes in the moisture, the color goes through the veins and into the leaves.

i. Show the children how different types of plants grow and which parts are edible: roots (carrots, turnips),

stalks (celery), leaves (lettuce, cabbage), blossoms (broccoli), ears (corn), and stems (asparagus, rhubarb). Use one type at a time and give accurate and appropriate information.

PROMOTING AREAS OF DEVELOPMENT

a. The teacher can promote psychomotor growth through helping the children with:

1. peeling fruit and vegetables
2. mashing potatoes
3. lifting and carrying items
4. straining vegetables, fruit
5. shaking cream to make butter
6. chopping vegetables, nuts
7. kneading and rolling dough
8. beating ingredients
9. hoeing, raking, and preparing soil for a garden
10. using a ladder to pick produce

b. The teacher can promote sensori-motor growth through leading the children to:

1. touch
2. taste
3. smell
4. feel
5. hear

c. The teacher can promote cognitive growth through assisting the children with:

1. problem solving
2. creative thinking
3. properly arranging sequence cards (seeds, produce, harvesting, cooking, eating—bread, from seed to loaf)

4. different ways of preparing and eating a fruit

5. sorting seeds (peas, beans, corn)

6. identifying pasta

7. making seed and picture collages

8. printing with vegetables

9. determining the plant parts that are edible

10. identifying growth above and below the ground

11. shopping—groceries, produce, bakery, dairy

12. growth from seeds, bulbs, tops, sprouts, eyes, and so on

13. learning terminology—equipment, recipe, ingredients

14. identifying changes that come with heat, moisture

15. contrasting and comparing food, coverings, colors, and so on

16. reading stories and books about food

17. taking field trips

d. The teacher can promote social/emotional growth through teaching the children about:

1. learning and using manners

2. following customs

3. setting the table

4. enjoying company

5. establishing feelings about different foods

6. identifying foods for different occasions (parties, holidays, religious events, and so on)

7. eating with peers for a social experience

8. making art projects from magazine pictures, seeds, and so on

9. singing songs, doing fingerplays, and so on

10. preparing and serving food

REFERENCES

Alles-White, M. L., and Welch, P. (1985). Factors affecting the formation of food preferences in preschool children. **Early child development and care,** 21:265–276.

Althouse, R. (1988). **Investigating science with young children.** New York: Teachers College Press.

Althouse, R., and Main, C. (1975). **Science experiences for young children: Food.** New York: Teachers College Press.

Birch, L. L. (1980). Effect of peer models' food choices and eating behavior on preschooler's food preferences. **Child development,** 51, 489–496.

Birch, L. L., Zimmerman, S., and Hind, H. (1980). The influence of social-effective contact on the formation of children's food preferences. **Appetite: Journal for intake research,** 3:353–360.

Carin, A. A., and Sund, R. B. (1980). **Discovery activities for elementary science.** Columbus, OH: Merrill Publishing.

Charlesworth, R., and Lind, K. K. (1990). **Math and science for young children.** Albany, NY: Delmar.

Cousins, J. (1988, Oct.). An apple for the teacher. **Science and children,** p. 32.

Eliason, C., and Jenkins, L. (1990). **A practical guide to early childhood curriculum,** 4th ed. Columbus, OH: Merrill.

Endres, J., and Rockwell, R. (1980). **Food, nutrition, and the young child.** St. Louis: Mosby.

Goodwin, M. T., and Pollen, G. (1980). **Creative food experiences for children** (revised). Washington, DC: Center for Science in the Public Interest.

Hack, K., and Flynn, V. (1985). Green beans: Gardening with two's. **Day care and early education,** 13(1), 14–17.

Herbert, D. (1980). **Mr. Wizard's Supermarket Science.** New York: Random House.

Javernick, E. (1988). Johnny's not jumping: Can we help obese children? **Young children,** 43(2), 18–23.

Jones, E.E., and Jones, S. M. (1983). A jarful of mystery. **Science and children,** (20)4, 18–19.

LeBow, M. D. (1984). **Child obesity.** New York: Springer.

Lipton, M. A., and May, J. P. (1983). Diet and hyperkinesis—an update. **Journal of American Dietary Association,** 83, 132–134.

Marotz, L., Rush, J., and Cross, M. (1985). **Health, safety and nutrition for the young child.** Albany, NY: Delmar.

Pessolano, J. (1986, May). Early childhood: Edible science. **Science and children,** 23(8), 40–41.

Phillips, M. G. (1986). Home economists and Head Start: A partnership to strengthen nutrition services to preschool children. **Journal of home economics,** 78(1), 34–43 (Spring).

Phillips, M. G. (1983). Nutrition education for preschoolers: The Head Start experience. **Children today,** 20, 20–24.

Pipes, P. (1985). **Nutrition in infancy and childhood,** 3d ed. St. Louis: Mosby.

Rogers, C. S., and Morris, S. S. (1986). Reducing sugar in children's diets. **Young children,** 41(5), 11–16.

Sucher, F., Manning, G., and Manning, M. (1981). **A parents' guide to early childhood: Education in the supermarket.** Provo, UT: Learning Development Systems IV.

Trostle, S. L., and Yawkey, T. D. (1990). **Integrated learning activities for young children.** Boston: Allyn and Bacon.

Whitener, C. B., and Keeling, M. H. (1984). **Nutrition education for young children: Strategies and activities.** Englewood Cliffs, NJ: Prentice-Hall.

Wishon, P., Bower, R., and Eller, B. (1983). Childhood obesity: prevention and treatment. **Young children,** 39(1), 21–27.

BOOKS FOR CHILDREN

Anglund, J. W. (1962). **Nibble, nibble mousekin.** New York: Harcourt Brace Jovanovich.

Asch, F. (1969). **George's Store.** New York: McGraw-Hill.

Brown, M. (1947). **Stone soup.** New York: Charles Scribner's Sons.

Carle, E. (1969). **The very hungry caterpillar.** New York: Philomel.

Carrick, D. (1985). **Milk.** New York: Greenwillow.

Cuyer, M. (1980). **The all-around pumpkin book.** New York: Holt, Rinehart and Winston.

Degan, B. (1983). **Jamberry.** New York: Harper & Row.

DePaola, T. (1978). **The popcorn book.** New York: Holiday House.

Ehlert, L. (1987). **Growing vegetable soup.** New York: Harcourt Brace Jovanovich.

Facklam, M. (1987). **I eat dinner.** Boston: Little & Brown.

Gibbons, G. (1985). **The milk makers.** New York: Macmillan.

Greene, C. (1958). **I want to be a storekeeper.** Chicago: Childrens Press.

Green, M. M. (1961). **Everybody eats.** New York: Wm. R. Scott.

Hines, A. G. (1986). **Daddy makes the best spaghetti.** Boston: Houghton-Mifflin.

Krauss, R. (1971). **The carrot seed.** New York: Scholastic.

Krementz, J. (1985). **The fun of cooking.** New York: Knopf.

Lynn, S. (1986). **Food.** New York: Macmillan/Aladdin.

McCloskey, R. (1948). **Blueberries for Sal.** New York: Viking.

McMillan, B. (1988). **Growing colors.** New York: Lothrop, Lee & Shepard.

Moncure, J. B. (1985). **What was it before it was orange juice?** Chicago: Childrens Press.

Ontario Science Center. (1987). **Foodworks—over 100 science activities and fascinating facts that explore the magic of food.** Reading, MA: Addison-Wesley.

Pluckrose, H. (1986). **Think about tasting.** New York: Watts.

Rockwell, A., and Rockwell, H. (1982). **How my garden grew.** New York: Macmillan.

Rylant, C. (1984). **This year's garden.** Scarsdale, NY: Bradbury.

Selsam, M. E. (1981). **The plants we eat.** New York: Wm. Morrow.

Selsam, M. E. (1976). **Popcorn.** New York: Wm. Morrow.

Selsam, M. (1972). **More potatoes.** New York: Harper & Row.

Selsam, M. (1959). **Seeds and more seeds.** New York: Harper.

Selsam, M., and Wexler, J. (1980). **Eat the fruit, plant the seed.** New York: Wm. Morrow.

Sendak, M. (1970). **In the night kitchen.** New York: Harper.

Sexias, J. S. (1986). **Vitamins: What they are, what they do.** New York: Greenwillow.

Seixas, J. S. (1984). **Junk food—what it is and what it does.** New York: Greenwillow.

Sharmat, M. (1980). **Gregory the terrible eater.** New York: Four Winds.

Showers, P. (1985). **What happens to a hamburger?** New York: Harper/Crowell.

Smaridge, N. (1982). **What's on your plate?** Nashville, TN: Abingdon.

Spier, P. (1981). **The food market.** New York: Doubleday.

Titherington, J. (1986). **Pumpkin, pumpkin.** New York: Greenwillow.

Tresselt, A. (1951). **Autumn harvest.** New York: Lothrop, Lee & Shepard.

Webber, I. E. (1943). **Up above and down below.** Boston: Addison-Wesley.

COOKBOOKS FOR CHILDREN

Alpha-Bakery Children's Cookbook. Gold Medal Alpha-Bakery Children's Cookbook, P.O. Box 5401, Dept. 836, Minneapolis 55460 ($1.00 per copy).

Bater, K. (1981). **Come and get it: A natural foods cookbook for children.** Ann Arbor, MI: Children First Press.

Children's cookbook. (n.d.) Minneapolis: Gold Medal Alpha-Bakery.

Christenberry, M. A., and Stevens, B. (1984). **Can Piaget cook?** Atlanta: Humanics Ltd.

Faggella, K., and Dixler, D. (1985). **Concept cookery.** Bridgeport, CT: First Teacher Press.

Ferreira, N. (1982). **Learning through cooking: A cooking program for**

children two to ten. Palo Alto, CA: R and E Associates.

Johnson, B., and Plemons, B. (1983). **Cup cooking: Individual child portion.** Early Educators Press, P.O. Box 1177, Lake Alfred, FL 33850.

Kendrick, A. S., Kaufmann, R., and Messenger, K. (eds) (1988). **Healthy young children: A manual for programs.** Washington, DC: National Association for the Education of Young Children.

Scherie, S. (1981). **Stuffin muffin: Muffin pan cooking for kids.** Avon, CT: Young People's Press.

Teddlie, A. T., and Turner, I. M. (1984). **Lots of action cooking with us.** Ruston, LA: Louisiana Association on Children Under Six.

Wanamaker, N., Hearn, K., and Richarz, S. (1979). **More than graham crackers.** Washington, DC: National Association for the Education of Young Children.

Wishik, C. S. (1982). **Kids dish it up . . . Sugar-free.** Port Angeles, WA: Peninsula Publishing.

RECORD SOURCES

(See Appendix C or preschool educational catalogues.)

Palmer, H. **Learning basic skills through music—Health and safety.** #EA-AR526R.

Palmer, H. "Kinds of food," on **Learning basic skills through music—Vocabulary.** #AR521 or #AC521.

The Carrot Seed. The Children's Record Guild, #1003.

Health

CONCEPTS AND ACTIVITIES

The health and welfare of young children is very important and there are many ways to teach science and health together. Parents and teachers need to be continually aware of eating, sleeping, playing, and protection patterns of the children in their daily environments.

Health of the young children will mostly depend upon decisions made by the parents. An increase in communicable diseases among young children has been alarming, mainly due to lack of immunizations. (Some states and school districts insist on evidence of immunization before a child can enter the program.) Parents should be strongly encouraged to have their children immunized at proper times and to keep the immunizations current. Parents with particular concerns should seek advice from their doctors.

Children who have been exposed to communicable diseases or common illnesses should be watched closely for signs of illness. When illness occurs, the child should get plenty of rest and drink more liquids than usual. Rest is as important for the individual child as isolation from spreading the illness to others. Parents and teachers need to be alert to side effects from diseases and illnesses.

Following are suggestions that could be used or modified in teaching health science concepts to young children: general information, nutrition, clothing and grooming, group living, exercising, and resources for adults and children.

GENERAL INFORMATION

a. Parents and children should be informed about the importance of immunizations. Teachers can help prepare children for these experiences. Sometimes when children talk about frightening or painful experiences, they accept them easier than when adults try to explain them.

b. Toddlers (and many preschoolers) put everything into their mouths because that is one of their most keen sensory organs. Adults should be alert to any dangerous things which the children could mouth or swallow (small objects, household and garden chemicals, poisonous leaves and berries, plastic bags, balloons, and so on).

c. Young children take things literally; therefore, using abstract concepts, over dramatization, and fear tactics confuse rather than instruct the child.

> Example: "Calcium in milk builds strong bones," "Little bugs get into your teeth and make holes," or "If you don't eat your vegetables, you'll never grow big." Instead, say such things as "Drinking milk and eating vegetables helps your body when you are playing," "Brushing your teeth keeps them clean and helps you chew your food."

d. Many food advertisements on television and in magazines are designed to appeal to children (shoes that make you run faster, food that makes you bigger and stronger, and so on). Young children believe everything they see and all they hear so adults need to do some monitoring and interpreting.

e. Invite a parent or guest in a related health field (nurse, dentist, doctor, nutritionist, aerobics instructor, and so on) to interact with the children on their level of understanding and development. This would also be a good opportunity to teach about roles being either male or female. (Screen and coach the person carefully.)

f. Talk to the children about immunizations and visits to a doctor or clinic when they are ill. Shots *do* hurt, but they can prevent disease and they can help one to recover from an illness.

g. Encourage parents to have physical examinations for their children at appropriate intervals. Discuss any health concerns with a physician.

h. As part of the intake information from parents, ask if the child has any food allergies or strong dislikes. This information could eliminate future problems.

i. Talk with the children about handling and interacting with pets. Help them to determine if a pet is healthy and friendly or if it should be avoided.

j. Talk with the children about how people in different occupations help to keep people healthy.

k. Impress upon the children the importance of an adult administering medicines and of the children not ingesting things which may be harmful, such as cleaning compounds.

NUTRITION

a. Food and liquid consumption will vary with the age of the child, the weather, the emotional environment, the skeletal structure, and the physical condition of the child. Adults should familiarize themselves with the normal development of the child so they can make adjustments at appropriate times.

b. Avoid coaxing, threatening, and bribing children to eat. Provide *nourishing* food and let them eat the amount they want or need. (Severe eating problems like overeating, refusal to eat, food jags, junk food, and other problems are likely to be promoted by adults. Medical or psychological help may be needed to help both adults and children.)

c. Involve the children in food preparation and serving. They are generally more willing to taste the food and will eat more if they have been involved with it. Try making some of their favorites, such as peanut butter from peanuts, pasta, or a dip or spread for crackers or vegetables, etc.

d. Cut pictures of food from magazines, newspapers, or other sources. Help the children to determine which are nourishing foods and which are not. Paste the nourishing food on an unwaxed paper plate and junk food on a piece of paper. (If you throw away the junk food the children do not have it as a referent for making good decisions.) This exercise may be difficult for some of the children because they like things that are sugary, fatty, and salty. (Young children do need calories for growth spurts, but they should begin to form good eating habits in order to avoid obesity, malnutrition, disease, and later health problems.)

e. Make and post a chart of good food. Encourage the children to look at the chart and match the food served in the classroom to the chart. If the food isn't on the chart, should it be served at school?

CLOTHING AND GROOMING

a. Talk about and show the kinds of clothing that promote independence, good toilet habits, body support, body hygiene, and unrestricted movement.

b. Prepare a mini-lesson on the importance of good shoes (cleanliness, warmth, good posture, safety in running and climbing, and weather appropriateness).

c. Talk about the different types of clothing worn for different activities (swimming, hiking, sleeping, exercising, warmth or coolness, and so on).

d. Have examples of clothing worn during different seasons and different types of weather. (Why do people wear boots or carry an umbrella in the wet season? How would a person feel if he wore a heavy coat during hot weather? What happens if you don't protect yourself from heat or cold?)

e. Introduce the reasons for wearing properly fitting clothes and for changing them frequently.

f. Show and discuss protective clothing during certain activities to protect the body from harm (snug clothing to prevent getting caught in things, protective goggles, and so on).

g. Talk about good health practices, including brushing teeth after eating, washing hands before handling or eating food and after toileting, covering the mouth and nose when sneezing or

coughing, wiping one's nose, washing one's hair, not sharing things that are put into the mouth, chewing food before swallowing it, keeping objects out of one's mouth, cleaning and caring for injuries, avoiding sharp or broken toys and objects, getting proper rest and sleep, eating good food, and others.

h. Have personal items so each child can perform good grooming and health measures (individual tooth brush, comb, wash cloth, towel, and so on).

i. On a table or tray have a variety of brushes—some for body care (tooth, hair, nail) and some for other care (pets, shoes, vegetables) Talk about the uses of each brush and practice using them when possible.

j. Talk about good physical care of animals to ensure the health of the pet and also people.

GROUP LIVING

a. Make water sources readily available for children for drinking, washing, and cleaning.

b. Where young children are gathered in groups, there should be a daily health check to determine the physical condition of each child for the benefit of the child as well as other children in the group. Briefly check eyes, face color, nose, and inside the mouth. An ill child will benefit more from home rest and care, while children at the center will benefit from not being exposed to illness. (Provide a procedure and place for children who become ill at school to wait until they can be picked up.) In other words, practice good health procedures in the classroom.

c. Weigh and measure each child periodically and post their statistics on a chart. This is mainly for a child to follow her own growth.

d. Prepare and eat good foods at snack and meals.

e. In the classroom, have areas and activities for action and rest, noise and quiet. Divert children to appropriate areas as their behavior indicates they need a change.

f. Check the landscaping on the playground for noxious or poisonous plants. Have them removed.

g. Show pictures and talk about different emotions. Encourage the children to make different emotions with their faces. Use a mirror for them to see their expressions. Discuss the healthiness of sharing their feelings with others verbally rather than physically.

h. Post the phone numbers of services needed in an emergency.

i. Sing songs, do fingerplays, tell stories, display pictures, and have books available for the children related to health topics. Involve the children in first-hand experiences for better understanding and opportunities to practice the concepts. Sing "This is the way we _____," using body parts and hygiene tools.

j. Caution the children to avoid harmful objects and to show the teachers toys and equipment that need to be repaired.

k. As a related art activity, provide items such as tongue depressors, cotton balls, and Band-Aids for the children to make a collage. Talk about the use of each item.

l. Assist the children to make eye glasses out of pipe cleaners. Discuss

with them how good eye sight adds to the person's health.

m. Provide doctor kits, cots, bandages and other items for the children to reenact experiences with medical people.

EXERCISING

a. Do some simple exercises daily with the children. Make them fun, successful, slightly challenging, and spontaneous rather than, "Now it's time to exercise our bodies."

b. Do activities that strengthen large muscles, such as running, jumping, throwing, crawling, climbing.

c. Do activities that strengthen small muscles: grasping small objects, cutting, drawing, and making puzzles.

d. Do activities that strengthen coordination, such as pouring, looking at books, threading, skipping, and catching.

e. Plan opportunities for each child to be successful in physical activities. Have each child work against himself rather than competing with others. ("You ran faster than last time." "You worked with blocks longer today than you have before." "Last time you threaded four beads and today you did seven.")

f. Provide a variety of opportunities for children to learn new and more challenging muscular activities.

g. Ask the children to tell what they do with their families to help keep them healthy.

REFERENCES

Center for Science in the Public Interest, 1501 16th St., NW, Washington, DC, 20036–1499. (Bulletin: **Nutrition Action Health Letter.**)

Child Health Alert, Box 338, Newton Highlands, MA, 02161. (Monthly publications.)

Child Health Talk, National Black Child Development Institute, 1463 Rhode Island Ave., NW, Washington, DC, 20005. (Newsletter.)

Herr, J., and Libby, Y. (1990). **Creative resources for the early childhood classroom.** Albany, NY: Delmar.

Kendrick, A. S., Kaufman, R., and Messenger, K. P. (1988). **Healthy young children: A manual for programs.** Washington, DC: National Association for the Education of Young Children.

Lind, K. K. (1985). The inside story. **Science and children,** 22 (4), pp. 122–123.

Child care center disease and sick child care. (1987). National Association for the Education of Young Children. Washington, DC: Author.

Trostle, S. L., and Yawkey, T. D. (1990). **Integrated learning activities for young children.** Boston: Allyn & Bacon.

BOOKS FOR CHILDREN

Bains, R. (1985). **Health and Hygiene.** Mahwah, NJ: Troll Associates.

Burmingham, J. (1978). **Time to take a bath, Shirley.** New York: Crowell.

Cole, Wm. (1963). **Frances face-maker.** New York: World Publishing.

Kalman, B., and Hughes, S. (1986). **The food we eat.** New York: Crabtree Publishing.

Jacobsen, K. (1982). **Health.** Chicago: Childrens Press.

Matsuoka, K. (1989). **There's a hippo in my bath!** New York: Doubleday.

Numeroff, L. J. (1977). **Phoebe Dexter has Harriet Peterson's sniffles.** New York: Greenwillow.

Quackenbush, R. M. (1975). **Too many lollipops.** New York: Parents Magazine Press.

Rockwell, A., and Rockwell, H. (1982). **Sick in bed.** New York: Macmillan.

Seixas, J. S. (1984). **Junk food—what it is and what it does.** New York: Greenwillow.

Showers, P. (1982). **You can't move without muscles.** New York: Crowell.

Showers, P. (1980). **No measles, no mumps for me.** New York: Crowell.

Watson, J. W., Switzer, R. E., and Hirschberg, J. C. (1987). **My friend the doctor.** New York: Crown.

Wolf, B. (1980). **Michael and the dentist.** Locust Valley, NY: Four Winds Press.

RECORD SOURCES

(See Appendix C or preschool educational catalogues.)

Caesar, I. **Health—cleanliness—safety.** Songlets for Project Head Start, Cleanliness Bureau.

Children's body awareness and movement exercises. Stallman Records.

Johnson, L. **Fun activities for toddlers.** Kimbo Educational Records.

Stewart, G. L. **Aerobics for kids.** Kimbo Educational Records.

Machines

CONCEPTS AND ACTIVITIES

Prior to any elaborate teaching about machines, find out what the children already know about some simple and familiar machines. Use caution in interpreting their words and actions. One possible preassessment would be to ask, "Here is a heavy toy and we want to take it outside today. What could we do to make it easier to move it?" Possible replies, might be to push it, get someone to help, leave it where it is, take some things out, lift it, and so on. Pick up on the suggestions of the children. If one works, use it! For safety's sake, have some props which can be used to try to move the toy. Encourage the children to work together in solving the problem.

a. Help the children define what a machine is. "Point out that a chair is not a machine; a machine has at least one moving part and does a task" (Lind, 1988, p. 32).

b. Encourage the children to look around the room and identify all the machines they can. If it is difficult for them to identify machines in the classroom, have a tray of objects—some classed as machines and some not. Is a car a machine? Is a puzzle? Is a child? Discuss with the children which objects are machines and why. Examples of machines are a pencil sharpener, clock, door hinge, light switch, water faucet, wheels and axles on pull toys, record players, and so on.

c. Provide old curriculum catalogues and let the children cut or tear out pictures of machines. They could then paste them on a sheet of paper or make a class mural.

d. Provide simple machines for the children to take apart and put together. There are some commercial toys for this purpose, but clocks, a simple food grinder, flour sifter, egg beater, and other kitchen utensils would be good.

e. Sing songs, do fingerplays, use puzzles, and provide books and pictures that focus on machines, wheels, inclined planes, and pulleys.

f. Provide opportunities to use machines with which the children are familiar—transportation, construction, dramatic play, and so on.

MACHINE CHARACTERISTICS

There are many different aspects of machines; however, this section will consider only wheels, pulleys, inclined planes, and movement.

Wheels
a. Wheels can make it easier to move things.

b. Using a box or block, ask the children how they could move it without lifting it up. Let some of the children try to move it by rolling it or pushing it. Then place the box or block inside a wheeled toy or wagon. Then ask them if they can move it without lifting it up. Talk about how much easier it is to move when wheels are added.

c. Talk a walk with the children through the outdoor play area and see how many wheels you can find. How many wheels do some of the objects have (one—wheelbarrow, unicycle, stick horse; two—scooter, bicycle; three—tricycles, cart; four—wagon, buggy). How can you use an object when one or more of the wheels are missing?

d. Take a walk with the children through the classroom (including the kitchen) and see how many wheels you can find. Some wheels will be easy for them to identify (toys, chair, serving cart, and so on), and some will be more difficult (where the wheel is a part of the object or is not visible or where wheels turn together).

e. Using a number of shapes (square, triangle, circle, oval, hexagon), encourage the children to experiment and decide which shape is the best for a wheel. Why?

f. Give the children a variety of sizes of spools. Brainstorm with them what uses the spools could have; try some ideas.

g. Using equipment or toys, help the children to see how some wheels move separately and how some move together (gears). Note the cogs in the gears.

h. Sing "The Wheels on the Bus." Make up new verses to include transportation vehicles that also have wheels.

i. For snack or lunch have round objects (crackers, buns, fruit, and so on) to stimulate discussion about wheels.

j. Borrow a wheelchair and help the children to push each other and to steer it.

Pulleys

a. Make or purchase a drapery rod with a pulley. Attach it securely to a surface. Encourage the children to use the pulley. Attach a basket to the rod and let the children raise and lower the basket.

b. A pulley has wheels. In the presence of the children, construct and use a pulley.

c. Provide toys with a pulley (a tow truck, a crane) and observe the children using them. Talk with the children about what is happening.

Inclined Planes

a. An inclined plane makes it easier to move things.

b. Try to roll some marbles through the clear vinyl tube while it is flat on the floor or ground. Then build a ramp from blocks and a board. Changing the incline of the board frequently, help the children to note the rate of speed at which the marbles roll through the tube.

c. Show pictures or objects and help the children identify which ones have inclined planes (road going up a hill, ramp for handicapped individuals, gangplank, stairway, and wedge are examples; level road, most bridges, table top, a lake, and table toys are non-examples, but could be elevated to become inclined). Give the children plenty of time and opportunities to practice using inclined planes. When are inclined planes helpful? When would inclined planes not be desirable?

d. Have a variety of balls (tennis, golf, foam, football, ping-pong, and so on). Help the children predict which balls will roll down an inclined plane the fastest. Try the balls. Change the pitch of the plane. Predict again. Try it.

e. Provide a variety of objects that are round and flat (buttons, hoops, bottle caps, poker chips, coins, and so on). Predict how fast they will roll down an inclined plane. What is the secret of their rolling at all?

f. Ramps can help lift objects. While on the playground with the children, note the riding surfaces for wheeled toys. Imagine that a tricycle went off the edge of the riding surface into a ditch. Brainstorm with the children how they could get the tricycle back on the road if it was too heavy to lift. Find a board, place it under a wheel and encourage the children to ride back onto the surface.

g. Take the children to a building (probably your school) where ramps have been built for wheelchairs. Talk about the ease with which the person can get the wheelchair from one level to the next by using the ramp.

h. With blocks, build an elevated road. Query the children as to how they could get their cars and trucks up and down from the high road. If necessary, assist them in building a ramp.

i. Borrow a wheelchair. Assist the children over difficult elevations. Provide boards for easier transitions. Take the children outside where a ramp is provided for wheelchair occupants. See if the ramp aids the person.

MOVEMENT

The Random House Dictionary (1980) describes a machine as an apparatus consisting of interrelated parts with separate functions, used in the performance of some kind of work; a mechanical, electric, or electronic contrivance; a device that transmits or modifies force or motion, as a lever or pulley.

Possibly it is the movement or power of a machine that makes it so intriguing to children. They want to know how it moves, how powerful it is, and what they can do with it. The main object of introducing power to the children is to show different means of creating movement, *not to deal with the specifics of each type*. Depending on the knowledge and experience of the children, consider introducing the following:

Type of Power	Suggested Activities
Batteries	Use selected cars, toys, and games without batteries. Then install and use the same objects with batteries.
Electricity	Try using electrical appliances before and after they are plugged into an electrical outlet.
Fuel	Show vehicles using model gas stations, fuel pumps, tow truck, and so on.
Friction	Use cars or objects with friction motors.
Man Power	Demonstrate and use *hand* tools (saw, screw driver, sander), and *manual* appliances (egg beater, potato masher, food grinder, juicer, and so on).
Solar	Note some buildings (or pictures) that have solar panels installed.
Tension	Observe and use wind-up toys, clocks, elastic bands on airplanes, and so on.

Type of Power	Suggested Activities
Water	Build dams in dirt or sand.
Wind	Make simple windmills. Blow or fan sail boats. Make and fly paper airplanes. Observe or look at pictures of gliders. Note the force of an electric fan.

REFERENCES

Carin, A. A., and Sund, R. B. (1980). **Discovery activities for elementary science.** Columbus, OH: Merrill Publishing.

Eliason, C., and Jenkins, L. (1990). **A practical guide to early childhood curriculum,** 4th ed. Columbus, OH: Merrill Publishing.

Harlan, J. (1988). **Science experiences for the early childhood years** 4th ed. Columbus, OH: Merrill Publishing.

Herr, J., and Libby, Y. (1990). **Creative resources for the early childhood classroom.** Albany, NY: Delmar.

Kamii, C., and Lee-Katz, L. (1979, May). Physics in preschool education: A Piagetian approach. **Young Children,** pp. 4–9.

Lind, K. K., and Milburn, M. J. (1988). Mechanized childhood. **Science and children,** Feb., 32–33.

Lind, K. K., and Milburn, M. J. (1988). More for the mechanized child. **Science and children,** March, 39–40.

Scarry, H. (1980). **On wheels.** New York: Philomel.

Sprung, B., Forschl, M., and Campbell, P. (1985). **What will happen if. . . .** New York: Education Equity Concepts.

BOOKS FOR CHILDREN

Bains, R. (1985). **Simple machines.** Mahwah, NJ: Troll Associates.

Baker, B. (1981). **Worthington Botts and the steam machine.** New York: Macmillan.

Barton, B. (1987). **Machines at work.** New York: Crowell.

Barton, B. (1979). **Wheels.** New York: Thomas Crowell.

Chapman, C. (1967). **Wings and wheels.** Niles, IL: Whitman.

Fitzgerald, F. (1980). **Little wheels, big wheels.** New York: Golden Press.

Gibbons, G. (1982). **Tool book.** New York: Holiday House.

Gibbons, G. (1975). **Willy and his wagon wheel.** Englewood Cliffs, NJ: Prentice Hall.

Henroid, L. (1982). **Grandma's wheelchair.** Niles, IL: Whitman.

Hoban, T. (1983). **Round and round and round.** New York: Greenwillow.

Hoban, R. (1959). **What does it do and how does it work?** New York: Harper.

Hooker, Y. (1978). **Wheels go round.** New York: Gosset & Dunlap.

Keats, E. J. (1973). **Skates.** New York: Franklin Watts.

Koren, E. (1972). **Behind the wheel.** New York: Holt, Rinehart & Winston.

Owen, W. (1967). **Wheels.** New York: Time Inc.

Rey, H. A. (1973). **Curious George rides a bike.** New York: Scholastic.

Rockwell, A., and Rockwell, H. (1972). **Machines.** New York: Macmillan.

Rockwell, A., and Rockwell, H. (1971). **The toolbox.** New York: Harper.

Scarry, R. (1974). **Cars, trucks, things that go.** New York: Golden Press.

Scarry, R. (1968). **What do people do all day?** New York: Random House.

Silver, R. (1983). **David's first bicycle.** New York: Golden.

Numbers

CONCEPTS AND ACTIVITIES

A three-year-old was asked to count to five. With his left index finger he counted the fingers on his right hand—"one, two, three, four, and five." He was then asked, "Can you count higher?" "Yes," he said, climbed up on a chair, raised his hand and began pointing to his fingers and counting, "one, two, three, four, five." He was asked further, "Can you count backwards?" "Yes," was the reply. He climbed down off the chair, turned his back to the requestor, pointed to his fingers and counted, "One, two, three, four, five."

Young children use their settings and play activities to develop coordination skills related to numbers. Through meaningful practice they learn to use numbers in a variety of useful ways. "Learning about math, science, social studies, health, and other content areas are all integrated through meaningful activities" (Bredekamp, 1986, p. 52). However, to be successful in teaching number concepts, "the teacher must know the level of understanding of the individual children" (Eliason and Jenkins, 1990, pp. 449–450).

WORKSHEETS/WORKBOOKS

More and more classrooms for young children include the extended use of worksheets and workbooks (Manning and Manning, 1981, p. 85). "Most early childhood educators are well aware that young children learn better with hands-on activities than with workbooks," write Williams and Kamii (1986, p. 23). Stone (1987, p. 16) has listed possible reasons for worksheets in early childhood programs as: 1. being less expensive than manipulative materials; 2. being more convenient than manipulative activities; 3. evidence of accountability—something to take home as evidence; and 4. providing a quiet, controlled, structured, and academic atmosphere. Her discussion and references clearly show these reasons to be invalid. Those who believe and support these reasons need to review how young children learn and observe the kinds of activities and materials that capture the attention of children—mostly items that are easily accessible and low in cost. They also should observe the actions and comments of the children as they interact with manipulative items. There doesn't need to be chaos in the classroom, but the children who converse and interact learn far more than those who sit quietly, isolated, and are restricted in their use of materials. Most teachers could find manipulative materials in their classrooms, in their homes, and from parents that could stock their classrooms for a long period of time and with great diversity.

LITERATURE AND NUMBERS

There is no lack of books on the market to introduce prenumber skills. Parents and teachers must exercise caution to select only the best of those available. Ballenger, Benham, and Hosticka (1984) believe some counting concept books are inappropriate for children, because the illustrations are unclear, the content is too advanced for the age group intended, or the cardinal or ordinal numbers are misused.

Harsh reports:

These findings strongly suggest the need for teachers of young children to be critical reviewers of counting books and of other types of books selected to enhance math education. Criteria such as the following need to be considered: 1) Book illustrations and written text should be accurate and portray mathematical ideas correctly. 2) Book illustrations should be attractive and appeal to young children. 3) Book illustrations should be appropriate in size and detail in keeping with developmental characteristics of the young child. 4) Written text of the books should be easily understood and interesting to young children. (1987, pp. 24–25)

In general, math concept books provide experiences in classification, comparison, ordering, one-to-one correspondence, cardinal numbers, ordinal numbers, number recognition, conservation of numbers, and rational counting.

"In the early years of childhood, when the development of language skills is of paramount importance and when the young child's curiosity creates an interest in all the relationships and categories of a complex world, one of the more difficult areas to master is that of the abstract concept. . . . Time, distance, size, mass, color, shape . . . need to be clarified and amplified in books as well as in conversation." (Sutherland and Arbuthnot, 1986, p. 99, quoted in Harsh, 1987, p. 28)

GENERAL EXPECTATIONS

Here are some general things one can expect of children in specific age groups related to number concepts:

Two-Year-Old
a. may be able to count a number or two

b. may raise two fingers to indicate his age

c. may try to say numbers—in and out of sequence

d. can count body parts with help

Three-Year-Old
a. may count to ten or higher, but may skip around

b. may know age and show it with appropriate number of fingers

c. does one-to-one correspondence

Four-Year-Old
a. knows own age

b. may count to ten or higher in rote fashion

c. may know own phone number and others

d. may be able to count objects and match with a number

e. uses one-to-one correspondence

f. uses numbers in fingerplays, but may have some difficulty with descending numbers

g. counts objects in books and in play activities

h. may confuse number symbols with letter symbols

i. may be able to count backwards from five or ten

j. may recognize a symbol for a number

k. can use a recipe of pre-measured in-gredients

l. matches dominos—may use pattern, or count dots

m. likes to match objects, make things equal

n. learns about zero

o. talks about size relationships

p. can measure with a string, ruler, or tape

q. can match quantities

r. seriates objects

s. likes stories, fingerplays, poems, nursery rhymes, and so on, with number repetition

Five-Year-Old

a. may count to 25 or higher

b. knows own phone number and others

c. may know own address

d. may recognize coins, and may know value of each

e. may do simple addition of sums

f. may be able to tell time—digital is easier

g. may recognize calendar and repeat the month, day, and year

h. measures and makes a food product from a recipe

i. matches dominos with purpose

j. may recognize and name number symbols

k. tries to write number symbols

l. sings "Number Pops" and recognizes the symbols

m. matchs numerals on various media

n. can classify items as an exercise in division

o. may collect stickers

p. can measure with string, ruler, or tape with some meaning

q. seriates objects

r. learns ordinal and cardinal numbers and differences

s. plays store using tokens or money—matches cost of item to symbol

t. does simple addition and subtrac-tion

u. talks about size, weight, length and other relationships

The following are ideas to promote number awareness:

CLASSIFICATION

Classifying is a process of putting simi-lar items into different categories or groups. Young children usually classify items by one dimension only (size *or* color). With experience they can find multiple ways to group items. Expect them to use one or two categories, such as color *and* size, but avoid getting too many dimensions beyond their abilities.

a. Following a nature walk where mate-rials were collected, help the children sort the materials into categories, count the number of items and categories, and make a picture or mural.

b. Using cans, cartons, or objects of the same size, write the numbers from zero to nine. Let the children arrange them in different, but logical, ways (ascending, descending, odd or even numbers, symbols with loops or straight lines, and so on).

c. Set out a flannel board and adhering objects (felt, flannel, sticky, and so on). Have some numerals and objects of varying quantity (one cat, two dogs, three birds). Note how the children place the objects (by quantity, with a symbol, or by category) Suggest other ways to group objects.

d. Match items (coins, thread, tees, keys, stickers, and so on); try different groupings (metal, wood, round, and so on).

e. Display pictures or use replicas of adult and baby animals. Ask the children to put all the "adults" in one pile and all the "babies" in another one. Then ask them to match the baby with the parent. (All one size together, then like animals together.)

COUNTING

a. Make parents aware of number experiences at school and encourage the parents to observe and assist children in simple number experiences at home (cooking, counting, measuring, identifying, finger plays, temperature, time, allowance, purchasing, games, birthdays, and so on). Encourage parents to use spontaneous situations and to avoid pressure or rote situations.

b. Play a game like "Mother May I?" or follow the leader (2 hops, 3 jumps, and so on).

c. Set up a bowling activity. Show the children how to place the numbered pins. Help them count their scores (usually one frame per score).

d. Make fishing poles by attaching a string and magnet onto the end of a dowel. Make fish shapes out of heavy paper or light cardboard and attach a paper clip (or two). The children can count the fish they "catch." An alternate would be to attract metal bottle caps out of a sack or box.

e. Take a piece of styrofoam at least six inches square. Provide colored golf tees. Suggest that the child stick the tees into the styrofoam and count the number inserted. Or the child can use various colors and amounts (one red, two yellow, three, orange, and so on).

f. In a non-pressured situation, help the children count to five or ten. Then help them count five or ten objects.

g. Make a situation where numbers are used in proper sequence, such as a floor game or card game. Ask the children to identify a certain number. Then give further instructions about movement from that number (move ahead four, move back two). Instructions can be more complicated as children are ready.

h. Using objects, children, toys, other materials, and verbalization, practice simple addition and subtraction exercises.

i. Provide a container, such as a box, bucket, or wastebasket, and bean bags. Encourage the children to toss the bean bags into the container and keep score mentally or on paper.

j. Use a magnetic board with magnetic objects to place different numbered

0123456789

objects or use objects and numerals together.

k. Use a calendar, numbered links in a paper chain, or other method to count the days until a special event (a holiday, special program, eggs hatching, and so on).

l. Do finger plays, poems, nursery rhymes, stories and other activities where numbers are used. (Baa, Baa, Black Sheep; Hickory, Dickory, Dock!; One, Two, Buckle My Shoe; One, Two, Three, Four, Five; This Little Pig Went to Market; Three Blind Mice; and so on). "Because the correct number sequence is 1, 2, 3, 4, 5 . . . these songs and finger plays should utilize this particular ordering, rather than . . . 5, 4, 3, 2, 1" (Eliason and Jenkins, 1990, p. 451).

m. Attach both ends of a heavy string or light rope to a stationary object. Give children numbered clothes pins and encourage them to clip them onto the string or rope in the proper sequence.

n. Prior to an outdoor walk, pairs of children are given paper sacks and assigned specific sets to collect: two pine cones, six leaves, eight rocks, and so on (Stone, 1987).

o. For an art activity, provide numerals made of fabric or paper, glue, scissors, and paper. Encourage those children who can to cut out predrawn numerals; have precut ones for those who lack cutting skills. Suggest a number collage, but note how different children use and arrange their numbers.

p. Encourage number printing by providing stamps and pads or numbers cut on potatoes or wood. (Reverse the cut numbers so they will appear correctly when printed.)

q. When they show readiness, introduce coins to the children. Point out that the size of the coin and the number of coins do not indicate value. (Pennies and nickels appear to be of more value than dimes.) In some cases, it may appear that store clerks are giving money to patrons rather than change. "Money becomes meaningful to a child only when he has opportunity to use it," states Hurlock (1972, p. 360). Many young children do not have the opportunity or experience to make purchases.

r. Make some large flash cards with numbers from zero to nine so the children can arrange them in a particular order—forward, backwards, even, odd. Make all numerals the same size and color so as not to associate size or color with a number.

s. The concept of zero is difficult for young children to comprehend. Try some simple games or activities where zero is introduced. If the children are confused, save this activity until they are older, more mature, have an increased vocabulary, or are more experienced.

t. Clap or use rhythm instruments. Count to the rhythm.

MEASUREMENT

Charlesworth and Lind state that the concept of measurement develops through five stages, and they summarize, in part, that preoperational children (those included in the focus of this text) use play, imitation, and comparing through naturalistic and informational experiences as they explore and discover, while children of six years and older use arbitrary units and standard units (1990, p. 227).

Measurement can be studied through various means. This section will provide information and activities to introduce linear measurement, volume, weight, time, and temperature to young children.

Linear Measurement

a. The numbers on yardsticks, rulers, and tapes may not matter to young children at first, but eventually they will recognize and utilize the numbers. They can measure with string, dowels, their feet, or other unnumbered items and determine which of two items is larger or smaller. Numbered rulers, tapes, and so on can be added when they have meaning for the children. Talk about people using measurements (seamstress, carpenter, builder, baker, community helpers, and so on).

b. Place on the floor a piece of white paper several inches longer than the height of the child. Have the child lay down on the paper. Using a marker or crayon, trace the outline of the child's body. Let the child fill in the details (face, hair, clothes, and so on). This gives the child an idea of her body size.

c. Using a tape, measure the various parts of the child's body (head, arm length, foot, waist, and so on). Record the information where the child has access to it.

Volume

a. In a sensory table or tub, set up opportunities for the children to practice liquid measurement by providing measuring cups, spoons, graded and ungraded containers (how many cups to fill a container?). Younger children will find joy in pouring and spilling while older children may predict, try, and evaluate.

b. Using beakers or containers of different sizes and shapes, encourage the children to guess which one holds the most liquid, then fill and measure them.

c. Ask the children if it will take more liquid to fill a tall slender container or a short fat one. Encourage them to experiment.

d. At snack or lunch time, encourage the children to pour their own beverages. Are they more interested in pouring, in filling the glass, or whether they will spill?

e. In a sand area or sensory table, provide containers for the children to measure and pour. Help them estimate how many times they will have to fill certain containers in order to fill one once—or how many smaller containers they can fill from one larger container.

f. In a sensory table, provide flour for the children to sift and measure. Does sifted flour fill more or less containers than unsifted flour?

g. When putting away toys, help the children estimate the size of the container or shelf space the toys will require.

Weight

a. Have a number of objects on a table. Visually determine with the children which ones would weigh the most or least. Predict a ranking on a specific dimension, like weight. Using a scale, weigh each object and determine if the ranking was correct. Then rank each object as to size. Again weigh each object and see how size and weight correlate. For children who are ready, separate the objects as to composition (wood, metal, plastic, and so on). Decide which composition will weigh the most. Weigh them and see if predictions were accurate. This activity could also be used to determine which objects would sink and float. Does weight, size, or composition influence buoyancy?

b. Periodically weigh and measure the children. Show each child how much he has grown in height and weight.

c. Fill small metal or plastic containers with different weights of the same material (sand, rocks, rice, and so on). Write the weight on the outside of the container (two oz., four oz.). Apply lids. Using a pan balance, encourage the children to weigh differing combinations of containers to make the scale balance.

d. Use the type of scale with weighted numbers so the children can combine the numbers to balance the scale.

e. Using a large scale, encourage the children to see how many items they can carry (blocks, for example) and then help them determine the weight they carried. Avoid competition between children, but see if the child's ability to lift and carry increases over a period of time.

f. Weigh empty containers, fill them with different things and then weigh them again. Note if the weight changes slightly or greatly.

Time

Young children hear and use terms related to the passage of time. Some words they understand, others are foreign—but are used because they hear them used by others.

> Example: One child was telling another, "Today our team won the game, tomorrow it won, and if it will win yesterday, we will be in the play-offs!"

Relational words, such as soon, sometime, later, tomorrow, yesterday, a long time ago, and once upon a time, seem inconsistent to children because they vary in their meaning. At one time "later" may be soon and at another time it may almost mean "never."

Young children usually know the basic periods of the day: morning, afternoon, night, and perhaps noon. At a preschool group they may know and anticipate different activity times (outside, story, snack, and so on).

It is through informal and natural experiences that the child learns about time and sequences. He relates passage of time to personal experiences. For sure, young children learn about special events like birthdays, holidays, trips, or visits. Perhaps it is adults who get them excited in advance and help them count down the days—or hours. Beginning with Piaget's stage of concrete operations (six years and older) the child learns to use units of time more like adults use them—numbers related to clocks, calendars, and addresses.

Some children have difficulty in learning to tell time because of their physical environment and experiences.

> Example: One parent was frustrated because her child couldn't look at the clock and report the present time. The parent finally realized the only model for the child was a modernistic, abstract face on the clock. There was nothing to relate numbers to! Another parent was pleased when her child could tell the exact time—4:22. Then she realized the model for her child was a digital clock and the child knew his numbers but could not make the transfer to a clock with hands and numbers.

a. Observe with the children how time changes situations or objects (plant and grow seeds, temperature, personal growth, and so on).

b. Instead of using vague time terms with young children, help them establish a sequence, for example, "After lunch and a story, it will be rest time," "After we pick up the toys, we will go to the grocery story and then Daddy will come home."

c. When playing or working, set a timer to let the children know that it is almost time to finish one activity and begin another. However, when this is done, use the timer to verbalize about what will soon occur. Don't let the sound of the timer take away from verbalization!

d. When a child is wanting to use a toy or object that is being used by another child, help both children to build a time reference. To the child using the toy, say, "Finish your turn soon so that Eddie can have a turn." To the child waiting say, "Stephen is not quite through with his turn. After he rides the bike around the circle two more times, it will be your turn." Also assure the child who gives up the toy or object that he will have another turn. Follow through and offer him another turn—whether or not he accepts.

Temperature
a. Use a thermometer in a cooking experience to show the children how to measure the heat in the food.

b. Use a thermometer to show the children the temperature of the classroom, the outdoor area, and other areas. Discuss ways to increase the heat on cold days and how to reduce the heat on hot days.

c. Have a thermometer in the room throughout the year and make a chart of the temperature.

d. Talk with the children about how doctors, nurses, and parents take a person's temperature to see if she is well or sick. Talk with them about appropriate measures to reduce a fever in a person.

NUMBER IDENTIFICATION
a. With or without the help of the children, make a bulletin or flannel board that has objects and numerals. Encourage the children to match the objects and numerals. Make it easy for the children to manipulate the materials.

b. Using Piaget's conservation tasks (two sets are equal even if they are arranged to look unequal), give the children opportunities to practice the concept that the arrangement of items does not change the number.

c. At snack time and other activities involve number experiences.

d. For children who know and recognize written numbers, draw a dot-to-dot number design for them to follow.

e. On a piece of plastic, canvas, or cardboard, draw or paste pictures of animals or objects. Ask the child to point to or stand on a picture representing a number, for example, one cow, or three pigs. As children get older, use number symbols or increase the number of picture objects.

f. Take an empty egg carton. Write a number in the bottom of each cup. In the lid of the carton, provide objects which will fit into the cups and which can be counted. Notice if the children actually count and try to put in the corresponding number of objects or if they merely try to put objects into each cup.

g. Use dial and push-button telephones. Note the arrangement of numbers on each type of telephone.

h. Use number and interlocking puzzles. This is a little more difficult than using puzzles or interlocking parts alone.

i. Provide newspapers or magazines and scissors. Encourage the child to cut out numbers from advertisements.

j. Play games that require a spinner, dice, or numbered cards to inform the players.

k. Involve children in making things from recipes (creative materials and food, for example).

l. Have numbers visible throughout the environment (speed signs in the blocks, symbols on the walls, clocks, scales, and so on). Use a calendar (day, month, and year) with children who are ready. Help children to count items when appropriate.

m. Place a calculator or adding machine where children have access to it.

n. Have a large clock in the room for children to notice the numbers, the movement of the hands, and relate them to the sequence of activities.

o. Display a large directory showing the names, birth dates, addresses, and phone numbers of each individual.

p. Make some flash cards with simple objects and the corresponding numeral so children can play games with them, put them in ascending or descending order, or match the objects and symbols.

q. Provide opportunities where numbers are displayed (telephones, games, cash registers, or coupons).

r. Mark a number (2, 3, . . . 10) on a card. Children can use paper clips, staples, hole punches, reinforcements, or clothespins to create sets—five staples on a five card, eight holes on an eight card, and so on (Stone, 1987).

s. Encourage adults to explain simply and show children how numbers are used in various settings (home, office, bank, post office, grocery store, service station, library, school, weather, sport uniforms, scoring, and so on).

t. Decide how temperature and weather could be introduced to the children.

u. Make some small books. For younger children, write a numeral between one and five on each page. Provide pictures and glue for the child to paste a corresponding number of objects, but don't be surprised if it is merely a pasting opportunity. For older children, encourage them to paste a certain number of objects on each page and then to print the corresponding number. Write in a message if the children are inclined to tell about their books.

v. Using a stop watch, time some activities. Avoid competition of one child against another.

NUMBER VOCABULARY

Hurlock writes that, "Words relating to numbers are used soon after the child starts to speak," and that, "The development of number concepts appears to be a function of age and of educational development" (1972, p. 358).

Very early children are taught to say the number corresponding to their age and to hold up the appropriate number of fingers. Just because they can perform one or both of these activities does not indicate an understanding on the part of the child, as was evidenced by the child who held up five fingers and said, "Now I three!"

a. Two- and three-year-olds are ready for some mathematical terms such as *some*, *few*, *more*, and *many*. Four- and five-year-olds are ready for more advanced vocabulary providing they have opportunities for hands-on practice with the concept (pair, single, double, triple, first, second, last, same as, more than, less than, and so on). Provide many opportunities for the children to use numbers.

b. Help children to determine when there are "enough" or "not enough" objects for an activity (cookies for snack, toys for the number of children).

c. Encourage comparison. "Are there more _____, more _____, or are there the same number?" Note the way the problem is resolved (one-to-one comparison, counting groups separately, retreating, and so on).

ONE-TO-ONE CORRESPONDENCE

Many young children try to count—in or out of sequence—and feel it is a mark of accomplishment. But it is in later development that the cognitive functioning helps them get a grasp on one-to-one correspondence. According to Katz, "Young children's understanding of numbers develops as they match, compare, sort or group, and order" (1983, p. 5).

According to Gelman (1978), a child must master a one-to-one correspondence before she can count items correctly. The child can verbalize the number sequence and rote count, but to count one per item is more difficult. Very often a young child will count two numbers for one item or two items while verbalizing only one number. Children need time and practice to learn to count correctly.

a. Let the children assist in preparing food and in setting the table.

b. Set up a store or shopping area. Provide tokens, coins, and paper money. Mark items with same denomination (price) as the money used. Encourage the children to purchase items and to exchange money.

c. Make available several bean bags and a large cardboard game with selected holes labeled with different denominations. Note if the children just aim for the holes or if they select those with the highest number. Is the skill or the score more important to them?

PARTS/WHOLE

a. In the presence of a few children, decide how many pieces you would have to cut an object in order for each child to have an equal piece. Review with the children how you decided to cut the object. This introduces fractions, problem solving, and a social experience (language, sharing, belonging, working together, and so on).

b. In the block area help the children note the dimensions of the blocks (two of one size equal one of another size, two triangles make one square, a circle can consist of four smaller blocks, and so on).

c. Use toys with removable parts. Talk about the different parts and how they help to make the toy complete.

d. Use construction toys (logs, plastic bricks, and building sets) to make complete objects.

e. Talk about puzzle pieces and how they make a completed puzzle when they are inserted in the correct places.

SERIATION/SEQUENCING

Seriation is comparing or ordering objects. It involves finding similarities and differences between objects; some are subtle, some more obvious. Charlesworth and Lind (1990) report four basic types of ordering activities: size, one-to-one matching, from the least to the most, and by ordinal number (first, second, and so on). They also state, "Patterning is related to ordering and includes auditory, visual, and physical motor sequences that are repeated. Patterns may be copied, extended, or verbally discussed" (Charlesworth and Lind, p. 215).

Sequencing refers to objects or ideas in a logical order. It could be done mentally or physically; however, young children relate to sequencing better when they are personally involved—lining things up, putting cards in a pictorial sequence, measuring and placing objects, demonstrating a sequence, and so on.

a. Match designs or numbers (such as picture or dot dominoes).

b. Sing songs or tell stories that include sequencing. If sequencing is difficult for the children (going back through all the animals on "Old Mac-Donald's Farm," for example), try a

simple modified version where children remember the sequence of the animals (without going through all the sounds the animals make) or just sing about the animals as the children suggest them.

c. Use cylinders, boxes, and other containers of various sizes. Encourage the children to stack and store them correctly.

d. Using two similar items but of different sizes (cans, blocks, string, and so on), talk with the children about "small," and "large." When the children show readiness, introduce a third length, "middle." Assist the children to understand these three sizes. Again, when readiness appears, these three sizes can be used to show "small, smaller, and smallest" or the opposite "large, larger, and largest." Use other examples for clarity (height, toys, cookies, and so on).

e. Using a variety of sizes of clothing (socks, for example), ask the children to identify who would wear them (baby, dad) and to line them up according to a specific dimension (smallest to largest, or vice versa).

SHAPES

a. Make, use, and discuss the characteristics of shapes: squares have four equal straight lines; triangles have three equal straight lines; rectangles have four straight lines, but two long equal lines and two shorter equal lines; a circle has one continuous round line; and so on.

b. Place four to six objects in front of the children. Tell them to look at them carefully because you are going to remove one and see if they can remember which one you removed. If the experience is too difficult, reduce the number of objects. If it is too easy, add two more objects.

c. Using blocks, give the children experiences in combining shapes to make additional shapes.

d. After the children learn to identify selective shapes, have them look around the room to see how many items of the same shape they can find.

e. For an art activity, supply many items of different shapes. Encourage the children to combine shapes to make new ones.

f. Use fingerplays, stories, poems, and other language experiences to discuss shapes.

SPACE

a. Do some physical activities or exercises with the children so they get the feel of having their own personal space.

b. Teach the children about prepositions by having them use their own bodies in relationship to something (get *under* the table, walk *around* the chair, put your finger *in* the water, and so on). Later reinforce the concepts by using objects.

c. Talk with the children about body positioning to do certain feats, such as catching or throwing a ball, or jumping over something.

d. Give each child an area outlined by a hoop, rope, or string. Give instructions about what to do within the area (hop, sit down, and so on).

e. Play ''Twister.'' The child needs to identify the color and shape required, and then put the correct body part onto it (''Put your hand on a blue square'').

REFERENCES

Almy, M. (1976). Piaget in action. **Young Children,** 31(2), 93–96.

Ballenger, M., Benham, N., & Hosticka, A. (1984). Children's counting books: Mathematical concept development. **Childhood Education,** 61(1), 30–35.

Baratta-Lorton, M. (1972). **Workjobs.** Menlo Park, CA: Addison-Wesley.

Baratta-Lorton, M. (1979). **Workjobs II.** Menlo Park, CA: Addison-Wesley.

Baroody, A. J. (1987). **Children's mathematical thinking: A developmental framework for preschool, primary, and special education teachers.** New York: Teachers College Press, Columbia University.

Beaty, J. J. (1990). **Observing development of the young child,** 2d ed. Columbus, OH: Merrill.

Bredekamp, S. (ed.) (1987). **Developmentally appropriate practice in early childhood programs serving children from birth through age 8** (expanded ed.). Washington, DC: National Association for the Education of Young Children.

Bredekamp, S. (ed.) (1986). **Developmentally appropriate practices: A position statement.** Washington, DC: National Association for the Education of Young Children.

Brown, S. E. (1982). **One, two, buckle my shoe: Math activities for young children.** Mt. Rainier, MD: Gryphon House.

Burke, E. M. (1986). **Early childhood literature—For love of child and book.** Boston: Allyn & Bacon.

Burton, G. M. (1985). **Towards a good beginning: Teaching early childhood**

mathematics. Menlo Park, CA: Addison-Wesley.

Charlesworth, R., and Lind, K. K. (1990). **Math and science for young children.** Albany, NY: Delmar.

Clements, D. H., and Callahan, L. G. (1983). Number or prenumber foundational experiences for young children: Must we choose? **Arithmetic teacher,** 31 (3): 34–37.

Copeland, R. W. (1984). **How children learn mathematics: Teaching implications of Piaget's research.** New York: Macmillan.

Cruikshank, D. E., Fitzgerald, D. L., and Jensen, L. R. (1980). **Young children learning mathematics.** Boston: Allyn & Bacon.

Eliason, C., and Jenkins, L. (1990). **A Practical Guide to early childhood curriculum.** Columbus, OH: Merrill.

Gelman, R. (1978). Counting in preschoolers: What does and does not develop. in R. S. Siegler (ed.), **Children's thinking: What develops?** Hillsdale, NJ: Lawrence Erlbaum Assoc.

Gelman, R., and Gallistel, C. R. (1986). **The child's understanding of number.** Cambridge, MA: Harvard University Press.

Harlan, J. (1988). **Science experiences for the early childhood years,** 4th ed. Columbus, OH: Merrill.

Harsh, A. (1987). Teaching mathematics with children's literature. **Young Children,** 42(6), 24–29.

Holt, B. (1989). **Science with young children.** Washington, DC: National Association for the Education of Young Children.

Honig, A. S. (1980). The young children and you—learning together. **Young Children,** 35(4), 2–10.

Hurlock, E. B. (1972). **Child development.** New York: McGraw-Hill.

Kamii, C. K. (1986). How do young children learn by handling objects? **Young Children,** 42(1), 23–26.

Kamii, C. K. (1985). **Young children reinvent arithmetic.** New York: Teachers College Press.

Kamii, C. (1982). **Number in preschool and kindergarten: Educational implications of Piaget's theory.** Washington, DC: National Association for the Education of Young Children.

Kamii, C., and DeVries, R. (1980). **Group games in early education: Implication of Piaget's theory.** Washington, DC: National Association for the Education of Young Children.

Katz, L. (1983). **Getting involved: Your child and math** (DHHS Publication No. OHDS 83–31144).

Kennedy, L. (1984). **Guiding children's learning of mathematics** (4th ed.). Belmont, CA: Wadsworth.

Manning, M., and Manning, G. (1981). The school's assault on childhood. **Childhood Education,** 58(2), 84–87.

Matthias, M., Platt, M., and Thiessen, D. (1980). Counting books: The children's choice. **Teacher,** 97(5), 103–104.

Moffitt, M. W. (1981). Play as a medium for learning. In M. Kaplan-Sanoff and R. Magid (Eds.), **Exploring early childhood education: Theory and practice.** New York: Macmillan.

Pratt-Butler, G. K. (1975). **The three-, four-, and five-year-old in a school setting** (pp. 163–169). Columbus, OH: Merrill.

Price, G. G. (1989, May). Mathematics in early childhood. **Young Children,** 44(4), 53–58.

Radebaugh, M. R. (1981). Using children's literature to teach mathematics. **The Reading Teacher,** 34(5), 902–906.

Schickedanz, J. A. (1986). **More than the ABCs: The early stages of reading and**

writing. Washington, DC: National Association for the Education of Young
Children.

Schultz, K. A., Colarusso, R. P., and Straw-
derman, V. W. (1989). **Mathematics for
every young child.** Columbus, OH: Merrill.

Smith, N. J., and Wendelin, K. H. (1981).
Using children's books to teach mathematical concepts. **Arithmetic Teacher,**
29(3), 10–15.

Stone, J. I. (1987). Early childhood math:
Make it manipulative! **Young Children,**
42(6). 16–23.

Sutherland, Z., and Arbuthnot, M. H.
(1986). **Children and books** (7th ed.).
Glenview, IL: Scott, Foresman.

Taylor, B. J. (1991). **A child goes forth** (7th
ed.). New York: Macmillan, pp. 201–214.

BOOKS FOR CHILDREN

Anderson, L.C. (1983). **The wonderful
shrinking shirt.** Niles, IL: Albert Whitman.

Anno, M. (1982). **Anno's counting book.**
New York: Philomel Books.

Bang, M. (1983). **Ten, nine, eight.** New
York: Greenwillow Books.

Barton, B. (1981). **Building a house.** New
York: Greenwillow.

Baum, A., and Baum, J. (1962). **One bright
Monday morning.** New York: Knopf.

Calmenson, S. (1985). **Ten items or less.**
New York: Golden Books.

Carle, E. (1987). **1, 2, 3 to the zoo.** New
York: Philomel Books.

Carle, E. (1981). **The very hungry caterpillar.** New York: Philomel.

Cohen, M. (1971). **Best friends.** New York:
Collier Books.

Cohen, M. (1967). **Will i have a friend?**
New York: Collier Books.

Conover, C. (1976). **Six little ducks.** New
York: Crowell.

Crews, D. (1986). **Ten black dots.** New
York: Greenwillow.

Crews, D. (1978). **Freight train.** New York:
Greenwillow.

Cromwell, L. and Hibner, D. (1976). **Finger
frolics.** Livonia, MI: Partner Press.

Doolittle, E. (1988). **World of wonders: A
trip through numbers.** Boston: Houghton Mifflin.

Ehlert, L. (1990). **Color farm.** New York:
HarperCollins.

Feelings, M., and Feelings, T. (1971). **Moja
means one: Swahili counting book.**
New York: Dial Press.

Freeman, D. (1968). **Corduroy.** New York:
Viking.

Friskey, M. (1964). **Chicken little, count-to-
ten.** New York: Childrens Press.

Garland, S. (1986). **Going shopping.** New
York: Viking Penguin.

Giganti, P., Jr. (1988). **How many snails?: A
counting book.** New York: Greenwillow.

Glazier, T. (1973). **Eye winker, Tom tinker,
chin chopper.** Garden City, NY: Doubleday & Co.

Hoban, T. (1972). **Count and see.** New
York: Macmillan.

Hoban, T. (1974). **Circles, triangles, and
squares.** New York: Macmillan.

Hutchins, P. (1986). **The doorbell rang.**
New York: Scholastic.

Keats, E. J. (1978). **The trip.** New York:
Scholastic Books.

Kellogg, S. (1977). **The mysterious tadpole.** New York: Dial.

Kitamura, S. (1986). **When sheep cannot
sleep? The counting Book.** New York:
Farrar, Straus, and Giroux.

Kitchen, B. (1987). **Animal numbers.** New York: Dial.

Kruss, J. (1963). **3 x 3: Three by three.** New York: Macmillan.

Lacharias, T., and Lacharias, W. (1968). **But where is the green parrot?** New York: Delacorte Press.

Langstaff, J. (1956). **Over in the meadow.** New York: Harcourt.

Lionni, L. (9160). **Inch by inch.** New York: Astor-Honor.

Livermore, E. (1973). **Find the cat.** Boston: Houghton Mifflin.

Matthews, L. (1978). **Bunches and bunches of bunnies.** New York: Scholastic.

McClosky, R. (1941). **Make way for ducklings.** New York: Viking.

McDermott, G. (1972). **Anansi the spider.** New York: Holt, Rinehart & Winston.

McLeod, E. W. (1961). **One snail and me.** Boston: Little, Brown, and Company.

Moncure, J. B. (1985). **My one book.** Chicago: Childrens Press. (Also a separate book for each number through ten, 1985 or 1986; same publisher.)

O'Brian. T. C. (1971). **Odds and evens.** New York: Crowell.

Pragoff, F. (1986). **How many?** New York: Doubleday.

Raskin, E. (1966). **Nothing ever happens on my block.** New York: Scholastic Book Services.

Rockwell, H. (1984). **My nursery school.** New York: Puffin Books.

Russo, M. (1986). **The line up book.** New York: Greenwillow.

Shannon, G. (1981). **Lizard's song.** New York: Greenwillow Books.

Suess, Dr. (1960). **One fish, two fish, red fish, blue fish.** New York: Random House.

Tafuri, N. (1984). **Have you seen my duckling?** New York: Greenwillow.

Tafuri, N. (1986). **Who's counting?** New York: Greenwillow.

Wahl, J., and Wahl, S. (1976). **I can count the petals of a flower.** National Council of Teachers of Mathematics, 1906 Association Drive, Reston, VA 22091.

Wolkstein, D. (1981). **The banza.** New York: Dial Press.

Yerian, M. (1976). **My little counting book.** Racine, WI: Western Publishing

RECORD SOURCES

(See Appendix C or preschool educational catalogues.)

Number fun. Melody House Records.

We all live together series—Vols. 1 and 2. Youngheart Records.

Numbers. Sesame Street Records.

Plants

CONCEPTS AND ACTIVITIES

Plants are very interesting to young children. They are anxious to touch them, to pull them out of soil, to investigate them, and even to eat them. Adults need to be sure that safe plants are in the young children's environment. Children can learn many things from their exposure to plants.

I especially like Fulghum's statement about kindergarten learning: "Be aware of wonder. Remember the little seed in the Styrofoam cup: The roots go down and the plant goes up and nobody really knows how or why, but we are all like that" (1989, p. 7).

Following are some categories that could be useful in helping young children learn about plants:

PLANTS/GARDENING

a. Have plants in the natural environment of children so they can see them, learn about them, and appreciate their beauty and usefulness in their daily lives.

b. Show the children some tools used in gardening. Let the children practice using hoes, shovels, and rakes in a safe situation. Talk about some general rules of safety.

c. In five- or eight-ounce clear plastic cups, encourage the children to place soil, large seeds (or bulbs) next to the plastic, and to water and care for their plants. Note how the roots grow down and the stems go upward.

d. Make a terrarium of plants in the classroom. Assign different children to water and care for the plants.

e. Conduct an experiment in the classroom where plants have varying amounts of light, water, soil, and temperature. Remind the children that plants need three things in order to grow: light, food, and water. Most plants make seeds for new plants.

f. If garden and planting space is limited, let the children put soil into the cups of empty egg cartons and then plant grass seed in each. When the plants begin to grow, they can be transplanted into other containers.

g. Make a background on a bulletin board showing the ground level. With the help of the children, place pictures of plants that grow above the ground and those that grow below the ground.

h. In about one inch of water in a shallow dish or ice cube tray, place kernels of Indian corn. Change the water daily. Notice the changes each day.

i. Cut a carrot about one inch below the top. Place the top in a saucer or container of water. Watch how the carrot top grows over a period of time.

j. Stick toothpicks into the sides of a sweet potato or avocado pit so the object will be partly immersed in a jar of water. Note the growth of the potato or pit.

k. Plant bulbs in a low bowl. Put the bowl in a dark room and let the bulbs grow; check growth periodically.

FOOD

a. For snack have vegetables and fruits. Casually talk about how and where the produce grows (above or below ground, on vines, bushes, and so on). Introduce these topics gradually and over a period of time.

b. Help the children prepare, plant, cultivate, and harvest a garden at school.

c. Invite the children to shell peas, snip beans and prepare other food items for snack or lunch.

d. Sprout seeds and eat them at snack or lunch.

e. In a container or on a table, place a variety of nuts and some nut crackers. Encourage the children to examine the shells, then crack and eat the nuts. How do the shells differ in size, texture, and thickness? Do the nuts taste different? Use the shells for a collage. Make some peanut butter in the classroom.

f. Have each child bring a fruit or vegetable from home. Let the children assist in making a fruit salad or soup for snack or lunch.

g. If possible, take a field trip to a grocery store or produce market. Note the many kinds of fruits and vegetables. Purchase a few items. Prepare and use them for snack or lunch.

h. All corn kernels have starch in them. They have a little water in them, too.

But popcorn kernels have a thick skin. When you heat the popcorn kernels, the water inside turns to steam. As it turns to steam, the steam expands and starts to push against the tough skin. The hotter the steam gets, the more it pushes. Soon the kernels explode and you suddenly see the white starch. Explain to the children that is how popcorn pops.

i. Have common fresh fruit to be cut in the presence of the children. Note each fruit and seed or pit. Put all fruit on one tray and all seeds or pits on another one. Help the children to match the seeds and pits with the corresponding fruit. Use only a few fruit at a time and plan to repeat the experience at other times. Good fruits for the exercise include: peach, apple, apricot, cherry, orange, grapes, watermelon, pear, and cantaloupe.

j. Provide samples of food prepared in different ways (juice, raw, cooked, with peeling, and so on).

k. Show and discuss with the children the different covering on food—some edible and some not.

l. Talk with the children about the kinds of plants different animals eat. Have examples. Observe some animals eating.

LANDSCAPING/AESTHETICS

a. Call the children's attention to the flowers and plants around the school by noting their colors, how they grow (individually, in clusters, on bushes, on trees, and so on), and their common names.

b. Have a vase of flowers in the classroom frequently. Talk with the children about the different colors of flowers and their different characteristics (thorns, clusters or single blossoms, fragrances, and so on).

c. Talk about pleasures we get from plants (shade, food, fragrance, beauty, flavor, and nutrition).

d. Talk with the children about the parts of plants we eat (stalk, root, leaves, blossoms, and so on). Do this over a period of time so the children will not be bombarded with information (Carin and Sund, 1980, p. 313).

e. Take a walk with the children through the playground and caution the children against eating plants, shrubs, and other vegetation. Invite a landscape person to carefully go through the yard and remove any plants that are toxic or poisonous.

f. Let the children help rake leaves and grass clippings and place them in containers to be removed from the grounds.

g. Take a nature walk to see the different kinds of leaves and flowers. If possible, collect some plants that are going to seed, such as dandelion or milkweed pods. Notice how the seeds scatter when gently blown. How else can seeds be scattered (water, man, animals)?

h. Point out how leaves, flowers, grass, and so on change as the weather and seasons change.

SUPPORTING ACTIVITIES

a. Use leaves, petals, twigs, and stems in a nature collage.

b. Have cut-outs of different plant parts. Encourage the children to put them together and glue them on a paper plate or piece of paper.

c. Sing songs, read stories, do finger-plays, have puzzles, display pictures, and use other curriculum items that refer to plants.

d. On a table, display a variety of seeds and pictures of their corresponding produce. Help the children match the seeds with the products, noting the size, shape, color, and texture of the seeds.

e. Use the record or book, *The Carrot Seed.*

f. Place a white carnation or a stalk of celery in a jar that has food coloring added to the water. Note how the color goes into the blossom and through the veins. Talk about how the plants get water.

g. Make some small books for the children to cut and paste pictures of flowers, plants, trees, and other vegetation. If possible, have some seeds that could be pasted by the plants. (Use old seed catalogues, magazines, newspaper ads, and so on).

h. Help the children gather large leaves to use for a creative art experience. The children paint the leaves with tempera paint and then press the painted side down on a piece of paper. Or children can place the leaves on a firm surface, cover them with a piece of paper, and color over the leaf with a crayon held length-wise.

i. Children can make a colorful collage using seeds.

REFERENCES

Althouse, R. (1988). **Investigating science with young children.** New York: Teachers College, Columbia University, pp. 124–135.

Althouse, R., and Main, C. (1975). **Science experiences for young children: Seeds.** New York: Teachers College Press.

Beller, J. (1985). **Experimenting with plants.** New York: Simon & Schuster.

Brown, S. E. (1981). **Bubbles, rainbows and worms.** Mt. Rainer, MD: Gryphon House.

Carin, A. A., and Sund, R. B. (1980). **Discovery activities for elementary science.** Columbus, OH: Merrill.

Charlesworth, R., and Lind, K. K. (1990). **Math and science.** Albany, NY: Delmar.

Cobb, V. (1972). **Science experiments you can eat.** New York: J. P. Lippincott.

Cooper, E. K. (1965). **Science in your own back yard.** New York: Harcourt Brace Jovanovich.

Eliason, C., and Jenkins, L. (1990). **A practical guide to early childhood curriculum,** 4th ed. Columbus, OH: Merrill.

Foote, I., and Frank, M. (1982). **Puddles and wings and grapevine swings.** Nashville, TN: Incentive Publications.

Furman, E. (1990, Nov.). Plant a potato—Learn about life (and death). **Young Children,** 46(1), 15–20.

Great beginnings in science, series cards. (1985). Lakeshore Catalog #LC433.

Hackett, J. K., Moyer, R. H., and Adams, D. K. (1989). **Merrill science: A natural in your classroom.** Columbus, OH: Merrill.

Harlan, J. (1988). **Science experiences for the early childhood years.** Columbus, OH: Merrill.

Herr, J., and Libby, Y. (1990). **Creative resources for the early childhood classroom.** Albany, NY: Delmar.

K and L Cactus Nursery, 12712 Stockton Blvd., Galt, CA 95632. (Send $3.00 to order a cactus egg complete with soil and approximately fifty cactus seeds.)

Moore, J. E., and Evans, J. (1987). **Learning about plants: Resource book.** The Evan-Moor Corp., 9425 York Road, Monterey, CA 93940.

Pugh, A. F., and Dukes-Bevans, L. (1987, Nov/Dec.). Planting seeds in young minds. **Science and children.** 19–21.

Russell, H. R. (1973). **Ten-minute field trips: Using the school grounds for environmental studies.** Chicago: J. G. Ferguson.

Sierra Club, Public Affairs, 730 Polk Street, San Francisco, CA 94109. (Send $1.00 for booklet entitled "School Gardens.")

Trump, R. F. (1981). Children with roots. **Children's World,** 133, 16–19.

Victor, E. (1985). **Teaching science in the elementary school.** New York: Macmillan.

BOOKS FOR CHILDREN

Ahlberg, J., and Ahlberg, A. (1979). **Each peach, pear, plum.** New York: Viking.

Bancroft, H. (1961). **Down come the leaves.** New York: Harper.

Brandt, K. (1982). **Discovering trees.** Mahwah, NJ: Troll Associates.

Brown, M. (1981). **Your first garden book.** Boston: Little, Brown and Co.

Bulla, C. R. (1973). **A tree is a plant.** New York: Harper.

Carle, E. (1987). **The tiny seed.** Natick, MA: Picture Book Studio.

Chevalier, C. (1981). **Little green pumpkins.** Niles, IL: Albert Whitman.

Coats, L. J. (1987). **The oak tree.** New York: Macmillan.

Cobb, V. (1981). **Lots of rot.** Philadelphia: Lippincott.

Darby, G. (1960). **What is a plant**? Chicago: Benefic Press.

dePaola, T. (1978). **The popcorn book.** New York: Holiday House.

Domanska, J. (1969). **Turnip.** New York: Macmillan.

Downer, M. L. (1955). **The flower.** New York: Wm. R. Scott.

Ehlert, L. (1988). **Planting a rainbow.** San Diego: Harcourt Brace Jovanovich.

Foster, W. K., and Queree, P. (1963). **Seeds are wonderful.** Chicago: Melmont.

Ginaburg, M. (1974). **Mushroom in the rain.** New York: Macmillan.

Goldin, A. (1967). **How does your garden grow**? New York: Harper.

Howell, R. (1970). **A crack in the pavement.** New York: Atheneum.

Jordan, H. J. (1960). **How a seed grows.** New York: Crowell.

Krasilovsky, P. (1970). **The shy little girl.** Boston: Houghton Mifflin.

Krauss, R. (1971). **The carrot seed.** New York: Scholastic.

Ladislav, S. (1976). **Dandelion.** New York: Doubleday.

Lobel, A. (1984). **The rose in my garden.** New York: Greenwillow.

McCloskey, R. (1948). **Blueberries for Sal.** New York: Viking.

McIntyre, M. (1984). **Early childhood and science.** Washington, DC: N.S.T.A.

McMillan, B. (1988). **Growing colors.** New York: Lothrop, Lee & Shepard.

McMillan, B. (1979). **Apples, how they grow.** Boston: Houghton Mifflin.

Marcus, E. (1982). **Amazing world of plants.** Mahwah, NJ: Troll Associates.

Miles, M. (1969). **The apricot ABC.** Boston: Little, Brown.

Miner, I. (1981). **Plants we know.** Chicago: Childrens Press.

Oechsli, H. and Oechsli, K. (1985). **In my garden: A child's gardening book.** New York: Macmillan.

Podendorf, I. (1981). **Weeds and wild flowers.** Chicago: Childrens Press.

Podendorf, I. (1972). **The true book of plant experiments.** Chicago: Childrens Press.

Rockwell, A., and Rockwell, H. (1982). **How my garden grew.** New York: Macmillan.

Romanova, N. (1985). **Once there was a tree.** New York: Dial.

Selsam, M. I. (1981). **The plants we eat.** New York: Wm. Morrow.

Selsam, M. I. (1978). **Play with plants.** New York: Wm. Morrow.

Selsam, M. I. (1976). **Popcorn.** New York: Wm. Morrow.

Selsam, M. I. (1969). **Peanut.** New York: Morrow.

Selsam, M. I. (1957). **Play with seeds.** New York: Wm. Morrow.

Selsam, M. I. (1959). **Seeds and more seeds.** New York: Harper.

Selsam, M., and Wexter, J. (1980). **Eat the fruit, plant the seed.** New York: Morrow.

Selsam, M. E., and Hunt, J. (1978). **A first look at the world of plants.** New York: Walker & Co.

Titherington, J. (1986). **Pumpkin, pumpkin.** New York: Greenwillow.

Tresselt, A. (1951). **Autumn Harvest.** New York: Lothrop, Lee & Shepard.

Thompson, E. (1963). **What shall I put in that hole I dig**? Racine, WI: Whitman.

Udry, J. (1956). **A tree is nice.** New York: Harper.

Wahl, J. (1985). **I can count the petals of a flower.** 2d ed. Reston, VA.: NCTM.

Webber, I. E. (1953). **Up above and down below.** New York: Wm. R. Scott.

Webber, I. E. (1953). **Travelers all: How plants go places.** New York: Wm. R. Scott.

Zion, G. (1959). **The plant sitter.** New York: Harper.

RECORD SOURCES

(See Appendix C or preschool educational catalogues.)

Little seeds. On **Singing fun.** Bowman-Noble.

Tick, tock, the popcorn clock. The Child's World.

Safety

CONCEPTS AND ACTIVITIES

Behavior to Prevent Accidents and Injuries

a. Through role playing, stories, informal discussions, and other means, help the children to learn about common courtesies, appropriate behaviors, expected guidelines, and other ways to prevent accidents and injuries. Practice good social behaviors informally. (Children usually model the behavior of adults!)

b. Talk about possible consequences of misbehavior or inappropriate actions toward others. (''What do you think we ought to do if _____ happens?'')

c. When children are harming themselves, others, or destroying property, teachers must step in and stop the behavior. Teachers of young children must have a repertoire of responses to help children reduce fear and anger and at the same time build appropriate releases for these feelings. Teachers may suggest individual physical activity—running, throwing a ball, punching a bag, marching or moving to music; expression with art materials—pounding clay, large brush strokes on paper, or water play; a quiet spot for reflection—not punishment; or verbal means—singing, talking over the situation, or verbalizing feelings. The teacher's responses must help reduce the intensity of the child's feelings and suggest a pattern for future responses to frustrating situations.

d. Plan appropriate activities for the children to reduce the possibility of harm or danger.

e. Be aware of each child and the stress they may feel. Plan activities that help to release stress, such as fingerpainting, movement to music, large muscle activities, or whatever helps each child to reduce tension.

f. As prevention, look for and discuss possible problems before they occur—smoke, cords, sharp objects, unsafe places and things in the environment. Decide on appropriate action with the children to rectify the problems.

With Peers

a. Sing songs, read stories, display pictures, use puzzles and other curriculum to teach the children about safety.

b. Use appropriate records to help the children practice safety measures. Role play situations.

c. Use follow-up activities to help children understand and follow safety rules.

d. When accidents do happen, help the children handle them with calmness and security. Model calm behavior yourself.

e. With the help of the children, propose some safety rules for indoors. Help the children understand what the problems are and how to resolve them.

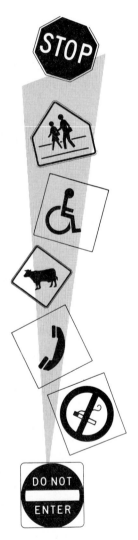

f. Walk around the playground with the children and make a list of potential hazards. Together suggest some solutions. Implement as many suggestions as possible. (Adults may need to point out some hazards not mentioned by the children.) Help the children to know how to safely use the playground equipment.

g. With the help of the children, propose safety rules for the playground. Help the children understand what the problems are and how to resolve them.

h. Before preparing food for snack or lunch, instruct the children in the proper ways to use the utensils, ensure cleanliness, and behave.

i. Ask parents about food likes, dislikes, and allergies of the children. Help the children learn to like a variety of foods and to assist in the preparation and serving of food.

With Pets

a. Introduce the children to classroom pets which are tame, friendly, and free from disease. Check with the local health department for animals to avoid having in the classroom (live or deceased wild animals, certain turtles, those that might carry disease, stray animals, those that are temperamental, and so on).

b. When caring for an appropriate pet in the classroom, help the children to learn about the proper diet, housing, handling, and habits of the animal. Hand washing is important after handling pets. Check school policies about pets.

c. Avoid having incompatible pets in the classroom at the same time. Only owners should handle pets in the classroom.

d. If a child is afraid of a certain type of pet, help the child to learn about the animal at a safe distance.

With Older Children and Adults

a. Propose certain situations and suggest people who could help the children when they are frightened, lost, or injured.

b. Talk about community people who protect us from harm and accident.

c. Introduce a policeman puppet who tells the children about safety, reviews traffic and street signs, notes signs on the bulletin board or in the block area, tells children what they will see on a short walk and then accompanies them on the walk. Try to introduce signs and procedures the children will encounter on the walk (school crossing, railroad, one way, exit, stop, cross walk, and so on)

d. Without alarming the children, talk with them about people who might harm them (kidnap, abuse, and so on) and what they should do under certain situations.

Using Tools

a. Rather than avoid using tools that could be harmful, teach the children how to use the tools appropriately and how using the tools can be fun, interesting, and helpful. Spend a day on woodworking and have a knowledgeable person demonstrate the proper use of tools and then help the children build something simple. Set rules about how many children can be at the activity at one time, how to use the tools, how to get out and return the tools, and so on. Young children will probably be more interested in the use of the tools than in making a product. Take precautions to make sure the tools are of appropriate weight, construction, are workable, and within the understanding of the children.

b. Provide extra supervision when the children are involved in a potentially dangerous activity. Avoid fear, and teach in the positive.

c. When using cooking tools in cooking experiences, show the children how to manipulate the tools to perform the desired task safely (peelers for fruit and vegetables, knives for spreading and cutting).

d. In food preparation, use appliances that are safe, supervised, familiar, and help accomplish tasks easily. Heat, speed, cords, moving parts, and complicated appliances can be used safely when the activity has been well planned.

Care and Storage of Toys and Equipment

a. By helping with the care and storage of toys and equipment, children can learn much about space, cooperation, independence, work habits, and other valuable ideas.

b. How toys and equipment are stored contribute to the longevity of the items. Children should be shown where to put items used for play (balls, trikes, sand toys, blocks, art materials, and so on).

c. Items that are stored correctly last longer and prevent accidents. Help the children make up a story about taking care of items (avoiding moralism or threats). Role play some possible situations.

d. Safety practiced on the playground and in the classroom will help the children develop a sense of responsibility.

Talk about toys lasting longer, being able to find them easily, avoiding accidents and problems, and having fun because of children helping and caring about them.

School Policies
a. Check school policies related to health and safety of the children and others on the premises. If such policies do not currently exist, volunteer to compile some for consideration.

b. If not already provided, make a list *and post in obvious and handy places* emergency services, phone numbers, and how to proceed with expected or common accidents or injuries.

c. Insist that those bringing or picking up the children sign the children into and out of the classroom *every day*. Do not let the children go with unauthorized or unfamiliar individuals. Remember that under certain conditions even family members may be restricted from picking up a child.

d. Prepare and distribute a ''Parent's Manual'' related to the child's attendance and performance in the classroom. Accept suggestions that contribute to the safety of the children and the classroom.

e. Frequently meet with parents, colleagues, and others who interact with young children and plan for their safety. Include information about what to expect and how to react, prevent or avoid dangerous situations.

f. Review (or initiate) school policies about field trips, materials and activities within the classroom, harmful teaching aids (inappropriate pets or plants) possible reduction or prevention of hazards, and illness of children or teachers.

g. Consider a cursory daily inspection before the children are admitted to the group. Ill children will recover faster at home and will reduce spreading infection and disease if they are excluded from the group during onset of sickness.

h. Formulate and evaluate a policy about serving and using food in the classroom. When edibles are used for purposes other than just consumption (in dramatic play, art activities, or the sensory table), how can the safety and health of the children be protected? When food is served, should children be required to eat *all* of it, can they refuse it, or what is to be done when children cannot eat it for religious, health, or personal reasons?

i. Talk about and refresh procedures to be used in situations where first-aid is required. Are teachers required to have specific training? If so, what and how often? Role play medical situations that are possible. Invite trained personnel to interact with teachers on a periodic schedule.

j. Design, understand, and practice procedures for serious emergencies (fire, earthquake, injuries). Talk about them frequently but in a non-threatening way. Designate a flow-chart, a method of accounting for all the children, a meeting place, a procedure during the emergency, and how to return to the classroom and activities. By instructing the children what to expect and how to react to catastrophes that may occur while they are at school, the children should be less fearful and more responsive than with no warning or instruction. Be calm yourself! An alarmed adult can cause the children to become afraid, apprehensive, and untrusting.

Proper Care of Body During Activities

The teacher should demonstrate, discuss, and provide opportunities for children to practice good care of their bodies. This might include:

a. protection of eyes (sun glasses, visor, prescription glasses)

b. proper use of clothing (less in hot weather except to avoid direct sun; more when weather is cold because layered clothing gives more warmth than a single article); use of head covering (scarf, hat, ear muffs)

c. good places to play (shelter during extreme hot or cold weather, where they can be observed, with non-harmful equipment, and so on)

d. safe activities and equipment—avoiding activities with potential danger or equipment that is in disrepair or improperly set up or supervised, knowing when to run or walk from situations

e. development of good health habits—brushing teeth, washing hands, bathing, being immunized, preventing colds and diseases

f. avoiding common but potentially dangerous materials—putting items into their ears or noses (beans are especially dangerous); mouthing small toys, buttons, balloons, marbles, puzzle pieces, and many other items that could cause choking or suffocation.

Field Trips and Visitors

a. Help the children to understand about safety rules by introducing and discussing a traffic light. Children practice the concepts of stopping, being cautious, and going as indicated by the appropriate colors—red, yellow, and green. This can be done on the playground by using traffic signs, in the block area by using small signs, in dramatic play while walking, and so on. This could be further reinforced by assisting the children to make traffic signs using dark construction paper for the background and cellophane or tissue for the color windows.

b. Before taking a walking field trip, talk with the children about what they may see, how to behave, and other items of importance to a successful walk.

c. If the children are transported for any reason, make sure each one is secured by a seat belt and that the children know the rules for good behavior.

d. Review school policies. How will children be transported? How is the cost covered? How will permission be obtained—written, verbal, or blanket for the year. Who will make a pre-visit to ensure the route is safe, the trip is on the developmental level of the children, and the time and efforts are well utilized? How is the visit expected to further the knowledge of the children? Could a better experience be planned right in the classroom? What about a follow-up experience?

e. In a positive, healthy way, teach children precaution about going with strangers or about letting a familiar or strange person touch certain parts of their bodies.

REFERENCES

Aronson, S. S. (1983, September). Injuries in child care. **Young Children,** pp. 19–20.

Hardin, J. W., and Arena, J. M. (1977). **Human poisoning from native and cultivated plants.** Durham, NC: Duke University Press.

Herr, J., and Libby, Y. (1990). **Creative resources for the early childhood classroom.** Albany, NY: Delmar.

Safety in the elementary science classroom. National Science Teachers Association, Stock #471–14750. Washington, DC: NSTA. 1742 Connecticut Avenue, N.W. #20009 ($2.00 for pamphlet.)

Pratt-Butler, G. K. (n.d.). **How to care for living things in the classroom.** Washington, DC: National Science Teachers Association.

BOOKS FOR CHILDREN

Chacon, R. (1985). **You can say "NO!"** Huntington Beach, CA: Teacher Created Materials, Inc.

Chlad, D. (1982). **Strangers.** Chicago: Childrens Press.

Chlad, D. (1982). **When there is a fire . . . Go outside.** Chicago: Childrens Press.

Chlad, D. (1982). **When I cross the street.** Chicago: Childrens Press.

Chlad, D. (1983). **When I ride in a car.** Chicago: Childrens Press.

Chlad, D. (1987). **Playing on the playground.** Chicago: Childrens Press.

Hoban, T. (1983). **I read signs.** New York: Greenwillow.

Longman, H. (1968). **Watch out.** New York: Parents Magazine.

Maass, R. (1989). **Fire fighters.** New York: Scholastic.

Parker, M. J. (1989). **Night fire!** New York: Scholastic.

Rockwell, A., and Rockwell, H. (1985). **The emergency room.** New York: Macmillan.

Shapp, M., and C. Shapp (1975). **Let's find out about safety.** New York: Franklin Watts.

Viorst, J. (1970) **Try it again, Sam.** New York: Lothrop, Lee & Shepard.

RECORD SOURCES

(See Appendix C or preschool educational catalogues.)

Learning basic skills through music, health and safety. Freeport, NY: Educational Activity Records.

Senses

CONCEPTS AND ACTIVITIES

The most appropriate learning for the very young child is through the five senses: sight, sound, smell, taste, and touch. Therefore, opportunities to exercise and develop the senses are vital. Children who have deficiencies in any of these senses will have a more difficult time learning about their world than children whose senses are keen.

The senses should be utilized in all teaching for young children. Each topic addressed in this book calls for frequent use of the appropriate senses to clarify and present materials in an interesting and challenging way for the children.

Albers states, ''Students sometimes fall into categories that reflect which sense they rely upon most often in learning about their world. Visual learners, for example, rely primarily on the sense of sight, audial learners on hearing, tactile learners on touch, and so on'' (1988, p. 12). By discussing the senses individually, concentration can be on each sense; however, in real life, learning through a combination of senses is most often the case. Therefore, a bulletin board featuring the sense organs could be an introduction to this topic.

THE VISUAL SENSE

a. In the classroom or home, pictures are often good reminders for children to show where certain objects belong, such as a picture of blocks where the blocks belong (perhaps even showing the correct size or shape of blocks), a picture of clothes that belong in a certain drawer, or a picture of toys over a certain place where they belong. As children show interest in written symbols, a word could be written and posted on a few items (chair, bed, door, and so on, but don't overdo the pictures or word symbols).

b. Whether or not someone in the classroom wears glasses, a brief discussion could be appropriate. Demonstrate how magnifying glasses can make things look larger, sunglasses can prevent glare, or craftsmen use eye gear for protection.

c. Preschool children can be screened for eye problems. Early detection is important to the success and treatment of any problems. Teachers should bring possible problems to the attention of parents and advise them of community resources when appropriate.

d. Young children usually resent being blind-folded even for games. If you are talking about limited eyesight, have the children close their eyes for certain activities, or you could remove objects from their sight or cover them.

e. Provide a picture recipe. Help the children understand what to put into the recipe (either for art or for an edible snack or lunch) by comparing the size of cups or spoons, by matching the picture on the recipe with a bagged product on the table, and by doing things in sequence.

f. On the door to the classroom, the bulletin board, or a low wall, place a picture of each child. Encourage the children to look at the pictures, and identify the children by name and the activity in which the child is involved.

g. Provide name tags for each child. Upon arrival, assist the child in selecting her name tag and in fastening it on. At departure time, the child removes the tag and replaces it.

h. On the walls, bulletin board, and during activities, have pictures of children and activities posted. Talk with the children about the actions and feelings in the pictures.

i. Talk with the children about the things they like to see. Why are they pleasing?

j. Give the children some similar objects (sticks, blocks, socks, cars, and so on), and ask the children to line them up from the biggest to the smallest. Do other activities so children can practice seriation tasks.

k. Give the children some objects and ask them to put like things together. Then ask the children to put them together a different way. This activity helps the children practice classification.

l. Help the children learn to identify some common shapes (circles, squares, triangles, rectangles). As their interest increases, introduce additional shapes (hexagons, freeforms, trapezoids, and so on).

m. Help the children learn to identify some common colors, beginning with the primary colors.

n. For cleanup purposes, have containers so the children can replace the items they have used, for example, a juice can wrapped with blue paper for holding blue crayons, boxes with pictures of the toys contained, hooks for dress-up clothes, and trays for soiled glasses and dishes.

o. Let the children help mix paint for the easel and other art activities. Provide materials needed and a place to mix the paint and then a place to use them.

THE AUDITORY SENSE

a. Young children are keenly aware of sounds, evidenced by their startled reactions when loud noises are made. Some sounds are desirable and pleasant; others are frustrating and frightening. Talk with the children about things they do and do not like to hear. Why do they have preferences?

b. Sounds are made by people, animals, and moving objects. Behind a screen or on an audio tape, play different common sounds. Have the children guess the sounds and then imitate them.

c. Young children like to hear and make animal sounds. Use a picture to represent the animal and make the corresponding sound so the children will connect the animal and the sound.

d. Clear, repeated sounds are necessary for the children to form correct concepts. Use poetry, books, games, and other activities where sounds are repeated.

e. Take a walk around the classroom and tape some familiar sounds. As a group, see who can identify the sounds as they are replayed.

f. Take a walk around the playground and tape some familiar sounds. As a group, see who can identify the sounds as they are replayed.

g. Take a walk around the neighborhood and tape some familiar sounds. As a group, see who can identify the sounds as they are replayed.

h. Tape the voices of the children in the group. Replay the tape and see if the individual voices can be identified.

i. Tape some familiar sounds in the home (phone ringing, water running, toilet flushing, appliances, car horn, dog barking, and so on), and see if the children can identify them. Then create a story with the children using the various sounds.

j. Talk with the children about what sounds mean (car horn, siren, soft music, children laughing, and so on).

k. Fill duplicate small containers with the same contents, such as rice, beans, rocks, water, or cotton balls. Ask the children to find the matching container.

l. Help the children make musical instruments so they can play them at an appropriate time (shakers, drums, waxed paper over a comb, rhythm sticks, and so on). Encourage the children to use their instruments. Then add music and see if the participation changes.

m. Play different kinds of music on the piano or use a record. Ask the children to move as the music indicates to them. Change rhythms and see if the participation changes.

n. Sing songs, do fingerplays, provide puzzles and pictures, read stories, and use records that encourage the children to listen carefully or talk about aspects of hearing.

o. Use games or stories where whispering is an important part. Children usually attend well when the adult uses a lowered or quiet voice. Try it!

p. Ask the children to think of sounds that are frightening or that warn us of danger. Why do some sounds make us feel one way, while others make us feel the opposite?

q. Provide a quiet area where the children can look at books and make up stories. A flannelboard and characters can stimulate storytelling by the children.

r. Encourage the children to verbalize to resolve problems rather than using physical means, such as hitting or taking.

s. Tell the children to listen carefully while you tell a story or give instructions. Then ask them to retell the story or repeat the instructions.

t. Introduce new vocabulary to the children and provide a means for them to practice the words.

u. Introduce rhythm instruments to the children. Let them explore and experiment with all the instruments they desire. (You may want to introduce only a few instruments at a time.) Add music to the experience and note if the children can adequately handle the more complex experience. (For safety and health, mouth instruments should be avoided.)

v. Fill eight pop bottles with varying amounts of water. Blow gently across the bottles and note the different sounds made. See if you can create a tune. (Blowing may be too difficult for the children.)

w. Acquire a book that has an accompanying record. Rather than the adult telling the story, let the children listen to the record. Note the difference in response of the children when an adult tells a story and when a recording is used.

x. Play a tape or record that has sounds of different objects. Have pictures of objects (some on the tape and some not on the tape) and encourage the children to match pictures and sounds. Ask them to make the sounds of the pictures that were not on the tape.

y. Using a stringed instrument (autoharp, guitar, violin, or rubber bands on a box), show the children how the strings vibrate when they are plucked or played.

z. Talk about or sort toys, food, or items of the same color. Try to involve the children in sorting by different means. Note the verbalization.

aa. Tap out different rhythms and ask the children to repeat them.

THE OLFACTORY SENSE

a. Children have a sensitivity to smells, which can signal security (food or a caring person) or something undesirable. Encourage the children to talk about pleasant smells and why they like them.

b. Lay a clean bedsheet or piece of white paper on the floor. Show the children some kernels of corn and let them touch to feel their consistency. With a popcorn popper placed so that

the cord is away from the children, pop some popcorn. Tell the children to describe what is happening. They will probably talk about the corn being big and white, or that it is good to eat. But they will probably not mention the smell. Direct their attention to how the classroom smells differently now.

c. Frequently do hands-on cooking experiences with the children so they recognize that odors change when a product is changed. Note that moisture, heat, and mixing can change the smell and texture of products.

d. In duplicate containers, put some pleasant but familiar scents. Have the children smell and match the containers. Use such things as mint, perfume, extracts, fruit peel, onion, spices, and water. Or have individual containers of familiar products for the children to smell but not see or taste, such as catsup, mustard, toothpaste, and candy. See how many they can identify.

e. In a bag or box, place cotton balls that have different scents. See if the children can identify the scent and match it to a picture or product on the board.

f. If acceptable to the children, blindfold them one at a time and let them smell substances. Note how many they can correctly identify.

THE SENSE OF TASTE

a. Young children put everything into their mouths, not knowing whether they are tasty or harmful. Adults need to be continually alert to the environment within the reach of these young children. Avoid small objects, food, plastic, or objects that could clog the child's throat.

b. The mouth is an organ for tasting, but it is also a means of conversing with others. Once children have learned to talk and feel secure, they thrive on asking questions, hearing their own voices, and developing social skills. Give them full attention when they are speaking.

c. Young children have keen taste buds in their cheeks. They prefer food that is mildly seasoned, mildly flavored, warm (rather than hot or cold), familiar, and unmixed (separate items rather than casseroles or stews). Observe the kinds of food they like, the amount they consume, the food they talk about, and their use of utensils. Does the company of peers encourage or discourage eating in young children?

d. The four tastes are: salty, sweet, bitter, and sour. These flavors may be more intense for children than adults. Some children have difficulty in naming the tastes, but can show when food is undesirable. (Have a lesson on the placement of tastes on the tongue for older children. It is even hard for some adults to comprehend.)

e. Check with the parents about food preferences and allergies of the children. Some are highly sensitive to milk, wheat, strawberries, chocolate, and sugar. Should children be forced to eat or taste all food? Why or why not?

f. Where do you fit in the debate on the influence of sugar in the diet of children? Get to know the children in your group and watch their behavior before and after holidays and when foods highly concentrated with sugar are served. Does such an observation cause you to change activities or sugar consumption at special times?

g. If snacks or lunch are served in your classroom, do you try to serve foods that are low in fat, salt, and sugar as recommended by nutritionists and researchers? Do you encourage the children to build good eating habits by serving them nourishing food and a balanced diet?

h. On a science table or tray, place a variety of non-harmful products that look alike (sugars, baking soda, baking powder, cornstarch). Have the children taste each product and see if they can properly label it.

i. At snack (or unstructured time) have a tasting party where numerous fruit and vegetable pieces are prepared for children to taste. Also have some whole fruit and vegetables for the children to relate to.

j. Talk with the children about things they like to eat. Why are they pleasant? Is it flavor, texture, color or association?

THE TACTILE SENSE

a. Touching things sends messages to the children. Generally young children prefer items that are soft, cuddly, and warm. Make a touching bulletin board using fabrics, twigs, plastic, metal, wood, and any other things children like to feel. Encourage them to feel the objects, add items, and discuss how they feel—temperature, hardness, smoothness, and so on.

b. As an art activity, let the children draw or scribble with crayons on different textures (sandpaper, wallpaper, tissue, wood, plastic, and so on). Talk about the experience.

c. Make a texture board by pasting different textures onto heavy cardboard or wood. In a separate container, have duplicate samples of the textures. Suggest that the child put the matching samples onto the ones on the board. Have extra samples, some identical to the board and some slightly different, such as variation in sandpaper, different colors, and different weights so the experience will be successful but slightly challenging to children who are ready.

d. In a sensory trough or in tubs, provide frequent experiences for the children to handle, pour, and use different media, such as flour, rice, beans, cornmeal, and water. If the media is cared for, it will last for a long time.

e. Provide water opportunities for the children. Water is inexpensive, easily cleaned up, therapeutic, not commonly provided for children in the home, and it enhances many other activities, such as sand, housekeeping, and outdoor play.

f. Make a "feely" box in which the children place their hands, feel an object, guess what it is, and then withdraw it from the box to check their accuracy.

g. Make a book of different textured fabrics (velvet, satin, muslin, nylon net, corduroy, canvas, wool, and so on). Let the children look through other samples to match textures. They could make their own texture book.

h. Go for a nature walk. Take bags, gather objects, and make a nature collage upon your return. Talk about what was found, how it came to be there, and how it adds to the picture.

i. Encourage the children to feel a product that will be changed by another experience. For example, after they use rice in the sensory table, show

them how to soak and cook it. Serve it for snack or lunch. Note the difference in the consistency.

j. Fingerpaint with commercial or home-made fingerpaint, liquid starch, whipped soap flakes, pudding, or shaving cream. Add other items to change the consistency or feel, such as sand or glitter. Observe the children in the activity and in the clean-up process.

k. Have the children feel a variety of different objects. Then have them put on a pair of gloves and feel the same objects. How does the activity differ?

l. Talk about a variety of gloves and the purposes for which they are worn (sports, work, pleasure, weather, and so on). Have the children try on the gloves and imitate the behavior that accompanies each glove.

m. Provide opportunities for children to cover or seal different kinds of containers (plastic, snap lids, screw lids, and so on) to practice grip and finger dexterity.

n. Provide manipulative toys for the children's use (pegs and boards, puzzles, interlocking and put-together toys).

o. Assist children in dressing and undressing themselves. Use zippers, snaps, buttons, laces, etc. on dress-up clothing, doll clothing, learning frames, or other items.

p. Talk with the children about things they like to touch. Why are they pleasant?

q. Have the children remove their shoes and socks and wash their feet in a tub. Paint the bottom of their feet with tempera and let them walk on a canvas, sheet of paper, or cardboard.

Note the prints of the toes and the shape of the feet. Replace shoes and socks to prevent injury.

r. Provide containers of macaroni, both cooked and dry. Encourage the children to experiment with different textures of macaroni. Watch as cooked macaroni begins to dry out and as water is added to dry macaroni. Encourage the children to describe the different textures.

REFERENCES

Albers, D. S. (1988). Create a sense-ation. **Science and children,** Nov and Dec., pp. 12–13.

Althouse, R., and Main, C. (1975). **Science experiences for young children: Senses.** New York: Teachers College Press.

Cain, M. F. (1988). Follow your nose. **Science and children,** Sept., pp. 40–41.

Eliason, C., and Jenkins, L. (1990). **A practical guide to early childhood curriculum.** Columbus, OH: Merrill.

Forte, I. (1986). **I'm ready to learn about beginning science.** Nashville, TN: Incentive Publications.

Hackett, J. K., Moyer, R. H., and Adams, D. K. (1989). **Merrill science: A natural in your classroom.** Columbus, OH: Merrill.

Heinz, B. J. (1989). Touch me! **Science and children,** Jan., pp. 22–23.

Lind, K. (1984). The sense-able approach to science. **Science and children,** 22(2), 36–38.

Moore, J. E., and Evans, J. (1987). **Learning about my body: Resource book.** Monterey, CA: The Evan-Moore Corp. (Use as a teacher reference, not as worksheets for young children.)

Shirah, S., and Dorman, M. M. (1989). Developing sense-activities. **Science and children,** Feb., pp. 38–41.

Trostle, S. L., and Yawkey, T. D. (1990). **Integrated learning activities for young children.** Boston: Allyn & Bacon.

BOOKS FOR CHILDREN

Aardena, V. (1978). **Why mosquitoes buzz in people's ears.** New York: Dial Press.

Aliki. (1984). **Feelings.** New York: Greenwillow.

Aliki. (1966). **Keep your mouth closed, dear.** New York: Dial.

Aliki. (1962). **My five senses.** New York: Crowell.

Aliki. (1962). **My hands.** New York: Harper.

Ayres, P. (1987). **Guess who?** New York: A. Knopf.

Brandt, K. (1985). **My five senses.** Mahwah, NJ: Troll Associates.

Brandt, K. (1985). **Sound.** Mahwah, NJ: Troll Assoc.

Branley, F. M. (1975). **High sounds, low sounds.** New York: Harper.

Brown, M. W. (1976). **The country noisy book.** New York: Harper.

Brown, M. W. (1976). **The indoor noisy book.** New York: Harper.

Brown, M. W. (1976). **The winter noisy book.** New York: Harper.

Brown, M. W. (1943). **Shhh-h-h Bang!** New York: Harper.

Carle, E. (1986). **The secret birthday message.** New York: Harper.

Davis, G. (1985). **Katy's first haircut.** Boston: Houghton Mifflin.

Engvick, W. (ed.) (1985). **Lullabies and night songs.** New York: Harper.

Ets, M. H. (1963). **Gilberto and the wind.** New York: Viking.

Fowler, R. (1986). **Mr. Little's noisy car.** New York: Putnam.

Francoise, A. (1960). **The things I like.** New York: Charles Scribner's Sons.

Fulton, M. J. (1971). **Detective Arthur on the scent.** New York: Golden Press.

Gaeddert, L. A. (1965). **Noisy Nancy Norris.** Garden City, NY: Doubleday.

Garland, S. (1984). **Having a picnic.** Boston: Atlantic Monthly Press.

Gibson, M. (1968). **What is your favorite thing to see?** New York: Grosset & Dunlap.

Gibson, M. (1965). **What is your favorite thing to touch?** New York: Grosset & Dunlap.

Hazen, B. S. (1972). **Listen! Listen! A story about sounds.** New York: Golden Press.

Hoban, T. (1985). **Is it larger? Is it smaller?** New York: Greenwillow.

Hoban, T. (1988). **Look! Look! Look!** New York: Greenwillow.

Hughes, S. (1985). **Noisy.** New York: Lothrop, Lee & Shepard.

Iveson-Iveson, J. (1986). **Your nose and ears.** New York: Bookwright Press.

Isadora, R. (1985). **I touch.** New York: Greenwillow.

Joslin, S. (1980). **What do you say, dear?** New York: Scholastic.

Keats, E. J. (1964). **Whistle for Willie.** New York: Viking.

Keats, E. J. (1971). **Apartment 3.** New York: Macmillan.

Kline, S. (1985). **Don't touch.** Niles, IL: Whitman & Co.

Kline, S. (1984). **SHHHH!** Niles, Il: Whitman & Co.

Kunhardt, D. (1988). **Pat the bunny.** New York: Western.

Lemieux, M. (1985). **What's that noise?** New York: Morrow.

McGovern, A. (1967). **Too much noise.** Boston: Houghton Mifflin.

Marzzollo, J. (1978). **Close your eyes.** New York: Dial.

Mayer, M. (1968). **There's a nightmare in my closet.** New York: Dial.

My first look at touch. (1990). New York: Random House

Packard, M. (1985). **From head to toe; how my body works.** New York: Messner.

Pluckrose, H. (1986). **Think about hearing.** New York: Franklin Watts.

Plume, I. (1980). **The Bremen town musicians.** Garden City, NY: Doubleday.

Podendorf, I. (1970). **Things are alike and different.** Chicago: Childrens Press.

Pragoff, F. (1985). **Alphabet.** New York: Bantam Doubleday Dell.

Radlauer, R. S. (1960). **About four senses and five senses.** Chicago: Childrens Press.

Rice, M., and Rice, C. (1987). **All about me.** Garden City, NY: Doubleday.

Ruis, M., Parramon, J. M., and Puig, J. J. (1985). **The five senses: Hearing.** New York: Barron's.

Ruis, M., Parramon, J. M., and Puig, J. J. (1985). **The five senses: Sight.** New York: Barron's.

Ruis, M., Parramon, J. M., and Puig, J. J. (1985). **The five senses: Smell.** New York: Barron's.

Ruis, M., Parramon, J. M., and Puig, J. J. (1985). **The five senses: Taste.** New York: Barron's.

Rius, M., Parramon, J. M., and Puig, J. J. (1985). **The five senses: Touch.** New York: Barron's.

Showers, P. (1961). **Find out by touching.** New York: Crowell.

Showers, P. (1963). **Follow your nose.** New York: Crowell.

Showers, P. (1976). **Look at your eyes.** New York: Crowell.

Showers, P. (1961). **The listening walk.** New York: Crowell.

Spier, P. (1972). **Crash! Bang! Boom!** New York: Doubleday.

Testa, F. (1983). **If you look around you.** New York: Dial.

Tudor, T. (1966). **First delights: A book about the five senses.** Eau Claire, WI: E. M. Hale.

Udry, J. M. (1967). **Mary Ann's mud day.** New York: Harper.

Wells, R. (1973). **Noisy Nora.** New York: Dial.

Wilt, J., and Watson, T. (1977). **Listen.** Waco, TX: Creative Resources.

Wilt, J. and Watson, T. (1977). **Look.** Waco, TX: Creative Resources.

Wilt, J. and Watson, T. (1978). **Taste and smell.** Waco, TX: Creative Resources.

Wilt, J. and Watson, T. (1977). **Touch.** Waco, TX: Creative Resources.

Zolotow, C. (1989). **The quiet mother and the noisy little boy.** New York: Harper & Row.

Shape
CONCEPTS AND ACTIVITIES

The younger the child, the fewer and more simple the shapes should be. The first three shapes children learn are the circle, the square, and the triangle. There are some simple concepts that young children can learn about shapes. However, the concepts should be presented in the proper context so the children are exposed to the concepts and then have time for individual exploration to integrate information. Young children should not be forced to repeat or learn specifics. Following are some concepts young children might encounter:

a. A circle is round or curved.

b. Round objects roll.

c. A square has four straight sides of equal length and four corners.

d. A triangle has three straight sides of equal length, three corners, and a point at the top.

e. Shapes can be different sizes, colors, and materials. (Be cautious that the children see and use shapes of different colors so they do not associate "blue" with "circle" or "small," for example.)

f. Shapes can be different or the same.

g. Shapes can be flat or dimensional (for example, a poker chip is flat and round, a ball is spherical and round).

ACTIVITIES TO HELP CHILDREN UNDERSTAND SHAPES

a. Sing songs, use fingerplays, tell stories, provide puzzles and other items that name or display shapes.

b. Have objects of shapes on a table or tray. Have silhouettes of the objects for the children to match.

c. Talk about objects which can be found in different shapes: boxes, shoes, balls, hats, pets, houses, containers, and so on.

d. Talk about objects which can be found in the same shape, for example, boxes, books, crackers, scarves, checkerboard, tile, and windows can all be "squares."

e. Make and play games with shapes ("Old Maid," "Concentration," "Twister," "Dominoes").

f. Have a group of objects in which some are round, some are square, and some are triangular. Suggest that the child put all like items together and then name the group shape. For young children, use only circles, squares, and triangles. For older children, use the three basic shapes but also introduce a few other shapes, such as rectangle, oblong, oval, hexagon, or freeform as the children are ready for more information and experiences.

g. Focusing on one shape at a time, look around the environment and identify items of that shape. Then use a second shape to identify items in the environment. If the children are still interested, introduce the third shape and repeat the procedure. Make it fun and interesting—not a rote or dull activity. More advanced children can look for two dimensions—round and small, skinny and blue, and so on.

h. For an art activity, cut a variety of circles from paper or fabric for the children to make a collage. Another time introduce a variety of squares for the children to paste. Still another time introduce triangles for their use. Eventually use a combination of the three shapes for them to paste into a collage. Older children can cut their own shapes if outlines are drawn for them.

i. Provide sturdy shape stencils for the children to draw around.

j. Provide pliable materials (dough clay) so the children can experiment in making different shapes (balls, doughnuts, pancakes, snakes, and so on).

k. Provide toys and opportunities for the children to familiarize themselves with different shapes in dramatic play, block building, art materials, and outdoor environments.

l. Make cookie dough and cut the cookies into different shapes.

m. Serve commercial crackers of different shapes for snack or lunch and help the children identify them by name.

n. Cut sponges into different shapes, provide a thickened paint, and help the children make shape prints on absorbent paper.

o. For lunch or snack let the children prepare gelatin and set it in individual shape molds.

p. Play circle games indoors or outdoors ("Duck, duck, goose," "I have a little doggie," and so on).

q. With a variety of colored shapes and sizes, encourage the children to make them into different objects, such as wheels on a wagon, a lollipop, or a house.

r. Make a container or use a commercial one with different shaped holes and corresponding objects to fit into the holes.

s. On the bulletin board have objects—a boat, a house, a train, and so on— made out of circles, squares, and triangles. Have some extra shapes for the children to add to or change the objects.

t. On a pegboard, draw the outline of musical instruments, woodworking tools, or other items that can be hung on it. The children can put away the objects by matching the silhouette.

REFERENCES

Beaty, J. J. (1990). **Observing development of the young child,** 2d ed. Columbus, OH: Merrill, pp. 206–208.

Beaty, J. J. (1988). **Skills for preschool teachers,** 3d ed. Columbus, OH: Merrill.

Bredekamp, S. (ed.) (1988). **Developmentally appropriate practice from birth to age 8.** Washington, DC: National Association for the Education of Young Children.

Charlesworth, R., and Lind, K. K. (1990). **Math and science for young children.** Albany, NY: Delmar.

Eliason, C., and Jenkins, L. (1990). **A practical guide to early childhood curriculum.** Columbus, OH: Merrill.

Herr, J., and Libby, Y. (1990). **Creative resources for the early childhood classroom.** Albany, NY: Delmar.

Williams, C. K., and Kamii, C. (1986). How do children learn by handling objects? **Young children,** 42(1), pp. 23–26.

BOOKS FOR CHILDREN

Atwood, A. (1967). **The little circle.** New York: Scribner Press.

Barrett, P., and Barrett, S. (1972). **The line Sophie drew.** New York: Scroll Press.

Barrett, P., and Barrett, S. (1970). **The square Ben drew.** New York: Scroll Press.

Barrett, P., and Barrett, S. (1970). **The circle Sarah drew.** New York: Scroll Press.

Brown, M. (1979). **Listen to a shape.** New York: F. Watts.

Bruna, D. (1984). **I know about shapes.** Los Angeles: Price Stern.

Carle, E. (1974). **My very first book of shapes.** New York: Harper.

Feiss, J. (1974). **Shapes.** New York: Bradbury Press.

Fisher, L. E. (1984). **Boxes! Boxes!** New York: Viking Press.

Gardner, B. (1980). **The turn about, think about, look about book.** New York: Wm. Morrow.

Hoban, T. (1982). **A, B, See!** New York: Greenwillow.

Hoban, T. (1974). **Circles, triangles, squares.** New York: Macmillan.

Hoban, T. (1983). **Round and round and round.** New York: Greenwillow.

Hoban, T. (1986). **Shapes, shapes, shapes.** New York: Greenwillow.

Hoban, T. (1970). **Shapes and things.** New York: Macmillan.

Hooker, Y. (1982). **Round in a circle.** New York: Grosset & Dunlap.

Hooker, Y. (1981). **Wheels go round.** New York: Grosset & Dunlap.

Kohn, B. (1971). **Everything has a shape and everything has a size.** Englewood Cliffs, NJ: Prentice-Hall.

Lerner, S. (1970). **Square is a shape: A book about shapes.** Minneapolis: Lerner.

Newth, P. (1981). **Roly goes exploring.** New York: Philomel.

Petersham, M., and Petersham, M. (1949). **The box with red wheels.** New York: Macmillan.

Porter, A. W. (1974). **Shape and form.** Worcester, MA: Davis Publishing.

Russell, S. P. (1965). **Lines and shapes.** New York: Henry Walck.

Russo, M. (1986). **The line up book.** New York: Greenwillow.

Schlein, M. (1952). **Shapes.** Boston: Addison-Wesley.

Sesame Street book of shapes (1971). New York: New America Library.

Seuss, Dr. (1973). **The shape of me and other stuff.** New York: Beginner Books.

Shapur, F. (1963). **Round and round and square.** New York: Abelard-Schuman.

Shaw, C. G. (1947). **It looked like spilt milk.** New York: Harper.

Thole, D. (1977). **Tatum's favorite shape.** New York: Scholastic.

Wildsmith, B. (1981). **Animal shapes.** London, England: Oxford University Press.

Zolotow, C. (1976). **One step, two . . .** New York: Lothrop, Lee & Shepard.

RECORD SOURCES

(See Appendix C or preschool educational catalogues.)

My world is round. Melody House Records.

Palmer, H. Record Library. Learning with circles and sticks. One shape, three shapes. Triangle, circle, or square. On **Learning basic skills through music (Vol. 2).** #AR585 or #AC585.

Palmer, H. Record Library. Walk around the circle. On **Learning basic skills through music—vocabulary.** #AR521 or # AC521.

We all live together series—Vol. 1 and 2. Youngheart Records.

When I was very young. The Children's Record Guild, #1031.

Size

CONCEPTS AND ACTIVITIES

Size is a difficult concept for young children. The first sizes to learn are "small" and "large"—in comparison with something else and with definite distinctions between them.

a. Have the children find, suggest, and name things they think are "big." Another time have them do the same thing for "small." Until the children are well versed in one size, they will have difficulty with comparisons.

b. Avoid comparisons where one is preferable to another. Such terms as "big boy" and "little boy" give the child the impression that "big" is "good" or desirable, and "little" or "small" is "bad" or undesirable.

c. Give the children opportunities to compare opposites (big-little, tall-short, heavy-light) as a direct way of learning about relationships and sizes; however, they need to learn about one relationship before moving on to other relationships. Over-burdening the child with pairs may result in his inability to make distinctions.

d. Have picture cards of adult and baby animals. Help the child sort the pictures by size (all the adults in one pile and all the young in another). Talk about the differences between the adults and their offspring.

e. Provide a flannelboard and similar figures in different sizes. Watch and listen. Encourage the children to line up the "family" from baby to parent or by size.

f. Using a variety of balls, discuss their uses and then line them up according to size.

g. At an art period provide brushes with different bristle thicknesses. Encourage the children to make a picture using each size of brush.

h. Compare sizes of familiar items, such as rolls from paper towel or toilet paper; apples; dolls; trucks; shoes; socks; containers; eating utensils; pans; or clothing.

i. Assist the children in placing one block in one pile, two blocks in the next pile, three blocks in the next pile, and so on to see how the height increases. If children are more interested in just building with the blocks, consider using the piling activity for another time.

REFERENCES

Althouse, R. (1988). **Investigating science with young children.** New York: Teachers College Press.

Beaty, J. J. (1990). **Observing development of the young child,** 2d ed. Columbus, OH: Merrill.

Beaty, J. J. (1988). **Skills for preschool teachers.** Columbus, OH: Merrill.

Eliason, C., and Jenkins, L. (1990). **A practical guide to early childhood curriculum.** Columbus, OH: Merrill.

Forman, G. E., and Kuschner, D. S. (1983). **The child's construction of knowledge: Piaget for teaching children.** Washington, DC: National Association for the Education of Young Children.

Siegler, R. S. (1986). **Children's thinking.** Englewood Cliffs, NJ: Prentice-Hall.

Williams, C. K., and Kamii, C. (1986). How children learn by handling objects. **Young children,** 42(1), pp. 23–26.

BOOKS FOR CHILDREN

Anderson, L. C. (1983). **The wonderful shrinking shirt.** Niles, IL: Albert Whitman.

Barton, B. (1981). **Building a house.** New York: Greenwillow.

Berkley, E. (1950). **Big and little, up and down.** Reading, MA: Addison-Wesley.

Carle, E. (1976). **The tiny seed and the giant flower.** New York: Crowell.

Hoban, T. (1985). **Is it larger? Is it smaller?** New York: Greenwillow.

Kohn, B. (1971). **Everything has a shape and everything has a size.** Englewood Cliffs, NJ: Prentice Hall.

Kellogg, S. (1976). **Much bigger than Martin.** New York: Dial.

Krasilvsky, P. (1962). **The very little boy.** New York: Doubleday.

Krasilvsky, P. (1952). **The very little girl.** New York: Doubleday.

Krauss, R. (1947). **The growing story.** New York: Harper.

Krauss, R. (1987). **Big and little.** New York: Scholastic.

Lenski, L. (1959). **Cowboy Small.** New York: Henry Walck.

Lenski, L. (1979). **Big book of Mr. Small.** New York: McKay.

Lionni, L. (1968). **Biggest house in the world.** New York: Pantheon.

McClosky, R. (1976). **Blueberries for Sal.** New York: Viking.

McMillan, B. (1986). **Becca backward, Becca frontward: A book of concept pairs.** New York: Lothrop, Lee & Shepard.

Miller, J. P. (1975). **Big and little.** New York: Random House.

My first look at opposites. (1990). New York: Random House.

My first look at sizes. (1990). New York: Random House.

Russo, M. (1986). **The line up book.** New York: Greenwillow.

Shapp, M., and Shapp, C. (1975). **Let's find out about what's big and what's small.** New York: Franklin Watts.

Spier, P. (1972). **Fast-slow, high-low: A book of opposites.** Garden City, NY: Doubleday.

Walter, M. (1972). **Make a bigger puddle, make a smaller worm.** New York: M. Evans.

Ward, L. (1952). **The biggest bear.** Boston: Houghton Mifflin.

Transpor- tation

CONCEPTS AND ACTIVITIES

Following are some possible concepts to include in your teaching:

General

a. Things we ride in or use to carry objects are called "transportation vehicles."

b. Transportation vehicles can be grouped by use on land, on water, or in the air.

c. Transportation vehicles must be kept in good repair.

d. There are safety measures to take when travelling in any transportation vehicle.

e. Briefly discuss how different animals get around. Do they act similar to or different from humans? (Use only if children are ready for this extension.)

f. Check with local travel agents for posters of *transportation vehicles* of many types. Display these in your classroom periodically and have informal discussions from time to time.

Child Involvement

a. Young children use tricycles, wagons, scooters, and other wheeled toys in their play.

b. While young children must depend on adults to take them in motorized vehicles, the children can dramatize using transportation vehicles.

c. In a pile, in a box, or on a table have replicas of numerous modes of transportation. Ask the children to sort them according to their use (land, air, or water). Encourage a discussion about the different modes of transportation and have some replicas that are similar to and different from others.

d. If it is impossible to take the children on field trips to local sites to see transportation vehicles, suggest to the parents some interesting and valuable sites—perhaps at specific times (displays, demonstrations, celebrations).

e. Talk with the children about different occupations and opportunities that are available related to transportation. Provide props (uniforms, hats, badges, and so on), opportunities, and time to understand the roles. Be sure to discuss anti-bias and diversity in occupations.

f. Have the children imitate the sounds made by the various transportation vehicles and ask the other children to guess the vehicle (land, sea, or air).

LAND VEHICLES

General

a. The most common land transportation vehicles are cars, vans, recreation vehicles, trailers, trucks, busses, trains, and motorcycles. (First emphasize the ones most familiar to the children in your classroom. Later introduce other types.)

b. Most land vehicles travel on wheels.

    1. Wheels are round and flat.

    2. Wheels roll.

    3. A wheel turns on an axle, which keeps the wheel from falling off (Althouse and Main, 1975).

c. Most land vehicles have four wheels.

d. People can travel and live in some land vehicles.

e. Land vehicles have motors.

Child Involvement

a. Provide toy land vehicles to be used in block areas. Encourage the play and ideas of the children.

b. Sing songs, do fingerplays, use puzzles, post pictures, read stories, provide books, and stimulate dramatic play related to land vehicles.

c. Talk about the differences between the various kinds of land vehicles (motorhome and a motorcycle, moving van and a family van, school bus and commercial bus).

d. Practice safe land travel (seat belts, plenty of time, quiet voices, maintain speed limit).

e. If field trips are permitted, take a short one to a familiar place. Make a previsit to the site, prepare the children carefully, and provide dramatic play as a follow-up upon your return.

f. If possible, take the children on a bus ride.

g. Ask which children have been in or on the different types of vehicles. Listen to their comments and concerns and then set up some dramatic play.

h. Encourage the children to use safe driving skills and rules when using tricycles, wagons, and other outdoor vehicles. Set up a traffic route, post signs, and have a police officer, if convenient. There could be a car wash, a gas station, motor pool, and repair shop.

i. In the sand or outdoor area, encourage the construction of a town with vehicles and rules.

j. Make maps or use commercial ones with communities drawn on them. Provide cars, people, animals and other props to stimulate dramatic and cooperative play.

k. Use visuals to talk about different community vehicles such as ambulances, police cars, fire engines, and repair vehicles, and how they help us.

l. In the sand or dirt, set up a construction site using various construction vehicles, such as graders, dump trucks, loaders, cranes, and bulldozers. If possible, visit a site where construction is in process.

m. It is possible that some children are (or will be) transported in a school bus. Simulate a bus and let the children practice good bus behavior.

n. Use vehicles with one wheel (wheelbarrow, unicycle), two wheels (bicycle, scooter), three wheels (tricycle, some cars), and four wheels (wagon, cart, buggy, wheelchair).

o. Decorate tricycles, wagons, buggies, and other wheel toys with crepe paper, ribbons, and scarves. Have a parade!

p. Invite children to watch as tricycles, wagons, and other wheel toys are being repaired or assembled.

q. Borrow a child-sized wheelchair. Let the children take turns riding in it and trying to make it go themselves.

r. Have the children imitate how different animals move on land. How are animals and people similar and different in their means of getting from one place to another?

s. Have the children imitate different types of land vehicles. Then play varying music or rhythms and have the children imitate the same vehicles. Does music encourage movement?

AIR VEHICLES

General

a. The most common air transportation vehicles are commercial or private airplanes, hot air balloons, helicopters, and gliders.

b. Most air vehicles have wings.

c. Some air vehicles have jet motors.

d. Some air vehicles are operated by hot air.

e. Air vehicles have special safety features.

f. Most air vehicles travel faster than land or water vehicles.

g. Most air vehicles have wheels.

h. Some air vehicles land in the water.

i. Most air vehicles are noisy.

Child Involvement

a. Obtain junior wings from an airline. Set up chairs to resemble an airplane and suggest the children be pilots, attendants, or other airline workers. Demonstrate how people check into commercial airlines, how their bags are tagged and loaded, and how they retrieve their luggage at their destination.

b. Sing songs, do fingerplays, use puzzles, display pictures, read stories, provide books, and set up dramatic play to stimulate and dramatize children's ideas about air flight.

c. Using large or small blocks, include props related to air flight for dramatic play.

d. Set up an imaginary plane on the playground and encourage the children's participation.

e. Practice air safety by talking about seat belts, parachutes, radio contact, staying seated, and following instructions.

f. Talk about hot air balloons. Use pictures and replicas if a hot air balloon can not be seen.

g. Talk about the differences between air vehicles, such as a helicopter and a passenger plane, or a hot air balloon and a glider.

h. Ask which children have flown in an airplane. Listen to their comments and concerns and then set up some dramatic play. Simulate activities such as boarding, eating, and sitting.

i. Help the children cut out pictures of air vehicles and paste them.

j. Make and fly paper airplanes.

k. Make or use commercial kites. Fly them on days that there is a different amount of wind. How does the wind help them fly?

l. Talk about and show the differences between the wings on birds and the wings on airplanes.

m. Have the children imitate how animals that fly are similar to and different from humans travelling.

n. Have the children pretend to be different air vehicles. Add music or rhythm of different types and have the children imitate the same vehicles but in time with the music.

o. On the playground or large enough space, use a small parachute or sheet. Have the children move it up and down and note the air motion. Place a small toy (stuffed animal, puppet, or ball) on the parachute and try to make it bounce without falling off. Note the force of the parachute as it is waved and how the height of the toy can be changed by the force of the air.

WATER VEHICLES

General
a. The most common water transportation vehicles are boats—freighters, sail, passenger, and motor.

b. Most water vehicles have motors.

c. There are special safety features when travelling on water, including life preservers, where to sit, how to behave, signals, and sounds.

d. Water vehicles travel slower than air or land vehicles.

e. Some water vehicles travel a short distance and some travel a long distance.

f. Some water vehicles are for pleasure (cruises, boating, fishing, water skiing, companionship), and some are for working (commercial fishing, transport goods or people).

g. Most boats are heavy but can float because of buoyancy. Give simple explanations, but provide many opportunities for the children to discover this for themselves.

h. Some commercial equipment can be purchased, rented, or borrowed—consider storage when not in immediate use.

Child Involvement
a. Partially fill a sensory trough or tub with water. Provide boats, water wheels, cups, and so on for enjoyment.

b. Help the children to make boats out of a bar of soap. Make a sail with a toothpick and a triangle of paper.

c. In the sand area, help the children make a waterway. Provide boats and let the fun begin!

d. Sing songs, do fingerplays, post pictures, read stories, provide books, and set out puzzles and other manipulative toys which encourage learning of the concepts of water vehicles.

e. Provide a large box with the side about one foot high. Suggest it be used as a boat.

f. A rubber boat, oars, and life preservers may be obtained from a sporting goods store. Children will develop their own play here. The children might also enjoy seeing equipment that is used under water, such as snorkels, fins, and wet suits.

g. Sometimes it is possible to obtain an old boat for permanent placement

in the play yard. Consider for maintenance and safety having the boat sanded to remove splinters, painted for beauty and comfort, drilled to drain moisture, and covered from animals.

h. Make a boat out of chairs. Provide fishing poles made from dowels, a string, a magnet, and cardboard or paper fish with paper clips attached. Supervision will be necessary to keep lines untangled and poles pointed toward the fish.

i. Sing "Row, row, row your boat" while making the motions and pretending to move the boat at different speeds, with different loads, and with different weather conditions.

j. Practice water safety 1. in the water (swimming), 2. near water, 3. on a water vehicle, 4. alone and with others, and 5. combining a vehicle and sport, such as water skiing.

k. Make pictures of water activities and vehicles either by drawing or cutting and pasting.

l. Ask which children have travelled on water. Listen to their concerns and comments. Set up a dramatic play situation.

m. Talk about the differences between water vehicles, such as motor boat and a sail boat, or a small boat and a large boat.

n. Talk about and let the children practice the principle of buoyancy (things that sink and things that float).

o. Talk about and show how boats are loaded (manually from a small dock; cranes and loaders for large ships).

p. Have the children imitate how water animals are similar to and different from humans in getting from one place to another where large bodies of water are involved.

q. Have the children imitate different types of water vehicles. Add music or rhythm of different types and have them repeat their actions to the music.

r. Talk with the children about river transportation, including barges, houseboats, river boats, and show boats.

REFERENCES

Althouse, R., and Main, C. (1975). **Science experiences for young children: Wheels.** New York: Teachers College Press.

Berliner, D. (1987). **Airplanes of the future.** Minneapolis: Lerner.

Borden, E. J. (1987). The community connection—it works! **Young children,** 42(4), pp. 14–23.

Conquest of the sky. (1985). Chicago: World Books.

Derman-Sparks, L. (1989). **Anti-bias curriculum: Tools for empowering young children.** Washington, DC: National Association for the Education of Young Children.

Eliason, C., and Jenkins, L. (1990). **A practical guide to early childhood curriculum,** 4th ed. Columbus, OH: Merrill.

Fisher, L. E. (1979). **The railroads.** New York: Holiday House.

Herda, D. J. (1982). **Model railroads.** New York: Holiday House.

Herr, J., and Libby, Y. (1990). **Creative resources for the early childhood classroom.** Albany, NY: Delmar.

Hilton, S. (1980). **Getting there: Frontier travel without power.** Philadelphia: The Westminster Press.

Kendall, F. E. (1983). **Diversity in the classroom: A multicultural approach to the education of young children.** New York: Teachers College Press.

Ramsey, P. G. (1982). Multicultural education in early childhood. **Young children, 37,** pp. 13–24.

Rogers, D. L., and Ross, D. D. (1986). Encouraging positive social interaction among young children. **Young children, 41(3),** pp. 12–17.

Saracho, O. M., and Spodek, B. (1983). **Understanding the multicultural experience in early childhood education.** Washington, DC: National Association for the Education of Young Children.

Scarry, H. (1982). **Balloon trip—a sketchbook.** Englewood Cliffs, NJ: Prentice-Hall.

Smith, C.A. (1986). Nurturing kindness through storytelling. **Young children, 41(6),** pp. 46–51.

Trostle, S. L., and Yawkey, T. D. (1990). **Integrated learning activities for young children.** Boston: Allyn & Bacon.

Yawkey, T. D., and Aronin, E. L. (1988). **Activities for career development in early childhood curriculum.** State College, PA. (Copyright transferred to T. D. Yawkey and E. L. Aronin by U. S. Copyright Office.)

Yawkey, T. D., Dank, H. L., and Glosenger, F. I. (1986). **Playing inside and out: How to promote social growth and learning in young children including the developmentally delayed child.** Lancaster, PA: Technomics Publishers.

BOOKS FOR CHILDREN

Arnold, C. (1983). **How do we travel?** New York: Franklin Watts.

Baker, E. (1969). **I want to be a taxi driver.** Chicago: Childrens Press.

Barton, B. (1979). **Wheels.** New York: Crowell.

Behrens, J. (1984). **Sally Ride, astronaut: An American first.** Chicago: Childrens Press.

Bendick, J. (1982). **Airplanes.** New York: Franklin Watts.

Burton, V. L. (1939; 1977). **Mike Mulligan and his steam shovel.** Boston: Houghton Mifflin.

Burton, V. L. (1974). **Katie and the big snow.** Boston: Houghton Mifflin.

Bushy, J. (1984). **The barge boat.** Minneapolis, MN: Carolrhoda Books.

Cameron, E. (1970). **The big book of real trucks.** New York: Grosset & Dunlap.

Chapman, C. (1967). **Wings and wheels.** Niles, IL: Whitman.

Chlad, D. (1983). **When I ride in a car.** Chicago: Childrens Press.

Clymer, El. (1965). **Wheels.** New York: Holt, Rinehart & Winston.

Coombs, C. I. (1963). **Wheels, wings and water.** Cleveland: World.

Crews, D. (1978). **Freight train.** New York: Greenwillow.

Crews, D. (1980). **Truck.** New York: Greenwillow.

Dixon, M. (1983). **On the road.** New York: The Bookwright Press.

Fisher, A. (1973). **Going places.** Glendale, CA: Bowmar.

Fitzgerald, F. (1980). **Little wheels, big wheels.** New York: Golden Press.

Flack, M. (1977). **The story of Ping.** New York: Viking.

Geis, D. (1987). **Rattle-rattle dump truck.** Los Angeles: Price/Stern/Sloan.

Gibbons, G. (1985). **Fill it up! All about service stations.** New York: Crowell.

Gibbons, G. (1975). **Willy and his wagon wheel.** Englewood Cliffs, NJ: Prentice Hall.

Green, C. (1958). **I want to be a truck driver.** Chicago: Childrens Press.

Greene, C. B. (1978). **Policemen and firemen: What do they do?** New York: Harper.

Greene, C. B. (1967). **Truck drivers: What do they do?** New York: Harper.

Gunsten, B. (1978). **Canal and river transport.** New York: Macmillan Education Limited.

Hartford, J. (1986). **Steamboat in a cornfield.** New York: Crown Publishing.

Henroid, L. (1982). **Grandma's wheelchair.** Niles, IL: Whitman.

Hoban, T. (1983). **Round and round and round.** New York: Greenwillow Books.

Holl, A. (1970). **ABC of cars, trucks, and machines.** New York: McGraw-Hill.

Hooker, Y. (1978). **Wheels go round.** New York: Grosset & Dunlap.

Kehoe, M. (1982). **Road closed.** Minneapolis: Carolrhoda Books.

Kessler, E., and Kessler, L. (1964). **The big red bus.** Garden City, NY: Doubleday.

Kunhardt, E. T. (1985). **The taxi book.** New York: Golden Books.

Oppenheim, J. (1971). **Have you seen boats?** Reading, MA: Addison-Wesley.

Oppenheim, J. (1969). **Have you seen roads?** Reading, MA: Addison-Wesley.

Oxenbury, H. (1983). **The car trip.** New York: Dutton.

Petersham, M., and Petersham, M. (1973). **The box with red wheels.** New York: Macmillan.

Petrie, C. (1987). **Joshua James likes trucks.** Chicago: Childrens Press.

Piper, W. (1980). **The little engine that could.** New York: Platt & Munk.

Posell, E. (1957). **The true book of transportation.** Chicago: Childrens Press.

Provensen, A., and Provensen, M. (1983). **The glorious flight.** New York: Viking.

Rockwell, A. (1988). **Trains.** New York: Dutton.

Rockwell, A. (1986). **Things that go.** New York: Dutton.

Rockwell, A. (1986). **Fire engines.** New York: Dutton.

Rockwell, A. (1982). **Boats.** New York: Dutton.

Ross, P., and Ross, J. (1981). **Your first airplane trip.** New York: Lothrop, Lee & Shepard.

Sandak, C. R. (1984). **Roads.** New York: Franklin Watts.

Scarry, R. (1974). **Cars, trucks, things that go.** New York: Golden.

Scarry, R. (1974). **Richard Scarry's cars and trucks and things that go.** New York: Western.

Shapp, M., and Shapp, C. (1962). **Let's find out about wheels.** New York: Franklin Watts.

Silver, R. (1983). **David's first bicycle.** New York: Golden Press.

Sis, P. (1988). **Waving.** New York: Greenwillow.

Slobodkina, E. (1960). **Moving day for the Middlemans.** New York: Abelard-Schuman.

Yepsen, R. (1983). **Train talk.** New York: Pantheon Books.

Young, M. (1967). **If I drove a truck.** New York: Lothrop, Lee & Shepard.

Zaffo, G. (1968). **Airplanes and trucks and trains; fire engines; boats and ships;**

and building and wrecking machines.
New York: Grosset & Dunlap.

Zaffo, G. (1950). **The big book of real
trains.** New York: Grosset & Dunlap.

Zaffo, G. (1950). **The big book of real
trucks.** New York: Grosset & Dunlap.

Zeck, P., and Zeck, J. (1982). **Mississippi
sternwheelers.** Minneapolis: Carolrhoda
Books.

Zion, G. (1957). **Dear garbage man.** New
York: Harper.

RECORD SOURCES

(See Appendix C or preschool educational
catalogues.)

The small singer. Bowmar-Noble. Al-
bum 1.

More singing fun. Bowmar-Noble. Al-
bum 1.

Hopping around from place to place. Educational Activities.

Water

CONCEPTS AND ACTIVITIES

Water is a good medium for children to use because it:

- releases tension
- is readily accessible, inexpensive, and easily cared for
- stimulates curiosity and interest
- teaches about the properties of water
- provides great social interaction
- has a soothing effect
- encourages action, interaction, and reaction
- can be used spontaneously or planned
- can be combined with other materials and activities

If water is to be used in conjunction with another activity, the teacher should place the activity near the water source. If water is to be used in a specific place and activity only, the teacher must make sure the instructions are clear to the children. ("Sometimes you use water in the house, but today it will only be used in the sensory table or at the sink.")

Following are but a few of the ways water can enrich the lives of children:

a. For snack or lunch prepare food that absorbs water, such as rice or macaroni. Make soup.

b. Talk with the children about water safety (swimming, drinking, boating, wading, bathtubs, hoses, and so on).

c. Children enjoy a painting experience, but paint may not be desirable. Water can give this same kind of experience by using a bucket of clear water and a large paint brush on large boxes, metal surfaces, the cement, and other areas that water will not damage. Point out to the children how water looks on different surfaces and how it dries differently. Introduce the concept of evaporation and let the children practice it.

d. Blowing bubbles out of doors is a delightful experience for children. Let them help make the solution (½ c liquid detergent, 2 quarts of warm water, and 1½ T glycerine). Make different sized wands out of pipe cleaners, metal jar rings, or items that have a band.

e. During warm weather, have a hose running in the sand area or encourage the children to water the shrubbery and flowers with a watering can they can fill frequently.

f. Provide a wading pool when appropriate.

g. Have a hose running down the slide, but provide good supervision of the activity.

h. Cut large tires in half and fill them with water. Provide boats and floating objects.

i. On a science table or in a container nearby have different items. Let the children explore to see which items float, and which ones sink. Compare the objects that float and sink for likenesses and differences.

j. Provide tubs of water and items to wash. Have a small drying rack where objects can be placed to dry. Note which items dry faster than others (use different kinds of fabric, paper towels, sponges, and so on).

k. Using plastic squeeze bottles, let the children squirt at a target.

l. Have toys and water where children will be out of the traffic pattern and where clean-up can be easily done.

m. Provide household props (dolls, dishes, and so on) that the children can wash and rewash.

n. Provide materials and space for the children to help mix and make creative materials, such as mixing paint for the easel or other activities.

o. Make sure that clean-up materials are readily available and that they include tubs of water, sponges and necessary materials to complete the particular type of clean-up. Clean-up can be as fun as the activity—imagine the excitement of cleaning up fingerpaint made from soap flakes, or wiping up and wringing excess water from sponges!

p. Make it possible for the children to water plants indoors and to help care for animals when possible.

q. Talk with the children about the importance of personal cleanliness. Have individual tooth brushes, combs, brushes, and hand care items readily available. Teach the children the necessity of washing their hands carefully

after using the toilet and before handling food.

r. Point out to the children how water is a part of daily living for humans, animals, and plants. Note the changes in weather and the different forms of water: snow, rain, ice, hail, fog. Relate teaching to the immediate environment.

s. In a water trough, place measuring cups, spoons, and funnels so the children can explore and experiment.

t. Integrate other areas of the curriculum with water through singing songs, doing fingerplays, displaying pictures, reading stories, using puzzles, and so on

u. Introduce new terms and characteristics of water and let the children practice the concepts (''recycling'' using a water wheel, ''buoyancy'' using things that float or sink, ''weight'' through lifting containers filled with water, and so on).

v. Encourage the children to use water in cleaning up the room (washing tables, chairs, and toys), and on the playground (washing trikes, toys, paths, play areas).

w. On a rainy or snowy day, put some containers outside to catch the moisture. Bring containers inside and use the water for classroom activities.

x. If convenient, visit a nearby water source—lake, river, fountain, ocean, or storage tank.

y. Observe the playground being watered and cared for, or watch water trucks washing streets.

z. Talk about proper clothing in different types of weather. Why do we wear rubber or plastic boots?

aa. Take a nature walk following a rain storm. Note the trees and leaves, the cement, how fresh the air smells, if there are any worms or insects out now.

bb. Show the children how water takes the form of the containers it is in. Provide different shaped containers and give the children plenty of time to try this for themselves.

cc. Give the children opportunities to measure and pour. At snack, small containers should be provided and the children encouraged to pour a beverage for themselves.

dd. Water can be changed by adding heat (to make steam) or cold (to make ice). Try both of these situations with the children present. Talk about simple uses of steam and ice. If possible, use ice to make something for snack or lunch (beverage, gelatin, or ice cream).

ee. Provide containers of crushed and block ice. Call attention to both containers over a period of time. Note that the crushed ice melts faster.

ff. Using different kinds of surfaces (fabric, plastic, wood, and metal), note what the water does to each. Is it absorbed or repelled? How can this information assist children in the home or classroom?

gg. Encourage the children to stir different food products into water (salt, sugar in different forms, honey, flour, corn starch, liquid or solid oil, punch powder, and so on). Talk with the children about how easily the substances combine. Then stir other items into water, such as paint, dirt, sand, beans, or gravel. Do they combine as easily? How can we use food products combined with water and how can we use

other substances combined with water? (Introduce concept of dissolving and let the children practice it.)

hh. Go on a walk or take a pretend camping trip in which you must take water with you. How do you package, carry, and use the water?

ii. In the sand or appropriate area, attach a water pump for the children's drinking or playing uses.

jj. Do some simple experiments with siphons, using straws.

kk. Visit a fire station or have a fire fighter come into the classroom. Talk about clothing, vehicles, safety, and water.

ll. Invite a mother to bring a baby to class. Ask her to bathe and feed the baby in the presence of the children.

mm. Talk about animals that live in water. Visit some if possible, or have a goldfish in the classroom.

nn. Talk about or observe activities relying on water, such as fishing, logging, shipping, or boating.

oo. Relate water to weather and seasons.

pp. Talk with the children about the plumbing in the classroom and on the playground.

qq. Briefly talk about the local rainfall or moisture content. Also discuss the steps necessary for water conservation—in your area or elsewhere if it interests the children.

rr. ''Fill dishpans with water and set out clear detergent bottles, spoons, cups, and bowls. Try to include a clear plastic funnel. Watch how water, a *liquid* at room temperature, always takes the shape of its container. Get some ice. Does it take the shape of its container? Not as a *solid*. What if you let it melt? Boil water in a teakettle and you may be able to see water *vapor* escape as steam. Carefully collect the vapor on a shiny metal pot lid, making sure that children's hands don't come between the kettle and the lid—even when you can't see the vapor, it's more than hot enough to burn!" (Ziemer, 1987)

ss. If you live in an area where snow falls, during one of the storms make some small snowmen (12 to 15 inches will do) and place them in a freezer. When spring or summer comes, bring out the snowmen and let the children watch them melt. Relate the concepts of how snow in the mountains melts to give water to the valleys. (See Zion, *The Summer Snowman* in references at the end of this chapter.)

tt. Talk about how different animals use water. Note that some animals avoid water except for drinking while other animals live in the water continuously or frequently.

REFERENCES

Althouse, R. (1988). **Investigating science with young children.** New York: Teachers College, Columbia University.

Althouse, R., and Main, C. (1975). **Science experiences for young children: Water.** New York: Teachers College Press.

Branley, F. M. (1963). **Rain and hail.** New York: Crowell.

Carin, A. A., and Sund, R. B. (1980, 1985). **Discovery activities for elementary science.** Columbus, OH: Merrill.

Dempsey, M., and Sheehan, A. (eds.) (1970). **Water.** New York: World Publishing.

Dickenson, J. (1983). **Wonders of water.** Mahwah, NJ: Troll Associates (paperback).

Donalson-Sams, M. (1988). Surface tension: The ways of water. **Science and children,** Nov./Dec., pp. 26–28.

Eliason, C., and Jenkins, L. (1990). **A practical guide to early childhood curriculum,** 4th ed. Columbus, OH: Merrill.

Forman, G. E., and Kuschner, D. (1983). **The child's construction of knowledge.** Washington, DC: National Association for the Education of Young Children.

Forman, G. E., and Hill, F. (1980). **Constructive play: Applying Piaget in the preschool.** Menlo Park, CA: Wadsworth.

Fowlkes, M. A. (1985). Funnels and tunnels. **Science and Children,** March, pp. 28–29.

Harlan, J. (1988). **Science experiences for the early childhood years,** 4th ed. Columbus, OH: Merrill.

Harlan, J. D. (1975). From curiosity to concepts; from concepts to curiosity—science experiences in the preschool. **Young children,** 30, pp. 249–255.

Herr, J., and Libby, Y. (1990). **Creative resources for the early childhood classroom.** Albany, NY: Delmar.

Kotar, M. (1988). Firsthand experiences—firsthand knowledge. **Science and children,** 25(8), p. 40.

Moore, J. E., and Evans, J. (1987). **Simple science experiments: Resource book.** Monterey, CA: The Evan-Moor Corp.

Myers, B. K., and Maurer, K. (1987). Teaching with less talking: Learning centers in the kindergarten. **Young children** 42(5), pp. 20–27.

Ziemer, M. (1987). Science and the early childhood curriculum: One thing leads to another. **Young children,** Sept., pp. 44–51.

Zubrowski, B. (1981). **Messing around with water pumps and syphons.** Boston: Little, Brown & Co.

BOOKS FOR CHILDREN

Alexander, M. (1977). **No ducks in our bathtub.** New York: Dial.

Amos, W. H. (1984). **Exploring the seashore.** Washington, DC: National Geographic Society.

Amos, W. H. (1981). **Life in ponds and streams.** Washington, DC: National Geographic Society.

Arvetis, C., and Palmer, C. (1983). **Why does it float?** Chicago: Rand McNally.

Bains, R. (1985). **Water.** Mahwah, NJ: Troll Associates.

Blocksma, M. (1987). **Rub-a-dub-dub-what's in the tub?** Chicago: Childrens Press.

Brewer, M. (1976). **What floats?** Chicago: Childrens Press.

Bright, R. (1959). **My red umbrella.** New York: Wm. Morrow.

Brooks, R. (1976). **Annie's rainbow.** New York: Bradbury Press.

Burton, V. L. (1943). **Katy and the big snow.** Boston: Houghton Mifflin.

Busch, P. (1971). **Walk in the snow.** Philadelphia: Lippincott.

Cole, S. (1985). **When the tide is low.** New York: Lothrop, Lee & Shepard.

Cook, B. (1956). **The little fish that got away.** Reading, MA: Addison-Wesley.

Cristini, E., and Puricelli, L. (1984). **In the pond.** Saxonville, MA: Picture Book Studio.

Delgado, E. (1986). **Alex's adventures at the beach.** New York: Derrydale Books.

Fitzsimmons, C. (1987). **My first fishes and other water life: A pop-up field guide.** New York: Harper.

Flack, M. (1970). **The story of Ping.** New York: Viking.

Flack, M. (1946). **The boats on the river.** New York: Viking.

Freeman, M. (1970). **Do you know about water?** New York: Random House.

Freeman, D. (1961). **Come again, pelican.** New York: Viking.

Friskey, M. (1965). **Seven diving ducks.** Chicago: Childrens Press.

Gans, R. (1972). **Water for dinosaurs and you.** New York: Crowell.

Goldin, A. (1974). **Ducks don't get wet.** New York: Crowell.

Holl, A. (1965). **The rain puddle.** New York: Lothrop, Lee & Shephard.

Hooker, Y. (1981). **Splish, splash!.** New York: Gosset & Dunlap.

Jonas, A. (1987). **Reflections.** New York: Greenwillow.

Kalan, R. (1978). **Rain.** New York: Greenwillow Books.

Keats, E. J. (1962). **The snowy day.** New York: Viking.

Knotts, H. (1975). **Follow the brook.** New York: Harper.

Kuskin, K. (1957). **James and the rain.** New York: Harper.

Lionni, L. (1970). **Fish is fish.** New York: Pantheon.

MacDonald, G. (1964). **The little island.** New York: Doubleday.

McCloskey, R. (1952). **One morning in Maine.** New York: Viking.

McCloskey, R. (1957). **Time of wonder.** New York: Viking.

McGovern, A. (1971). **Stone soup.** New York: Scholastic.

McMillan, B. (1988). **Dry or wet?** New York: Lothrop, Lee & Shepard.

Milgrom, H. (1970). **ABC science experiments.** New York: Macmillan.

Milne, A. A. (1961). **Winnie-the-pooh.** New York: Dutton, Chapter 9.

Peters, L. W. (1988). **The sun, the wind, and the rain.** New York: Holt, Rinehart, & Winston.

Podendorf, I. (1954). **The true book of science experiments.** Chicago: Childrens Press.

Raffi. (1987). **Down by the bay.** New York: Crown Pub.

Reidel, M. (1981). **From ice to rain.** Minneapolis: Carolrhoda.

Sabin, F. (1982). **Wonders of the pond.** New York: Troll Associates.

Sargent, S., and Wirl, D. A. (1983). **My favorite place.** Nashville, TN: Abingdon Press.

Schulevitz, U. (1969). **Rain rain river.** New York: Farrar & Straus.

Shapp, M., and Shapp, C. (1962). **Let's find out about water.** New York: Franklin Watts.

Shartall, L. (1963). **Davey's first boat.** New York: Wm. Morrow.

Simon, S. (1969). **Wet and dry.** New York: McGraw-Hill.

Skofield, J. (1984). **All wet! All wet!** New York: Harper.

Spier, P. (1982). **Peter Spier's rain.** New York: Doubleday.

Stone, L. M. (1983). **Pond life.** Chicago: Childrens Press.

Tresselt, A. (1970). **The beaver pond.** New York: Lothrop, Lee & Shepard.

Tresselt, A. (1965). **Hide and seek fog.** New York: Lothrop, Lee & Shepard.

Tresselt, A. (1947). **White snow, bright snow.** New York: Lothrop, Lee & Shepard.

Tresselt, A. (1946). **Rain drops splash!** New York: Lothrop, Lee & Shepard.

Waterton, B. (1980). **A salmon for Simon.** New York: Antheneum.

Woodard, C. (1968). **The wet walk.** Philadelphia: Fortress Press.

Wyler, P. (1986). **Science fun with toy boats and planes.** New York: Julian Messner.

Yashima, T. (1958). **Umbrella.** New York: Viking.

Zion, G. (1976). **The plant sitter.** New York: Harper.

Zion, G. (1956). **Really spring!** New York: Harper.

Zion, G. (1955) **The summer snowman.** New York: Harper.

Weather

CONCEPTS AND ACTIVITIES

It is important to promote weather concepts related to where the children reside. Talking about the present conditions and season is much more valuable to them than trying to teach about all kinds of weather and the four seasons. Trying to teach them about the four seasons in four consecutive days is overwhelming to most young children. Teaching the name of the season as it occurs is more practical.

As children get older, they like to know about weather in other places; however, to understand what snow is like when the child lives in a hot climate or learning about the long sunny periods in Alaska when the child does not experience them is almost unbelievable.

Some activities depend upon different types of weather, such as entertainment, field trips, leisure, and sporting events. Children need help understanding that even though an important event is planned, it can depend as much upon weather as upon other things.

The following activities can help children learn about weather in the classroom:

a. Talk about and show the children the appropriate kinds of clothing for their environment. Does clothing worn in your area change with seasons? Older children can relate to clothing worn in other environments.

b. Talk about occupations related to the weather in your environment. Are they seasonal, for example, agricultural or sports oriented? Are they dependent upon hot or cold weather?

c. Make a wind sock or notice the movement of a flag to determine if the wind is blowing and from which direction. Help the children make windmills, wind chimes, or simple pinwheels. Talk about ways the wind helps people (energy from windmills, moving sail boats, drying clothes, grinding grain, and so on).

d. Each day note the weather and post a sun for sunny, clouds for cloudy, rain drops for rainy, and so on. Help the children to become aware of the daily weather.

e. Talk about how animals in your area prepare for different types of weather.

f. People do different things in different types of weather and during different seasons. How does their clothing change? How prominent are the seasons where you live?

g. Some children are frightened by storms and especially by lightening and thunder. Find a simple way to explain storms without being dramatic or teaching false concepts.

h. Notice and talk about the clouds. Read the story "It looked like spilt milk" by Shaw (See Books for Children).

i. Encourage the children to make "cloud" pictures by pasting cotton balls on blue paper, gray and white pieces of paper on either gray or blue paper, or drawing with white chalk on a piece of paper.

j. Sing songs, do fingerplays, provide puzzles, read stories, and display pictures and books about different kinds of weather.

k. Set up outdoor activities when weather permits. Avoid forcing outdoor play when weather is unusually hot or cold.

l. Provide creative art materials that coincide with the season so the children can make collages (blossoms in spring, leaves in spring or fall, snow pictures in winter).

m. Have some large cardboard boys and girls with clothing to fit them, or use commercial kits like "We Dress for the Weather" (see preschool educational catalogues). Watch and listen as the children dress and undress the figures.

n. Have a suitcase with clothing to be worn in two different seasons (winter and summer, for example). Tell the children you are packing for a trip, why you are going, and that you want them to help you decide what to take. After packing, discuss why you would or would not take different items. Listen carefully to the children's ideas.

o. Use spontaneous and planned experiences with poetry to learn about weather (A. A. Milne's *Now we are six*, Robert L. Stevenson's *A child's garden of verses*, and anthologies like *Poems children will sit still for*, and many others).

p. Talk about and celebrate holidays when they occur as long as the plans are based on developmentally appropriate knowledge, skills, and experiences of the children involved.

q. Take nature walks at different times of the year. Note the characteristic of the present season and weather (spring planting and new life; fall harvesting).

r. If the situation presents itself, call the children's attention to current weather (how the wind is blowing, the color changes in the sky, the rain on the windows and in puddles, rainbows in the sky, and so on).

s. If you are in an area where it snows, bring some snow inside the classroom. Encourage the children to look at the flakes with a magnifying glass and to check periodically to see what is happening and how fast the snow melts.

t. Observe icicles hanging from the building. Note the different shapes. Bring one into the classroom for the children to handle and watch it melt. Freeze some ice for classroom purposes (ice pack for injuries, cubes for beverages, ice for making ice cream, and so on).

REFERENCES

Berger, M. (1970). **Storms.** New York: Coward-McCann.

Bonsall, G. (1960). **How and why wonder book of weather.** New York: Grosset & Dunlap.

Bowden, M. (1989). **Nature for the very young: A handbook of indoor and outdoor activities.** New York: John Wiley & Sons.

Eliason, C., and Jenkins, L. (1990). **A practical guide to early childhood curriculum.** Columbus, OH: Merrill.

Knight, M. E., and Graham, T. L. (1984). What's so hard about teaching science? **Day Care and Early Education,** Winter, pp. 14–16.

Hackett, J. K., Moyer, R. H., and Adams, D. K. (1989). **Merrill science: A natural in your classroom.** Columbus, OH: Merrill.

Harlan, J. (1988). **Science experiences for the early childhood years,** 4th ed. Columbus, OH: Merrill.

Herr, J., and Libby, Y. (1990). **Creative resources for the early childhood classroom.** Albany, NY: Delmar.

Lambert, D., and Hardy, R. (1984). **Weather and its work.** London, England: Orbis Publishing Ltd.

Trostle, S. L., and Yawkey, T. D. (1990). **Integrated learning activities for young children.** Boston: Allyn & Bacon.

BOOKS FOR CHILDREN

Allington, R. (1981). **Autumn.** Milwaukee, WI: Raintree Children's Books.

Andrews, J. (1986). **Very last first time.** New York: Antheneum.

Arvetis, C. (1987). **Why do animals sleep through winter?** Chicago: Childrens Press.

Bahr, R. (1982). **Blizzard at the zoo.** New York: Lothrop, Lee, & Shepard.

Bauer, C. F. (1986). **Snow day stories and poems.** Philadelphia: Lippincott.

Blegvad, L. (1987). **Rainy Date Kate.** New York: Market K. McElderry Books.

Borden, L. (1989). **Caps, hats, socks, and mittens.** New York: Scholastic.

Brandt, K. (1982). **What makes it rain?** Mahwah, NJ: Troll Associates.

Branley, F. M. (1986). **Snow is falling: A let's read and find out science book.** New York: Crowell.

Branley, F. M. (1975). **Flash, crash, rumble and roll.** New York: Crowell.

Branley, F. M. (1963). **Snow is falling.** New York: Crowell.

Broekel, R. (1982). **Storms.** Chicago: Childrens Press.

Brooks, R. (1976). **Annie's rainbow.** New York: Bradbury.

Brown, M. W. (1976). **The winter noisy book.** New York: Harper.

Burton, V. L. (1978). **The little house.** Boston: Houghton Mifflin.

Busch, P. (1971). **A walk in the snow.** Philadelphia: Lippincott.

Cartwright, S. (1971). **Why can't you see the wind?** New York: Wonder Books.

Cartwright, S. (1974). **Sunlight.** New York: Coward, McCann & Geohegan.

Cole, S. (1985). **When the tide is low.** New York: Lothrop, Lee & Shepard.

Craig, J. (1977). **Questions and answers about the weather.** New York: Scholastic Book Services.

Delgado, E. (1986). **Alex's adventures at the beach.** New York: Drysdale Books.

Delton, J. (1982). **A walk on a snowy night.** New York: Harper.

de Paola, T. A. (1977). **Four stories for four seasons.** Englewood Cliffs, NJ: Prentice-Hall.

de Paola, T. A. (1975). **The cloud book.** New York: Holiday House.

Duvoisin, R. (1956). **The house of four seasons.** New York: Lothrop, Lee, & Shepard.

Ets, M. H. (1963). **Gilberto and the wind.** New York: Viking.

Fisher, A. (1973). **Now that days are cooler.** Glendale, CA: Bowmar.

Florian, D. (1987). **A winter day.** New York: Greenwillow.

Freeman, D. (1966). **A rainbow of my own.** New York: Viking.

Garelick, M. (1961). **Where does the butterfly go when it rains?** New York: Scholastic.

Gibbons, G. (1983). **Sun up, sun down.** New York: Harcourt Brace Jovanovich.

Goffstein, M. B. (1986). **Our snowman.** New York: Harper.

Goudy, A. (1961). **The day we saw the sun come up.** New York: Scribner's Sons.

Green, S. (1987). **Season.** New York: Doubleday.

Gundersheimer, K. (1982). **Happy winter.** New York: Harper & Row.

Hader, B., and Hader, E. (1972). **The big snow.** New York: Macmillan.

Hirschi, R. (1990). **Spring.** Cobblehill.

Hirschi, R. (1990). **Winter.** Cobblehill.

Johnson, C. (1979). **Time for spring.** New York: Harper.

Kalan, R. (1978). **Rain.** New York: Greenwillow.

Keats, E. J. (1973). **Over in the meadow.** New York: Macmillan.

Keats, E. J. (1962). **The snowy day.** New York: Viking.

Kessler, E., and Kessler, L. (1973). **Slush, slush.** New York: Parents Magazine Press.

Kroll, S. (1987). **I love spring.** New York: Holiday.

Lambert, D. (1983). **Weather.** New York: Watts.

Lowery, L. (1969). **Clouds, rain, clouds again.** New York: Golden Press.

McCully, E. A. (1985). **First snow.** New York: Harper.

McNaughton, C. (1984). **Autumn.** New York: Dial.

McNaughton, C. (1984). **Summer.** New York: Dial.

Moncure, J. (1977). **What causes it? A beginning book about weather.** Elgin, IL: The Child's World.

Moncure, J. (1975). **Spring is here.** Elgin, IL: Child's World.

Morgan, A. (1985). **Sadie and the snowman.** New York: Scholastic.

Parker, B. (1966). **Fall is here.** New York: Harper.

Parsons, E. (1971). **Rainy day together.** New York: Harper.

Pearson, S. (1988). **My favorite time of year.** New York: Harper & Row.

Rockwell, A., and Rockwell, H. (1987). **The first snowfall.** New York: Macmillan.

Ryder, J. (1979). **Fog in the meadow.** New York: Harper.

Santery, L. (1983). **Autumn—Discovering the seasons.** Mahwah, NJ: Troll Associates.

Santery, L. (1983). **Summer—Discovering the seasons.** Mahwah, NJ: Troll Associates.

Santery, L. (1983). **Winter—Discovering the seasons.** Mahwah, NJ: Troll Associates.

Schulevitz, U. (1969). **Rain, rain, rivers.** New York: Farrar, Straus, & Giroux.

Selsam, M., and Hunt, J. (1989). **Keep looking.** New York: Macmillan.

Shaw, C. (1947). **It looked like spilt milk.** New York: Harper.

Spier, P. (1982). **Peter Spier's rain.** New York: Doubleday.

Szilagyi, M. (1985). **Thunderstorm.** New York: Bradbury.

Tresselt, A. (1965). **Hide and seek fog.** New York: Lothrop, Lee & Shepard.

Tresselt, A. (1947, 1969). **White snow, bright snow.** New York: Lothrop, Lee & Shepard.

Whitby, J. (1984a). **Emma and grandpa (1) (January, February, March).** Essex, England: Longman.

Whitby J. (1984b). **Emma and grandpa (2) (April, May, June).** Essex, England: Longman.

Whitby J. (1984c). **Emma and grandpa (3) (July, August, September).** Essex, England: Longman.

Whitby J. (1984d). **Emma and grandpa (4) (October, November, December).** Essex, England: Longman.

Wildsmith, B. (1980). **Seasons.** New York: Oxford University Press.

Yashima, T. (1958). **Umbrella.** New York: Viking.

Zion, G. (1956). **Really spring.** New York: Harper.

Zion, G. (1955). **The summer snowman.** New York: Harper.

Zolotow, C. (1983). **Summer is . . .** New York: Crowell Jr. Books.

Zolotow, C. (1975). **When the wind stops.** New York: Harper.

RECORD SOURCES

(See Appendix C or preschool educational catalogues.)

Bowman-Noble. **More singing fun. The small singer.**

Jenkins, E. **Seasons for singing.**

Lyons Publishers. **All about spring.**

Melody House Records. **Raindrops.**

Palmer, Hap. **Modern tunes for rhythm and instruments.**

Wood, L. **Springtime walk.**

Appendix A

TWO-YEAR-OLDS

SOCIAL-EMOTIONAL DEVELOPMENT

Social

- Is unable to share—takes toys from others
- Engages in solitary play—ignores or watches others
- Behaves negatively at times—ignores some requests
- Seeks attention
- Expresses some fears
- Tries to verbalize feelings
- Sees others as barrier, but begins to see others' rights
- Enjoys small-group activities
- Imitates others
- Is self-involved, curious, energetic, explorative
- Begins dramatic play and games
- Likes to do things for herself

Emotional

- May display aggressive behavior
- Has mood shifts
- Shows pride in creations
- Shows empathy
- Has a strong sense of self—domineering, self-assertive
- Wants independence
- Is learning to trust parents and others
- May express feelings of jealousy
- Easily distracted
- Is impatient, impulsive and egocentric
- Has outbursts usually due to fatigue and hunger

INTELLECTUAL DEVELOPMENT

Language

- Has a speaking vocabulary of about 200 words
- Uses adjectives, adverbs and 2- or 3-word sentences
- Uses pronouns, past and future tense with errors
- Talks to self and toys
- Asserts independence—"me," "no"
- Shows and names objects
- Answers "yes/no" questions
- Can follow two commands
- Enjoys short stories and conversations

Cognitive

- Learns and names some colors
- Likes to count rote numbers or objects—mostly inaccurate
- Explores and learns through senses and by "doing"
- Follows simple requests
- Understands more than can express
- Beginning of cause and effect

PHYSICAL DEVELOPMENT

Fine Motor

- Has uncoordinated small-muscle control
- Can use peg boards, snap beads, crayons, paintbrushes
- Uses fingers and thumb in scooping motions
- Can complete simple puzzle with few pieces
- Turns pages in a book singly
- Tries drawing and coloring
- Enjoys simple finger play games
- Pokes fingers in openings

Gross Motor

- Tries riding a wheel toy
- Is clumsy in balance
- Stands and walks on tip toes
- Jumps in place
- Tries to alternate feet when climbing stairs
- Runs awkwardly
- Uses whole arm or whole leg motions
- Gets easily fatigued
- Is active or constantly on the move
- Enjoys musical activities, dancing, and moving
- Helps dress and undress self—undressing is easier
- Is developing hand-eye coordination
- Uses large strokes when painting or drawing
- Feeds self but is somewhat messy
- Can walk on a low balance beam

THREE-YEAR-OLDS

SOCIAL-EMOTIONAL DEVELOPMENT

Social

- May have short interest span, if uninterested
- Shows more independence, self-reliance, and assurance
- Can share easier, but it is still difficult
- Plays in small group—some parallel play
- Begins to take turns
- Is a "do-er"
- Likes to relive babyhood
- Does simple chores
- Enjoys dramatic play
- Enjoys finer plays, songs, and other activities
- Makes friends, but of short duration
- Plays with children of both sexes

Emotional

- Begins to test limits set by others
- Is egocentric
- Learns to make choices between two alternatives
- Depends on family members to provide sex role models, esteem, sense of security, values, and behavior control
- Likes to be near family or familiar people
- Anxious to please adults
- Expresses both positive and negative feelings
- Cries easily
- Uses "no" frequently
- Develops some independence and self-reliance
- Needs approval, encouragement, and support
- Needs guidelines and limits
- May strike out if thwarted or afraid—needs feelings defined
- Wants security

INTELLECTUAL DEVELOPMENT

Language

- Asks questions: how, what, when, and why
- Uses verbs and adverbs; articulation and grammar are immature
- Has limited, functional vocabulary
- Is developing hearing and sound discrimination
- Likes special words: secret, surprise
- Begins to use prepositions correctly
- Follows simple directions—use them sparingly
- Learns rote counting and some letters
- Enjoys talking; experiments with new words and sounds
- Enjoys short and simple stories, repetition, and surprise
- Talks as he acts; frequently a monologue
- Uses physical means to communicate (hits, takes, bites)

Cognitive

- Differentiates slightly between truth and make-believe
- Understands some pronouns
- Understands simple concepts, such as smaller/larger
- Begins to generalize from one situation to another
- Frequently has a short attention span
- Cannot deal with abstract ideas
- Is curious and inquisitive
- Misconstrues information and develops misunderstandings

PHYSICAL DEVELOPMENT

Fine Motor

- Cuts sharp, jagged lines with scissors
- Pastes with uncertainty
- Can pour from a pitcher
- Draws and colors crudely
- Constructs puzzles with more pieces than 2-year-old
- Holds drawing and writing implements awkwardly
- Can use fingers and thumb to pick up small objects
- Can string beads or objects; uses sewing cards
- Can use a knife to spread soft food
- Likes to do finger plays, songs with actions

Gross Motor

- Can catch a large ball
- Throws a ball (underhand)
- Does a somersault
- Rides a wheeled-toy (tricycle, wagon)
- Runs, walks, jumps, and moves faster (likes music)
- Hops on one foot
- Alternates feet when climbing stairs
- Has unstable coordination
- Advances faster in gross motor than fine motor development
- Can dress and undress self easier
- Needs to interpret world through body movement
- Needs practice with hand-eye coordination—expect awkwardness and messiness

FOUR-YEAR-OLDS

SOCIAL-EMOTIONAL DEVELOPMENT

Social

- Wants to be independent
- Enjoys group (cooperative) play; loves having a friend
- Is learning cooperation and sharing
- Bases friendships on shared activities
- Needs and seeks approval of friends—plays longer together
- Enjoys humorous stories; has a bubbling humor
- Creates and continues dramatic play; discusses roles, rules, and responsibilities
- Is enthusiastic and energetic; shows off
- Tests adult limits
- Develops qualities of leadership
- Is a tattletale
- Is interested in situations outside the immediate family
- Is highly competitive

Emotional

- Is assertive, boastful
- Shows off to gain attention
- Expresses displeasure loudly or aggressively
- Includes or excludes children according to activity
- Shows pride in achievement
- Expresses caring behavior toward others
- Has strong home and family feelings
- Begins to develop a sense of humor
- Is beginning to distinguish between right and wrong
- Uses verbal more than physical behavior to solve problems
- May be bossy, impolite, stubborn *or* cooperative and friendly
- May have an imaginary companion (human or animal)
- Is sometimes physically or verbally aggressive

INTELLECTUAL DEVELOPMENT

Language

- Shows great strides in quantity, quality and use of words
- Increases vocabulary by 1,200 to 1,500 words
- Challenges adults by asking questions, needs more supervision, and tests limits
- Uses language to solve problems more than physical means
- Increases in language; likes to talk; asks why and how questions, then listens to answers
- Shows more interest in books and printed word—likes some stories repeated frequently
- Begins to identify letters
- Exaggerates when practicing new words; loves silly words
- Repeats words which have emotional connotation (for adults)
- Enjoys playing with words (rhyming, repeating)
- Can tell a lengthy story

Cognitive

- Still experiences difficulty telling the difference between reality and fantasy
- Begins awareness of concepts of "bad" and "good"
- Enjoys simple card games
- Can follow three unrelated commands in proper order
- Can visually discriminate some shapes and colors
- Lives in the here-and-now, but is developing powers of abstracting, generalizing, and beginning reasoning
- Learns to take directions and follow rules
- Is curious and inquisitive about the world in general
- Requires concrete, sensory, firsthand learning experiences

PHYSICAL DEVELOPMENT

Fine Motor

- Still likes to do finger plays and finger actions with songs
- Shows more representation and symbolism in art work
- Cuts more accurately with scissors
- Uses brushes and crayons with more precision
- Completes more complex puzzles (six or more pieces)
- Can manage clothing better (buttons, zippers, fasteners, but tying is still a problem)
- Likes to use tools (woodworking, cooking)
- Enjoys stringing articles or using sewing cards

Gross Motor

- Plays direction games with change in actions
- Likes to copy letters and numbers
- Builds large block structures
- Rides a tricycle easily
- Loves climbing, jumping, running and other active activities
- Can walk on a balance beam
- Throws and catches a ball easier
- Has great amount of physical energy
- Demonstrates new physical skills and likes an audience

FIVE-YEAR-OLDS

SOCIAL-EMOTIONAL DEVELOPMENT

Social

- Prefers play in small groups; plays longer together
- Prefers friends of same sex and age; may have a best friend
- "Mothers" younger children
- Generally respects other people's property
- Is developing a sense of fairness and rules
- Is friendly and cooperative; shows empathy
- Works on new things with great gusto
- Acknowledges positive attitude and encourages acceptable behavior
- Likes to tease and will at times do unexpected things for attention
- Likes dramatic and pretend play
- Seeks approval; avoids disapproval of adults
- Is self-assured and conforming
- Brags about new accomplishments and skills
- Enjoys noise, music, rhythms, songs, and games, especially about real children or animals that behave like children

Emotional

- Has mood swings; may be assertive and bossy
- Has a sense of order; responds to some structure
- Begins to see importance of rules; criticizes non-conformers
- Is generally dependable
- Seeks sex role expectancies from parents
- Admires teacher; is eager to learn
- Tends to be obedient and cooperative
- Has frequent but short-lived quarrels
- Expresses feelings freely, often in extreme form
- Is relatively truthful
- Is delightful, easy to live and work with, and often sedate
- Tries to please
- Prefers the real world
- Often reminds others of truth and reality
- Is interested in family relationships
- Is becoming aware of own identity; may embarrass easily
- Shows strong awareness of right and wrong
- Is independent, dependable, self-reliant, obedient, happy, trustful, and proud
- Trusts others
- Enjoys humor, tricks, jokes

INTELLECTUAL DEVELOPMENT

Language

- Uses language easily for conversations, interaction, and discussion; uses full sentences, some clauses and idioms
- May mispronounce some words or sounds
- Understands more language than is able to use
- Names the days of the week
- Is using language more to settle differences
- Asks serious questions and expects answers
- Likes poetry and rhyming activities
- Follows verbal instructions with confidence
- Uses verbal aggression when angry
- Can retell details of stories
- Has vocabulary of 2,000 or more words
- Tells original stories and situations

Cognitive

- Focuses attention for longer periods—based on interest
- Initiates or repeats prior play
- Begins to work with abstract thoughts
- Has intense curiosity; is an eager learner
- Has an active imagination; distinguishes fantasy and reality
- Recognizes some written symbols (letters, numbers, words)
- Recognizes cause and effect of actions
- Follows three-step commands
- Recognizes shapes
- Decides beforehand the content of drawings and pictures
- Begins to understand number correlation
- Relates past and future events
- Remembers sequences of numbers, letters, and ideas

PHYSICAL DEVELOPMENT

Fine Motor

- Has established handedness and eyedness
- Is adept at coordinating hand-eye movements
- Shows great improvement in painting, pasting, drawing, cutting, and coloring
- Folds paper, copies shapes or designs, draws numbers and letters, traces objects, colors within lines, cuts smoothly
- Writes own name, numbers from 1 to 10, and other symbols
- Can lace, button, zip, and usually tie shoes

Gross Motor

- Has quite good body control; jumps, jumps from heights, jumps rope, runs, skips, climbs, throws, catches and kicks a ball
- Rides a two-wheeled bike
- Is adept at using wheeled toys; possesses improved balance
- Dresses self confidently—may need help with tying
- Can keep time to music and do rhythm activities
- Thrives on activity

Appendix B

REFERENCES

Abruscato, J. (1988). **Teaching children science.** Englewood Cliffs, NJ: Prentice-Hall.

Ainsworth, M. D. S. (1980). Attachment and child abuse. In G. Gerbner, C. J. Ross, and E. Zigler (eds.), **Child abuse: An agenda for action.** New York: Oxford University Press.

Allen, G., Giat, L., and Cherney, R. (1974). Locus of control, test anxiety and student performance in a personalized instruction course. **Journal of Educational Psychology,** 66, pp. 968–973.

Althouse, R. (1988). **Investigating science with young children.** New York: Teachers College Press.

Anthony, E. J., and Pollock, G. H. (1985). **Parental influences in health and disease.** Boston: Little, Brown and Co.

Bar-Tal, D., Kfir, D., Bar-Zohar, Y., and Chen, M. (1980). The relationship between locus of control and academic achievement, anxiety, and level of aspiration. **British Journal of Educational Psychology,** 50, pp. 53–60.

Barrow, L. H. (1989) A box of ideas. **Science and Children,** Feb., pp. 42–43.

Bazler, J. A., and Simonis, D.A. (1990). Are women out of the picture? **The Science Teacher,** Dec., pp. 24–26.

Beaty, J. J. (1990). **Observing development of the young child,** 2 ed. Columbus, OH: Merrill.

Beatty, J. J. (1988). **Skills for preschool teachers,** 3d ed. Columbus, OH: Merrill.

Belch, P. J. (1975, Winter). The question of teachers' questions. **Teaching Exceptional Children,** p. 47.

Benham, N., B., Hosticka, A., Payne, J. D., and Yeotis, C. (1982). Making concepts in science and mathematics visible and viable in the early childhood curriculum. **School Science and Mathematics,** 82(1), pp. 45–56.

Berlyne, D. E. (1970). Children's reasoning and thinking. In P. Mussen (ed.) **Carmichael's manual of child psychology** (Vol. 1).

Berlyne, D. E. (1960). **Conflict, arousal, and curiosity.** New York: McGraw-Hill.

Best books for children: Preschool through the middle grades. (1985). New York: Bowker.

The best science books for children. (1983). Washington, DC: American Association for the Advancement of Science, 1972.

Blackwelder, S. K. (1980). **Science for all seasons: Science experiences for young children.** Englewood Cliffs, NJ: Prentice-Hall.

Bloom, B. (1964). **Stability and change in human characteristics.** New York: Wiley.

Blough, G., and Schwartz, J. (1984). **Elementary school science and how to teach it.** New York: Holt, Rinehart and Winston.

Blough, G. (1971, Dec.). Some observations and reflections about science teaching in the elementary school. **Science and Children.**

Bowden, M. (1989). **Nature for the very young: A handbook of indoor and outdoor activities.** New York: John Wiley and Sons.

Bradbard, M. R., and Endsley, R. (1980, July). How can teachers develop young children's curiosity? What current research says to teachers. **Young Children,** 35(3), pp. 21–32.

Bradbard, M. R., Halperin, S. M., and Endsley, R. C. (1988). The curiosity of abused preschool children in mother-present, teacher-present, and stranger-present situations. **Early Childhood Research Quarterly,** 3, pp. 91–105.

Bredekamp, S., and Shepard, L. (1989, March). How best to protect children from inappropriate school expectations, practices, and policies. **Young Children,** 44(3), pp. 14–23.

Bredekamp, S. (ed.) (1987). **Developmentally appropriate practice in early childhood programs serving children from birth through age 8: Expanded edition.** Washington, DC: National Association for the Education of Young Children.

Bredekamp, S. (ed.). (1986). **Developmentally appropriate practices. A position statement.** Washington, DC: National Association for the Education of Young Children.

Bronson, W. J. (1974). Competence and the growth of personality, in K. Connolly and J. S. Brunner (eds.) **The growth of competence.** London, England: Academic Press.

Brown, B. (1981). **200 illustrated science experiments for children.** New York: William Collins and World.

Brown, C. C., and Gottfried, A. W. (eds.) (1985). **Play interactions: The role of toys and parental involvement in children's development.** Skillman, NJ: Johnson and Johnson.

Brown, J. F. (ed.) (1982). **Curriculum planning for young children.** Washington, DC: National Association for the Education of Young Children.

Brown, S. (1981). **Bubbles, rainbows, and worms: Science experiments for preschool children.** Mt. Rainier, MD: Gryphon.

Browne, N. (ed.) (1991). **Science and technology in the early years.** Philadelphia: Open University Press.

Bruner, J. (1960). **The process of education.** Cambridge, MA: Harvard University Press.

Bruner, J. S. (1961, Winter). The act of discovery. **Harvard Educational Review,** 31(1), pp. 21–32.

Buckner, L. M. (1988, July). On the fast track to . . . ? Is it early childhood education or early adulthood education? **Young Children,** 43(5), p. 5.

Caplan, T., and Caplan, F. (1983). **The early childhood years: The 2 to 6 year old.** New York: AGC/Perigee.

Carin, A. A., and Sund, R. B. (1980). **Discovery activities for elementary science.** Columbus, OH: Merrill.

Carin, A. A., and Sund, R. B. (1985a). **Teaching modern science,** 4th ed. Columbus, OH: Merrill.

Carin, A. A., and Sund, R. B. (1985). **Teaching science through discovery,** 5th ed. Columbus, OH: Merrill.

Carini, P. (1977, March). Building a curriculum for young children from an experiential base. **Young Children,** 33, pp. 14–18.

Carmichael, V. S. (1982). **Science experiences for young children.** Palo Alto, CA: R and E Research Associates.

Carson, R. (1956). **The sense of wonder.** New York: Harper and Row.

Cartwright, S. (1989). Kids and science—magic in the mix. **Exchange,** June, pp. 51–54. Reprinted from B. Neugebauer (ed.), **The wonder of it: Exploring how the world works: A beginnings book for teachers of young children.** Redmond, WA: Exchange Press.

Case, R. (1985). **Intellectual development: Birth to adulthood.** New York: Academic Press, Inc.

Charlesworth, R., and Lind, K. K. (1990). **Math and science for young children.** Albany, NY: Delmar.

Children's Defense Fund (1987). **A children's defense budget.** Washington, DC: National Association for the Education of Young Children.

Clark, B. (1986). **Optimizing learning: The integrative education model in the classroom.** Columbus, OH: Merrill.

Cobb, V. (1987). A little science, a little magic. **Parents,** Feb., pp. 97–102.

Cohen, S. (1989, May). Fostering shared learning among children and adults: The children's museum. **Young Children,** 44(4), pp. 20–24.

Coie, J. (1974). An evaluation of the cross-situational stability of children's curiosity. **Journal of Personality,** 42, pp. 93–116.

Connell, D. R. (1987, July). The first thirty years were the fairest: Notes from the kindergarten and ungraded primary (K-1-2). **Young Children,** 42(5), pp. 30–38.

Connolly, K., and Bruner, J. (eds.) (1974). **The growth of competence.** London, England: Academic Press.

Crandall, V. (1965). Achievement behavior in young children. In W. W. Hartup and N. L. Smothergill (eds.) **The young child: Reviews of Research,** Vol. 2, pp. 165–185. Washington, DC: National Association for the Education of Young Children.

Danilov, V. J. (1986). Discovery rooms and kidspaces: Museum exhibits for children. **Science and Children,** Jan., pp. 6–8.

Dawes, D. D. (1987). **Improving the attitudes of primary teachers and students towards science by using a hands-on approach.** Practicum for Ed.D., Nova University. December.

Day, H. I. (1968). Role of specific curiosity in school achievement. **Journal of Educational Psychology,** 59, pp. 37–43.

deCharms, R. (1984). Motivation enhancement in education, in R. Ames, and C. Ames (eds.) **Student Motivation,** pp. 275–310. New York: Academic Press.

Duckworth, E. (1987). **"The having of wonderful ideas" and other essays on teaching and learning.** New York: Teachers College Press.

Dunitz, Robin J. (1985, May/June). Interactive museums. **Media and Methods,** 21(8), pp. 9–11.

Dweck, C., and Goetz, T. (1978). Attributions and learned helplessness, in J. Harvey, W. Ickes, and R. Kidd (eds.) **New directions in attribution research** (Vol. 2). Hillsdale, NJ: Erlbaum.

Eaton, J. F., Anderson, C. W., and Smith, E. L. (1984, March). Students' misconceptions interfere with science learning: Case studies of fifth-grade students. **The Elementary School Journal,** 84(4), pp. 365–379.

Editor's Note. (1986, Jan.). Two viewpoints: A challenge to early childhood educators. **Young Children,** 41(2), p. 9.

DeVito, A., and Krockover, G. H. (1980). **Creative sciencing: Ideas and activities for teachers and children.** New York: Little, Brown.

Einstein, A. (1949). **The world as I see it.** New York: Philosophical Library.

Eliason, C., and Jenkins, L. (1990). **A practical guide to early childhood curriculum,** 4th ed. Columbus, OH: Merrill.

Elkind, D. (1988, May). From our president: Acceleration. **Young Children,** 43(4), p. 2.

Elkind, D. (1988, July). From our president: Play. **Young Children,** 43(5), p. 2.

Elkind, D. (1987a). **Miseducation: Preschoolers at risk.** New York: Knopf.

Elkind, D. (1987b, March). Superbaby syndrome can lead to elementary school burnout. **Young Children,** 42(3), p. 14.

Elkind, D. (1981a). **Children and adolescents,** 3d ed. New York: Oxford Press.

Elkind, D. (1981b). **The hurried child.** Reading, MA: Addison-Wesley.

Elkind, D. (1972, Nov). Piaget and science education. **Science and Children,** 10(3), p. 9–12.

Endsley, R. C., and Clarey, S. (1975). Answering young children's questions as a determinant of their subsequent question-asking behavior. **Developmental Psychology,** 11, p. 863.

Endsley, R. C., and Gupta, S. (1978). Group size as a determinant of preschool children's frequency of question asking. **Journal of genetic psychology,** 132, pp. 317–318.

Endsley, R. C., Hutcherson, M. A., Garner, A. P., and Martin, J. (1979). Interrelationships among selected maternal behaviors, authoritarianism, and preschool children's verbal and nonverbal curiosity. **Child Development,** 50, pp. 331–339.

Epstein, H. (1978). Growth spurts during brain development: Implications for educational policy and practice, in J. Chall and A. Mirsky (eds.) **Education and the brain** (77th Yearbook of NSSE, Part II, pp. 343–370). Chicago: University of Chicago Press.

Erikson, E. (1977). **Toys and reason: Stages in the ritualization of experience.** New York: Norton.

Erikson, E. (1950). **Childhood and society,** 2d ed. New York: Norton.

Esler, W. K., and Esler, M. K. (1984). **Teaching elementary science,** 4th ed. Belmont, CA: Wadsworth.

Feldman, W. W., and Nash, S. C. (1986). Antecedents of early parenting. In A. Fogel and G. F. Melson (eds.) **Origins of nurturance: Developmental, biological and cultural perspectives of caregiving.** Hillsdale, NJ: Lawrence Erlbaum Assoc.

Fowler, W. (1980). **Curriculum and assessment guides for infant and child care.** Boston: Allyn and Bacon.

Forman, G., and Kaden, M. (1986). Research on science education for young children, in C. Seefeldt (Ed.), **The early childhood curriculum.** New York: Teachers College Press, Columbia University.

Forman, G. E., and Kuschner, D. S. (1983). **The child's construction of knowledge: Piaget for teaching children.** Washington, DC: National Association for the Education of Young Children.

Franklin, M. B., and Biber, B. (1977). Psychological perspectives and early childhood education: Some relations between theory and practice. In L. G. Katz (ed.), **Current topics in early childhood education,** Vol. 1. Norwood, NJ: Ablex Publishing.

Friedl, A. E. (1986). **Teaching science to children: An integrated approach.** New York: McGraw.

Friedrich, W. M., and Boriskin, J. A. (1980). The role of the child in abuse: A review of the literature, in G. J. Williams and J. Money (eds.), **Traumatic abuse and neglect of children at home.** Baltimore: Johns Hopkins University Press.

Froebel, F. (1899). **The education of man.** Translated by W. N. Hailmann. New York: D. Appleton and Co.

Fulghum, R. (1989). **All I really need to know I learned in kindergarten.** New York: Villard Books.

Gagné, R. M. (1966). Varieties of learning and the concept of discovery, in L. S. Schulman and E. R. Keislar (eds.), **Learning by discovery: A critical appraisal.** Chicago: Rand McNally.

Galin, D. (1979, Oct.). Educating both halves of the brain. **Childhood Education,** 53(1).

Gelman, R. (1979). Preschool thought. **American Psychologist,** 34(10), pp. 900–905.

Gilbert, D. L. (1971). **National resources and public relations.** Washington, DC: Wildlife Society.

Gilbert, J. K., Osborne, R. J., and Fensham, P. J. (1982). Children's science and its consequences for teaching. **Science Education** 66(4), pp. 623–633.

Greenberg, (1989, May). Parents as partners in young children's development and education. **Young Children,** 44(4), pp. 61–75.

Gross, T. F. (1985) **Cognitive Development,** Monterey, CA: Brooks/Cole.

Hackett, J. K., Moyer, R. H., and Adams, D. K. (1989). **Merrill science: A natural in your classroom.** Columbus, OH: Merrill.

Haiman, P. E. (1986). There is more to early childhood than cognitive development, in J. B. McCracken (ed.), **Reducing stress in young children's lives** (p. 92). Washington, DC: National Association for the Education of Young Children.

Harlan, J. (1988). **Science experiences for the early childhood years,** 4th ed. Columbus, OH: Merrill.

Harlan, J. (1987, Sept). Rebuttal to Smith. **Young Children,** 3.

Harlan, J. D. (1975). From curiosity to concepts; from concepts to curiosity—science experiences in the preschool. **Young Children,** 30(4), pp. 249–255.

Harlen, W. (ed.) (1985). **Primary science: Taking the plunge.** Portsmouth, NJ: Heinemann.

Harris, J. R., and Liebert, R. M. (1991). **The child.** Englewood Cliffs, NJ: Prentice-Hall.

Henderson, B., and Moore, S. G. (1979). Measuring exploratory behavior in young children. **Developmental Psychology,** 15(2), pp. 113–119.

Hendrick, J. (1990). **Total learning: Developmental curriculum for the young child.** Columbus, OH: Merrill.

Hendrick, J. (1988). **The whole child: Developmental education for the early years,** 4th ed. Columbus, OH: Merrill.

Hendrick, J. (1987). **Why teach: A first look at working with young children.** Washington, DC: National Association for the Education of Young Children.

Henniger, M. L. (1987). Learning mathematics and science through play. **Childhood Education,** 63(3), pp. 167–171.

Herbert, D. (1980). **Mr. Wizard's supermarket science.** New York: Random House.

Hermann, N. (1981). The creative brain. **Training and Development Journal,** 35(10), pp. 10–16.

Hildebrand, V. (1991). **Introduction to early childhood education,** 5th ed. New York: Macmillan.

Holt, B. (1989). **Science with young children,** (rev.) Washington, DC: National Association for the Education of Young Children.

Holt, B.G. (1977). **Science with young children.** Washington, DC: National Association for the Education of Young Children.

Holt, B.G., Ives, W., Levedi, B. L., and von Hippel, C. S. (1983). **Getting involved: Your child and science.** (DHHS Publication NO. OHDS 83–31143), Washington, DC: U. S. Dept. of Health and Human Services.

Howe, A. (1975). A rationale for science in early childhood education. **Science Education,** 59, pp. 95–101.

Hunt, J. McV. (1986, June). The effects of variation in quality and type of early child care on development, in W. Fowler (ed.), Early experience and the development of competence. **New Directions in Child Development,** p. 32.

Hutt, C. (1970). Specific and diversive exploration, in H. W. Reese and L. P. Lipsett (eds.), **Advances in Child Development and Behavior** (Vol. 5). New York: Academic Press.

Hyson, M., Hirsh-Pasek, K., and Resorla, L. (1988). **The classroom practices inventory: An observation instrument based on NAEYC's guidelines for developmentally appropriate practices for 4- and 5-year-old children.** Chicago: Spencer Foundation.

Iatridis, M. D. (1986). **Teaching science to children: A resourcebook.** New York: Garland Publishing, Inc.

Iatridis, M. (1981, Oct.) Teaching science to preschoolers. **Science and Children,** pp. 25–27.

Ideas that work with young children (1988, May). Postive self-image: More than mirrors. **Young Children,** 43(4), pp. 57–59.

Johns, C., and Endsley, R. C. (1977). The effects of maternal model on young children's tactual curiosity. **Journal of Genetic Psychology** 131, pp. 21–28.

Kamii, C., and DeVries, R. (1978). **Physical knowledge in preschool education: Implications of Piaget's theory.** Englewood Cliffs, NJ: Prentice-Hall.

Kantrowitz, B., and Wingert, P. (1989). How kids learn. **Newsweek,** April 17, pp. 4–10. Reprinted in **Young Children,** September 1989, p. 3.

Klee, W., Bonstetter, R., McCloskey, S., and Falts, B. (1985). What research says: Science through discovery—Students love it. **Science and Children,** p. 23.

Knight, M. E., and Graham, T. L. (1984). **The leaves are falling in rainbows: Science activities for early childhood.** Atlanta: Humanics Ltd.

Knight, M. E., and Graham, T. L. (1984). What's so hard about teaching science? **Day Care and Early Education,** Winter, pp. 14–16.

Kotar, M. (1988). Firsthand experience—firsthand knowledge. **Science and Children,** 25(8), p. 40.

Lao, R. (1970). Internal-external control and competent and innovative behavior among Negro college students. **Journal of Personal Social Psychology,** 14, pp. 263–270.

Levenson, E. (1985). **Teaching children about science: Ideas and activities every teacher and parent can use.** Englewood Cliffs, NJ: Prentice-Hall.

Levy, J. (1985, May). Right brain, left brain: Fact and fiction. **Psychology Today,** pp. 38–44.

Lupkowski, A. E. (1985). Characteristics of gifted preschool children. Paper presented at the Annual Convention of the Council for Exceptional Children (63rd, Anaheim, CA, 15019 April, 1985).

Maccoby, E. E., and Jacklin, C. N. (1974). **The psychology of sex differences.** Stanford, CA: Stanford University Press.

McIntyre, M. (1984). **Early childhood and science: A collection of articles.** National Science Teachers Association, 1742 Connecticut Ave., NW, Washington, DC 20009.

McNamee, A. S. (1987, Feb). Museum readiness: Preparation for the art museum (ages 3–8). **Childhood Education,** 63, pp. 181–187.

Markle, S. (1988). **Hands-on science.** Cleveland, OH: The Instructor Publications.

Martin, H. P. (ed.) (1976). **The abused child.** Cambridge, MA: Ballinger.

Maslow, A. (1970). **Motivation and personality.** 2d ed. New York: Viking Press.

Maxim, G. (1989). **The very young,** 3d ed. Columbus, OH: Merrill.

Maw, W. M., and Maw, E. W. (1961). Establishing criterion groups for evaluating measure of curiosity. **Journal of Experimental Education,** 29, pp. 299–306.

Mintzes, J. J. (1984, November). Naive theories in biology: Children's concepts of the human body. **School Science and Mathematics,** 84(7), pp. 548–555.

Minuchin, P. P. (1971). Curiosity and exploratory behavior in disadvantaged children: A follow-up study. Paper presented at the meetings of the Society for Research in Child Development, Minneapolis, Minnesota, April, 1971.

Morrison, A., and McIntrye, D. (1971). **Schools and socialization.** Baltimore, MD: Penguin.

Morrison, G. S. (1990). **The world of child development.** Albany, NY: Delmar Publishers.

Mukherjee, R., and Preeti, J. (1987). Concept and curiosity development in pre-school children. **Psychological Research Journal,** 11, pp. 25–32.

Myers, B. K., and Maurer, K. (1987). Teaching with less talking: Learning centers in the kindergarten. **Young Children,** 42(5), pp. 20–27.

Neuman, D. B. (1978). **Experiences in science for young children.** Albany, NY: Delmar.

Nunnally, J. C., and Lemond, L. C. (1973). Exploratory behavior and human development, in H. W. Reese (ed.), **Advances in Child Development and Behavior** (Vol. 8).

Osborn, J. D., and Osborn, D. K. (1983). **Cognition in early childhood.** Athens, GA: Education Associates.

Osborne, R., and Freyberg, P. (1985). **Learning in science: The implications of children's science.** Portsmouth, NH: Heinemann.

Papalia, D. E., and Olds, S. W. (1990). **A child's world.** New York: McGraw-Hill.

Patterson, G. R. (1986). Maternal rejection: Determinant or produce for deviant child behavior?, in W. W. Hartup and Z. Rubin (eds.), **Relationships and development.** Hillsdale, NJ: Lawrence Erlbaum Associates.

Peltz, W. H. (1990). Can girls + science − stereotypes = success? **The Science Teacher,** Dec., pp. 45–49.

Phares, E. (1975). **Locus of control in personality.** Morristown, NJ: General Learning Press.

Piaget, J. (1929). **The child's conception of the world.** New York: Harcourt and Brace.

Piaget, J. (1952). **The origins of intelligence in children.** New York: International Universities Press.

Piaget, J. (1954). **The construction of reality in the child.** New York: Basic.

Piaget, J. (1962). **Play, dreams and imitation in childhood.** New York: W. W. Norton and Co.

Piaget, J. (1973). **To understand is to invent: The future of education.** New York: Grossman.

Piaget, J., and Inhelder, B. (1969). **The psychology of the child.** New York: Basic Books.

Pines, M. (1983). Can a rock walk? **Psychology Today,** Nov., pp. 46–54.

Pines, M. (1979, Sept.). Head start in the nursery. **Psychology Today,** 13(4), pp. 56–68.

Pitcher, E. G., Feinburg, S. G., and Alexander, D. A. (1989). **Helping young children learn,** 5th ed. Columbus, OH: Merrill.

Pugh, A. F., and Dukes-Bevans, L. (1987). Planting seeds in young minds. **Science and Children.** 25(3), pp. 19–21.

Radencich, M. C., and Bohning, G. (1988, Feb). Pop up, pull down, push in, slide out: Natural science action books. **Childhood Education,** pp. 157–161.

Ripple, R. E., and Rockcastle, V. E. (eds.) (1964). **Piaget rediscovered: A report of the Conference on Cognitive Studies and Curriculum Development:** Ithaca, NY: School of Education, Cornell University, p. 5.

Roche, R. L. (1977). **The child and science: Wondering, exploring, growing.** Washington, DC: Association for Childhood Educational International.

Rowe, M. B. (ed.) (1978). **What research says to the science teacher.** Washington, DC: National Science Teachers Assoc.

Rowe, M. B. (1978). **Teaching science as continuous inquiry: A basic.** New York: McGraw-Hill.

Rowe, M. B. (1974). Relation of wait-time and rewards to the development of language, logic, fate control: Part II, rewards. **Journal of Research in Science Teaching,** 11(4), pp. 291–308.

Sava, S. G. (1987, March). Development, not academics. **Young Children,** 42(3), p. 15.

Saxe, R. M., and Stollack, G. E. (1971). Curiosity and the parent-child relationship. **Child Development** 42: pp. 372–384.

Schmidt, V., and Rockcastle, V. (1982). **Teaching science with everyday things.** New York: McGraw-Hill.

Schools Council (1972). **Early experiences.** London, England: Macdonald Educational Ltd.

Schultz, C. (1985, May). Early childhood. **Science and Children,** 22(8), pp. 49–51.

Seefeldt, C. (1985). Tomorrow's kindergarten: Pleasure or pressure? **Principal,** 64, pp. 12–15.

Severeide, R. C., and Pizzini, E. L. (1984, May). What research says: The role of play in science. **Science and Children,** pp. 58–61.

Shymansky, J. A. (1978). How teaching strategies affect students: Implications for teaching science, in M. B. Rowe (ed.), **What research says to the science teacher,** Washington, DC: National Teachers Association, pp. 31–39.

Siegler, R. S. (1986). **Children's thinking.** Englewood Cliffs, NJ: Prentice-Hall.

Sisson, E. (1982). **Nature with children of all ages.** Englewood Cliffs, NJ: Prentice-Hall.

Smith, R. F. (1987, Jan.). Theoretical framework for preschool science experiences. **Young Children,** 42(2), pp. 34–40. Read also rebuttal by J. Harlan, **Young Children,** Sept. 1987, p. 3.

Smith, R. F. (1981). Early childhood science education: A Piagetian perspective. **Young Children,** 36(2), pp. 3–10.

Spodek, B. (1985). **Teaching in early years,** 3d ed. Englewood Cliffs, NJ: Prentice-Hall.

Springer, S. P., and Deutsch, G. (1985). **Left brain, right brain.** New York: W. H. Freeman, p. 237.

Sprung, B., Campbell, P. B., and Froschl, M. (1985). **What will happen if . . . Young children and the scientific method.** New York: Educational Equity Concepts.

Stewart, I. S. (1982, July). The real world of teaching two year old children. **Young Children,** 37(5), pp. 3–13.

Sunal, C. S. (1990). **Early childhood social studies.** Columbus, OH: Merrill Publishing Co.

Sunal, C. S. (1982). Philosophical bases for science and mathematics in early childhood education. **School Science and Mathematics,** pp. 2–10.

Thomas, G. (1986). Cultivating the interest of women and minorities in high school mathematics. **Science Education,** 70(1986), pp. 31–34.

Tipps, S. (1982). Making better guesses: A goal in early childhood science. **School Science and Mathematics,** 82(1), pp. 29–37.

Toole, A. L., and Boehm, E. (1983). **Off to a good start.** New York: Walker and Co.

Victor, E. (1985). **Science for the elementary school,** 5th ed. New York: Macmillan.

Wadsworth, B. J. (1984). **Piaget's theory of cognitive and affective development,** 3d ed. New York: Longman.

Wellman, H. H. (1982). The foundation of knowledge: Concept development in the young child, in S. G. Moore and C. R. Cooper (eds.), **The young child: Reviews of research,** (Vol. 3). Washington, DC: National Association for the Education of Young Children.

White, B. L. (1975). **The first three years of life.** Englewood Cliffs, NJ: Prentice-Hall.

White, R. W. (1968). Motivation reconsidered: The concept of competence, in M. Almy (ed.), **Early childhood play: Selected readings related to cognition and motivation.** New York: Simon and Schuster.

White, R. W. (1959). Motivation reconsidered: The concept of competence. **Psychological Review,** 66, pp. 297–333.

Whitehead, A. N. (1959). **The aims of education.** New York: Macmillan.

Whitehead, A. N. (1968). **Modes of thought.** New York: Free Press.

Williams, C. K., and Kamii, C. (1986). How do children learn by handling objects? **Young Children,** Nov., pp. 23–26.

Williams, G. J., and Money, J. (eds.) (1980). **Traumatic abuse and neglect of children at home.** Baltimore, MD: Johns Hopkins University Press.

Williams, R. B., Rockwell, R. E., and Sherwood, E. Z. (1987). **Mudpies to magnets: A preschool science curriculum.** Mt. Rainier, MD: Gryphon House.

Wittrock, M. C. (ed.) (1977). Learning as a generative process, in **Learning and Instruction.** Berkeley, CA: McCutcheon, pp. 621–631.

Wolfinger, D. A. (1984). **Teaching science in the elementary school: Content, process, and attitude.** Boston: Little, Brown and Co.

Worthy, W. (1989). Scientific literacy: Sweeping changes in teaching urged. **Chemical and Engineering News,** 67(9), p. 4.

Wrobel, G. (1986, May). Toddlers take to science. **New Scientist,** 29, p. 59.

Ziemer, M. (1987). Science and the early childhood curriculum: One thing leads to another. **Young Children,** (42:6) Sept., pp. 44–51.

Zubrowski, B. (1984). Of cabbages, science curriculums, and children's learning. **Science Education,** 68(1984), pp. 589–593.

Appendix C

RESOURCES

American Teaching Aids, P. O. Box 1406, Covina, CA 91722.

Bomar-Noble Publishers, 1901 North Walnut, P. O. Box 25308, Oklahoma City, OK 73125.

Child's World, P. O. Box 989, Elgin, IL 60121.

Children's Book and Music Center, 2500 Santa Monica Boulevard, Santa Monica, CA, 90406–1130.

Children's Record Guild, 225 Park Avenue So., New York, NY 10003.

Columbia Children's Record Library, CBS, Inc., 15 West 52nd Street, New York, NY 10019.

Conservation Foundation, **Aids to educators.** 1717 Massachusetts Ave., NW Washington, DC, 20036.

Creative Dimensions, P. O. Box 1393, Bellingham, WA 98227.

David C. Cook Publishing Co., School Products Division, Elgin, IL 60120.

Educational Activities, Inc., Box 392, 1937 Grand Ave., Freeport, NY 11520.

Educators guide to free science materials. (1987). Randolph, WI: Educators Progress Service, Inc.

Field Enterprises, World Book and Childcraft, Encyclopedia Division. **Teaching aids,** 510 Merchandise Mart Plaza, Chicago, IL 60654.

Folkways Records, Distributed by Scholastic Book Services, 906 Sylvan Ave., Englewood Cliffs, NJ. 07632. **OR** 632 Broadway, Ninth Floor, New York, NY 10012.

Hap Palmer Record Library, Educational Activities, Inc., 1937 Grand Ave., P. O. Box 87, Baldwin, NY 11510.

Insect Lore Products (the science and nature company), **Catalog,** P. O. Box 1535, Shafter, CA 93263.

Judy/Instructo, Educational Materials, 4325 Hiawatha Avenue South, Minneapolis, MN 55406.

Kimbo Educational, P. O. Box 477, 10 North Third Ave., Long Branch, NJ 07740.

Lyons Band, 530 Riverview Ave., Elkhart, IN 46514.

Melody House Publishing Co., 819 Northwest 92nd Street, Oklahoma City, OK 73114.

National Audubon Society, 950 Third Ave., New York, NY 10022.

National Dairy Council, **Educational aids,** 6300 North River Road, Rosemont, Il 60018–4233. OR 111 North Canal Street, Chicago, IL 60606.

National Geographic Society, 17th and M Streets, NW, Washington, DC 20036.

National Geographic Educational Services, Dept. 76, P. O. Box 1640, Washington, DC 20013.

National Science Resources Center, Smithsonian Institution, National Academy of Sciences. (1988). **Resources for teachers.** National Academy Press, 2101 Constitution Ave., NW, Washington, DC 20418. **Excellent resource: lists by grade level and grade level by category** (life science, health and human biology, earth science, physical science, multidisciplinary and applied science, activity books, and magazines).

National Science Teachers Assn. and Children's Book Council. (1987). **Outstanding science trade books for children in 1987.** (Free) Washington, DC: National Science Teachers Association.

National Science Teachers Assn, **Elementary science packets,** 1742 Connecticut Ave., NW Washington, DC, 20009. ($3 per packet.)

National Science Teachers Assn, **How to do it series** (ask the right questions, care for living things, and so on), 1742 Connecticut Ave., NW, Washington, DC 20009.

Richter, B., and Wenzel, D. (1986). **The museum of science and industry basic list of children's science books 1986 and 1987.** Chicago, IL: American Library Assoc.

Supt. of Documents, U. S. Government Printing Office, Washington, DC: 20402–9325. **Excellence in early childhood education: Defining characteristics and next-decade strategies,** publication #065-000-00415-1. ($1.75)

Teachers' Laboratory, Inc., **1991 Catalog for active learning in science and math** (focuses on ways to improve students' problem-solving skills in math and science. It includes resources for early childhood through eighth grade, selected from the United States and abroad), P. O. Box 6480, Brattleboro, VT 05302 (802–254–3457). (Free)

United Fresh Fruit and Vegetable Assn, **Educational aids,** Educational Services Div., 1019 Nineteenth St., NW, Washington, DC 20036.

U.S. Dept. of Health, Education and Welfare, **Sources of free and low-cost materials,** Supt. of Documents, Government Printing Office, Washington, DC 20402.

Young People's Records, Children's Record Guild, 100 Avenue of the Americas, New York, NY 10017.

PERIODICALS

Write for information or sample to determine if the magazine is appropriate for the children in your classroom before you enter a subscription.

Animal Kingdom, New York Zoological Society, Bronx, NY 10460.

Appraisal: Science books for young people (teacher resource). Boston University, School of Education, 605 Commonwealth Ave., Boston, MA 02215.

Chickadee, Young Naturalist Foundation, P. O. Box 11314, Des Moines, IA 50340.

Happy Times, Concordia Publishing House, 35585 Jefferson Ave., St. Louis, MO 73118.

Highlights for Children, 2300 West Fifth Ave., P. O. Box 269, Columbus, OH 43272.

Lollipops, Ladybugs and Lucky Stars, Good Apple, Box 299, Carthage, IL 62321-0299.

Sesame Street, Children's Television Workshop, P. O. Box 2896, Boulder, CO 80322.

Scienceland, Scienceland, Inc., 501 Fifth Ave., New York, NY 10017-6165.

Turtle: Magazine for Preschool Kids, Children's Better Health Institute, 1100 Waterway Blvd., P. O. Box 567, Indianapolis, IN 46206.

Your Big Backyard, National Wildlife Federation, 1412 16th St., NW, Washington, DC 20036–2266.

Zoobooks, Wildlife Education, Ltd., 930 West Washington St., San Diego, CA 92103.

INDEX